The Educational and Social Needs of
Children with Severe Handicap

Above: What fun they have in drama.

Left: It is opportunities they need.

Frontispiece photographs by kind permission of Mr. Ron Heavey (Dip.E.H.C.), Headmaster, Mill House School, Newton-le-Willows, Lancs.

The Educational and Social Needs of Children with Severe Handicap

MILDRED STEVENS M. Ed.

Matlock College of Education;
Honorary Lecturer, University of Manchester.

EDWARD ARNOLD

© Mildred Stevens 1976

First published 1971
by Edward Arnold (Publishers) Ltd
25 Hill Street, London W1X 8LL

Reprinted in paperback, with amendments, 1973
Second edition, 1976

ISBN: 0 7131 4265 0

Previously entitled *Educational Needs of Severely Subnormal Children*

Dutch translation, 1975

To all those who in the words of
my Swedish friend Ingvar Sandling (Malmö 1973)
'will change the environment to suit the
individual rather than conditioning the
individual to fit into a system' particularly,
I would like to add, when he cannot protest.

All Rights Reserved. No part of this publication may be reproduced, stored in a retrieval system, or transmitted in any form or by any means, electronic, mechanical, photocopying, recording or otherwise, without the prior permission of Edward Arnold (Publishers) Ltd.

Printed in Great Britain by Butler and Tanner Ltd., Frome and London.

Contents

Chapter		Page
	Acknowledgements	vi
1	Introduction	1
2	To be known as persons	17
3	Essentials for educational development	28
4	Pre-school education	43
5	Choosing their own activities	75
6	Structure in learning	84
7	Visits into the community	112
8	Play understood by the adults	117
9	A special kind of teacher	146
10	An interesting dynamic programme and curriculum	154
11	Planned systematic individual teaching	170
12	Education after 16 plus	189
13	Specially trained teachers	243
	Appendix 1 Suggested activities for stimulating very young handicapped children and some of those in special care units	262
	Appendix 2 A teaching notebook as an aid to observation assessment and systematic work with individuals and groups	264
	Appendix 3 Play as a two-way communication theme	266
	Appendix 4 Development of normal socialization	268
	Appendix 5 Rates of intellectual development in E.S.N.(S) children	271
	Appendix 6 Early attempts to evaluate teaching skills and initial suggestions to teachers for teaching practice assessment	272
	Appendix 7 Colleges of Education offering courses (Main/Optional/B.Ed) in mental handicap	292
	References	293
	Further useful reading	299

Acknowledgements

I shall always be deeply indebted to Mr. S. Jackson, M.ED., Principal Lecturer in the Education of Handicapped Children, Jordanhill College of Education, Glasgow; to Professor Eric Lunzer, PH.D., University of Nottingham; and to Mary Woodward, PH.D., University of Swansea, S. Wales. All have been responsible in one way or another for arousing my interest in the implications of some of Piaget's work for the education of severely subnormal children. Had I never met them nor read some of their work my thinking about Piaget would have been poorer.

My grateful thanks are ever given to all those students, colleagues and friends whose work, named and unnamed, in this book I have freely drawn upon to illustrate principles, theory and practice of education in this special field. They are all ever in my mind.

I should like to say a very special thank you to the families whose children I have worked with with such happiness as a teacher (1972-5) and who have given me much to share with others. In particular I shall mention Susan and Bill Walker, Congleton, Cheshire; Doreen and Jack Hayhurst (Alison, John and 'Villa' too) of Bury, Lancashire; Mary and Jack Taylor of N. Reddish, Manchester; and Mr. Fred Halliwell, who at 72 is excited at the development and improvement he has seen 'in the last two years in particular' in his handicapped son, George, because of his efforts and interest.

I should also like to say thank you:

to my friends Sheila Wigglesworth and Jean Dean for text scanning and proof reading;

to Miss F. Birkinshaw of Adlington who came the minute I needed her and waded through parts of a most difficult manuscript;

to Mrs. J. Knowles (Castle Priory College, Wallingford, Berkshire) and Dr. McAgerholme (Disabled Living Foundation) for suggesting a different kind of title;

to Uzgiriz and Hunt for allowing me to draw so extensively on their work in Chapter 3;

to Dr. Hannah Olechnowicz in Warsaw for sending me so many copies of her book to share with colleagues, and for the contribution she and her colleagues have made for the benefit of teachers and mentally handicapped children everywhere;

to Mary Lamb, the 'mum' of a seven-year-old mentally handicapped boy, who in using my book to find some ideas for playing with him wanted to know what the little numbers on the pages meant (the reference numbers). She reminded me that good teachers should take nothing for granted;

and to my husband for his continuous encouragement over nearly 30 years of friendship.

1 Introduction

Any relatively long acquaintance with mental subnormality shows that solutions solving its many problems are always in a state of 'becoming'. Ideas are always 'new' or 'recent' partcularly when new and recent people enter the field for the first time. The inevitable shocks they experience, the sense of guilt at not knowing that such children existed or where they were to be found inevitably cause them quite genuinely to desire TO DO SOMETHING NEW to bring about change in the lives of those less fortunate than themselves. The achievements of the past leave no impression for they are never enough.

Each decade seems to produce a band of workers wanting and needed to play a part, however small, in alleviating the incurable condition of mental subnormality and the unacceptable[1] life situation for parents who (because of the present lack of sufficient services) will clearly have life-long responsibility for their dependent handicapped offspring.

The 1950s was a growth period for workers in medical, psychological and social research.* This decade also saw the rise of voluntary societies concerned with the treatment and management of the mentally handicapped and the training of staff:

    The National Association for Mental Health
    The National Society for Mentally Handicapped Children
    The Spastics Society.†

The Mental Health Act of 1959 made it the duty of every local authority to provide some form of training for all mentally handicapped children. The Scott Report[11] described the kind of staff currently involved in work with the mentally handicapped and the future possibilities for training staff. These two documents heralded the decade of the educator's influence and contribution. Places looking like schools were built by local health authorities all over the

---

    * The names GUNZBURG,[2] CLARKE and CLARKE,[3] O'CONNOR,[4] GRAD,[5] TIZARD,[6] PENROSE,[7] KIRMAN,[8] WOODWARD,[9] and HOLT[10] being amongst the most well known in England.
    † N.A.M.H. now Mind, 22 Harley Street, London W.1.
N.S.M.H.C., Pembridge Hall, 17 Pembridge Square, London W2 EEP.
Spastics Society, 12 Park Crescent, London S.W.1.

country. These replaced the church halls and dilapidated buildings of previous decades where, with a few exceptions, child minding practices were generally the order of the day.

Concurrently with this growth in schools there was a growth in special courses for teachers. Teachers, some with higher degrees, some with advanced diplomas in special education and others with long teaching experience became Tutors to these special courses. They began to train teachers on initial one-, and then (1964) two-year courses (with one-year courses for mature women who had 'taught' in the schools for at least five years and needed training and a qualification). Whilst research in some instances influenced the thinking of these teacher trainers, they were largely influenced by their own educational expertise and knowledge of child development, and the shared thoughts and practices of colleagues, disseminated (i) by N.A.M.H. Tutors in quarterly reports to the responsible committee 1960–72; (ii) verbally at the professionally-formed Association of Tutors after 1964; (iii) to members of the Central Training Council* in annual reports; (iv) at the annual refresher courses organised by the N.A.M.H. and planned by their particular teacher trainers.

The mainstay of courses was innovation and 'action research' as Tutors with their students and the teachers they had trained grew in experience and came to know some of the needs of the children who were their mutual concern.

The work of these Tutors alongside the work of visiting specialists carefully selected by them from a number of allied disciplines demonstrated on a wider scale than ever before the educational possibilities for these children in the kind of curricula they developed. Unfortunately, training and research were not partners in this exciting educational adventure over a decade. Consequently much of the positive progress we saw made by the children in language, drama,

---

* This body under the umbrella of the D.H.S.S. was formed in 1964. A minimum of educationists was on the committee. Only in 1968, when the new Act bringing mentally handicapped children under education was imminent, was a Tutor, after much remonstrating, appointed to this committee. The Council approved the four pioneering courses (N.A.M.H.) and using their syllabuses and programmes as models and their Tutors as 'consultants' to interested newcomers in this teacher trainer group, it approved new courses, appointed assessors to the qualifying written examination, approved external examiners to the teaching aspects (always educationists) and awarded the nationally reconized Diplomas.

It will always be a matter of great concern to me that this body was not adequately consulted, as far as one can discover in conversation with some of those involved, when the D.E.S. plans for changes in this form of teacher training became compulsory in the early 'seventies.

art, physical education and social skills remained unmeasured and unrecorded. Much-needed practical changes were slowly brought about in the schools, sometimes painfully, by those directly responsible for training the teachers.

There were many drawbacks to their work. This meant that the quality of these changes was not spread evenly over the country. Acceptable professional standards of teaching could not be achieved let alone maintained in areas where schools were unsupported by a *continual* flow of ideas from students coming on teaching practice from the various courses. Some of these drawbacks included:

(a) students returning to schools where 'Headteachers' were untrained;
(b) the small number of specialised two-year courses (eight);
(c) the lack of follow-up for a teacher on qualifying by a supervised probationary year, informed continuous In-Service Training, inspection from specially chosen local advisers [five Advisory Welfare Officers (fortunately all educationists) at the D.H.S.S. had the gigantic unenviable task of advising in a growing number of schools — 400 in 1971 and about 100 hospital schools];
(d) the absence of teachers' centres to develop the various areas of the curricula introduced to and practised by students under skilled supervision during training;
(e) the lack of special teaching materials and aids in the schools and the inevitable fall in standards in providing these once training was over;
(f) the lack of support from the child health and schools guidance services;
(g) the job frustration for Tutors, engendered over a period of three years when specialised training as it had developed over a decade was not only unrecognised but criticised, was in jeopardy and in conflict with general policy, and with D.E.S. officials who saw opportunities in the already existing college courses and the particular expertise of the Tutors concerned to train teachers to work with other kinds of handicapped children (E.S.N.(M)) without ensuring that mentally handicapped children (E.S.N.(S)) would continue to be educated by specially trained teachers.

In November 1968 the Prime Minister announced that the responsibility for the education of severely subnormal children would be transferred from the Department of Health and Social Security to the Department of Education and Science. This step pleased those who were personally involved in the education of these children. Parents were also pleased, for it promised qualified teachers, adequate teaching equipment, the benefits of the School Health Service, peripatetic specialists such as teachers of the deaf and partially sighted, inspection of schools and an advisory service for the teachers of their children.

A year later the Secretary of State for Education announced that legislation to bring these children under the education service was to be speeded up and that teachers holding the diploma of the Training Council (equivalent to the N.A.M.H. Diploma pre-1964) would be recognised as fully qualified teachers after five year's acceptable post-diploma service.* Those we had trained deserved to be fully accepted by a profession still having one-year-, two-year- and three-year-trained members.

By 1970 the Education Act (Handicapped Children) was passed and in April 1971 education authorities began to administer the affairs of teachers and children in schools for the mentally handicapped. Thinking in terms of another decade (almost now half over) I am curious about the development that will take place. Undoubtedly educational research will play an important part in evaluating the achievements of the past; in refining the personal impressions which build up into assimilated knowledge when experienced teachers work with children. With the help of the teachers, research workers will give theoretical explanations to the sound practice existing in some schools. They might discover new techniques. They will certainly add to the structured teaching materials already being published.[12] Whilst welcoming teaching materials that leave the teacher more energy for forming relationships with the children, my only fear here is that too many teachers might use such materials by the book and ignore the interests and needs of individual children.

I am happy to see that some research is making good use of some of the skills we gave our teachers during their training in the 'sixties. I am referring here to the way in which researchers have trusted teachers to give the children objective tests as part of their surveys in language[13] and also the way in which my own pioneering work in training teachers to observe skilfully and systematically record[14] has now been extended in work with parents[15, 16] by the building of the Child Study Centre by the National Society for Mentally Handicapped Children at Westhill College, Birmingham; in other research work[17, 18]; and in the work carried out by my friend and colleague

---

* This meant that not only would they receive the Special Schools allowance in salary terms but their opportunities of a professional career structure were safeguarded. All Advanced Courses in Universities and Colleges of Education were open to them.

Olwen Gregory in assessing 120 children, some of them profoundly handicapped, in Day Centres in Glasgow.[19]

One of the very positive aspects of present research as I see it happening, in the North West at least, is that there is a genuine attempt by most of the researchers to do practical, useful research; to keep the teachers well supplied with written information about what is going on;* and to describe and interpret their findings simply. Perhaps this has occurred because the career opportunities of the 'sixties in mental subnormality attracted many people to research whose first professional qualification was in teaching.

As far as one can forecast, the 'seventies will see an increase in educational research by mature students on advanced diploma and M.Ed. courses. In this way they will bring the much-needed academic knowledge to their Tutors in the universities and the colleges. Much of it will undoubtedly concern itself with the provision of better services, the methodology of In-Service Training, the acquisition of language, assessment for remediation programmes, curriculum development and the education of the family. It seems imperative that when this happens the *content* of what students produce at least is always evaluated by those with knowledge and expertise in the sphere of mental subnormality practice and development. Upon reflection too, a useful strategy seemingly employed by Dutch researchers at a recent (1973) conference in The Hague might also be implemented in this country. As far as I can judge this means that all research workers in Universities receiving grants are expected to interpret and fully describe the *practical* implications of their work particularly when this is highly theoretical. For my part this is in no way implying that other professionals cannot do this for themselves but rather suggesting to researchers that by performing this exercise they will more readily be impelled to evaluate the value of their research to the community they are serving and to justify the large sums of money sometimes appearing to be spent.

If the efforts of those involved with the mentally handicapped in the 'seventies are successful the following features, considered advances, might be part of accepted practice:

(1) No one will be content to continue seeing profoundly handicapped children in bare, dull, unstimulating, institution-like envir-

---

* Teachers (and others), you have only to write to the Hester Adrian Research Centre, University of Manchester, Manchester, for the documents produced and you will get them. Perhaps *Parents Voice, Teaching and Training* and *Special Education* could be prevailed upon to publish relevant lists of available titles from time to time, say quarterly.

onments (and I have seen some of these schools even in 1974). Advisers, administrators, head teachers will prevail strongly upon their authorities and their staff to provide the kind of *lovely* environment we all know these children and those working with them should have. They might enlist community aid in designing and providing special aids and support to staff who have *the* most difficult task in the world to keep stimulating for such little return and very often for reasons which cannot be rationalized.*

(2) Parent workshops will be part of each school's responsibility and parent-teacher relationships as an essential *compulsory* part of special teacher training. In some areas the concept is accepted because fostering an interest in the homes has been part of training and an integral part of the philosophy of developing appropriate special education attitudes.[20-26] In other areas of Britain the concept has not even started to develop—indeed some hostility has been met when such relationships were suggested with the extra work it demands of the teachers.

(3) Family Teach-In Colleges[27] will be established by all local authorities so that parents can receive education, information and support, *as a right*, from the very moment they discover they have a handicapped child or are in any doubt whatsoever about their child's development. These will not be assessment centres but will supplement their work.

(4) More assessment units will be available and *directly accessible* to families in doubt. At the moment doctors (G.Ps) or local authorities can prevent a parent from having the full assessment service by denying them the necessary recommendation to the Unit. Of course one can sympathize with them because there are too few multidisciplinary assessment units available. After specialized assessment too there is often no machinery for the parents to receive the special help they seem to need if the findings of the various specialists are to be used meaningfully.

(5) Resource centres containing relevant teaching materials will exist in each authority for use by teachers and students preparing to work with these children. Such centres would encourage teachers to design materials and exhibit them for their colleagues.[23, 28]

(6) Educational suppliers might be prevailed upon to produce materials designed by teachers and others (in spite of an unknown

---

* I heard recently of one Headteacher (Ron Heavey of Mill House School, Newton-le-Willows, Lancashire) who has advertised in a local club for the services of 'ten intelligent, healthy, retired men' to help his teacher in the Special Care Unit.

commercial market). Firms doing this would be recognized as doing their bit in an area of life that needs all the support it can get.
(7) Student conferences on mental subnormality might be a regular feature for those in teaching, social work and nursing in order for cross-fertilization of ideas to take place and in order to foster understanding between members of these three professions.
(8) A return in some degree at least to the concept of specialized two/three-year training for teachers in this sphere of education in view of the admission already made (*Times Educational Supplement* 5.7.74) by the D.E.S. that there is a shortage in the country of trained specialists for mentally handicapped children.*
(9) A wide variety of examinable In-Service courses might be promoted.
(10) Results of research into PREVENTION OF MENTAL SUBNORMALITY will be quickly taught on the mass media and in all schools and colleges.
(11) The established voluntary agencies known to have had a long continuous interest and involvement with the handicapped might be linked up more closely with each other in a massive cooperative effort and with those seeming to have played a more prominent part in the lives of the Mentally Handicapped since 1970, viz:
  (a) Save the Children Fund;
  (b) Campaign;
  (c) King's Hospital Fund;
  (d) National Children's Bureau;
  (e) Pre-School Playgroups Association;
  (f) Dr. Barnardo's.
(12) Research workers and teachers will be discussing aspects of learning that the teachers want measurements for and the former will be:
  (a) compiling batteries of tests to measure such aspects so that more precise individual remediation programmes can be devised and evaluated;
  (b) giving these tests at the beginning and end of any one/two-year period;
  (c) discussing the results with the teachers and planning further programmes with them.
In this way research workers will be encouraged to recognize that

---

* MITTLER in a paper[29] presented in 1974 stated that only 50 per cent of those teaching the mentally handicapped have any kind of teaching qualification. In 1960 it was $33\frac{1}{3}$ per cent.

teachers have different but equally valuable skills; teachers will not be feeling that they are being used by research workers seeking academic career structures without recognition of their part in the work. Both will be developing a mutually recognized language.

(13) There will obviously be a number of experiments in integrating the mentally handicapped with normal children. Immediate attention will clearly need to be given in all Colleges of Education to methods of training likely to encourage ALL teachers to have positive attitudes to the handicapped and also to those wanting to work with them. This will inevitably mean that more courses about mental subnormality for the subject lecturers in the colleges will have to be arranged and paid for by the appropriate bodies.

(14) Medical and dental help will be immediately available to families of mentally handicapped children—without the parents having the extra burden of having to bully medical authority with all the attendant guilty feelings this entails. An example of this springs to mind where a small handicapped child of $3\frac{1}{2}$ years needed dental treatment and this in such a manner as to require an anaesthetic. The child was in dire pain and communicated this by banging her chin, her ear and her head. The parents had been told by the specialist concerned that the child needed a tooth extraction. They were given an appointment for six weeks ahead—pain, sleepless nights, for six weeks? When the mother complained and insisted, she got the appointment sooner *and* the treatment for her child; but in her own words—'no one came to me after my child's operation'—the mother felt the hostility because she had jumped the queue however legitimately. Why should she?

I have written this book to demonstrate the educative nature of the work that should be expected of teachers in schools for the severely subnormal. I have pointed out some of the difficulties teachers will encounter as well as some of the rewards. The methods and activities described are those which have been tried out by skilled, practising, qualified, teachers and found to be educationally possible and successful in terms of the children's happiness, interest, response and development.

I also wish to record that education in its broadest sense has in fact been a reality in many of the schools known to me since the early 'sixties. Particularly has this been so where teachers understood the necessity for a developmental approach to education and parents trusted them without pressures. I feel these facts should be noted even now by newcomers from the educational world who are largely ignorant of severely subnormal children and the special training needs of the teachers.

The methods implied are not new to teachers and educational psychologists but they do depend for their success on the teacher's ability to use the combined skills of systematic observing and recording of a child's *spontaneous* behaviour in structured and unstructured situations,[28, 29] and to relate her findings to a detailed knowledge of child development. Particularly is this the case if the management and handling of the children is going to be consistently positive and is for their benefit. She has also to understand fully that development although it can be promoted cannot be rushed. One of the job hazards of a teacher working with the mentally handicapped if one measures the results of one's work is intense frustration when one experiences the snail-like pace of the progress.

The methods described have two-way communication as a fundamental aim. I would like to suggest that one of the main aims of the teachers is to so contrive the programme and devise situations that purposeful communication in its many forms is paramount and that the child is helped towards understanding in as varied and interesting a way as possible. Silence and inactivity have little place in these schools. Wherever they exist to any large extent, teachers should question their approach, their methods, their own ability to communicate successfully.

The approach outlined is known to encourage the development of communication in all its forms. It was arrived at over a number of years by continual and careful observation on the part of a large number of well informed educationists and by personal involvement with these children in a variety of planned situations. Perhaps this book will remind specially qualified teachers of the severely subnormal of some of the features of their training; will stimulate others to evolve their own personal approach. It might be useful for:

(1) Adventurous teachers wishing to provide a sound learning environment for the children.
(2) Teachers who have not yet worked with these children and realized the possibilities for deepening their own thought about the meaning of education and the learning processes through contact with them.
(3) Lecturers in Colleges of Education and University Departments responsible for training and examining the teachers.
(4) Inspectors, Organizers and Advisory Teachers in Local Education Authorities now responsible for advising teachers in this work and for setting up In-Service courses.
(5) Wardens of the growing number of Teachers' Centres wishing to plan courses of In-Service training along the lines suggested in the

Chapter on teacher training.

(6) Research Workers interested in a child-centred approach to education and wanting to interpret their results well for teachers so that their work will supplement the practice of the best. I would like to emphasize that this will be done more successfully if the research worker familiarizes himself with the skills of the teachers concerned as well as with current educational attitudes reflected in the sound practice in schools generally. Too many young academic psychologists are perhaps becoming involved in this sphere of work without much practical experience of the normal child and his education.

(7) Nurses in Subnormality Hospitals. It is becoming more and more apparent that the work of the nurse and the teacher must go hand-in-hand if the children are to lead lives considered satisfactory within the limits of their handicap. Although the modern trend is away from large institutions and towards family group homes, it is a fact that thousands of children still live in institutions (where only 20–25 per cent of the nurses are qualified; where, as one nurse tutor informed me, only 10 per cent of these are in patient-contact, the others occupying higher positions of management) and are likely to do so for many years to come.

It is also well known that more tutors to mental subnormality nursing courses have taken a special teaching diploma additionally to their specialized nursing qualifications and regard themselves as teachers. These tutors are encouraging their students to see the educational role they have to play in their special function *in loco parentis*. Nurse/parent workshops might be a further extension of the work initiated by Jeffree and Cunningham in Manchester in 1970. It was exciting for me to hear one nurse tutor say to some young students 'you are not going there (a ward of a hospital) to please the matron but to bring some change about'. I can well remember saying a similar thing to my own students in 1961 when they were hesitant about 'treading on the Head's toes' in the junior training centres. There was little place for the 'you are a visitor to the school' attitude when one met some of the practices prevailing amongst workers in the field of mental subnormality both in this country and abroad.

(8) Parents wanting to know our expectations for their children and how we tried to enable the children to demonstrate these expectations and how they can become more purposefully involved in the education of their own child.

(9) House parents in the increasing number of hostels that are being

installed by voluntary and statutory bodies.
(10) Organizers of Opportunity Play Groups and Save the Children organizations. I know my previous edition was much used by the former.
(11) Peripatetic teacher/advisers of the pre-school child (cf. page 60).

Those training the teachers in the past had to work under the most challenging, inconceivable conditions. They had to rely to a large extent upon growing experience, consultation with a few well-informed colleagues and relevant research. The work of students reinforced theories and encouraged them to develop their thoughts. Those organizing courses under the auspices of The National Association for Mental Health were afforded opportunities for independent thinking, for experimenting and for educational innovation. Our work was exciting and rewarding for because of our work we saw countless severely subnormal children having opportunities for development and an increased quality of life.

In a short pamphlet entitled *The Mentally Retarded as Human Beings* collected during my travels in Holland in 1973* I found a very relevant description of the attitudes developing towards this now recognized group of human beings:

'Beliefs and principles which have stood the test of time and seemed unalterable are now viewed in a more relative perspective or are being reconsidered. There is still a great measure of uncertainty but a new movement is growing which gives grounds for hope and expectation. A revaluation of the mentally handicapped as human beings is taking place. They are no longer regarded as being ill or incomplete or deficient people but rather as members of our society who have the right to lead their own lives to the fullest extent. It is the duty of us—the not mentally retarded—to create those circumstances that will allow them to do so.'

This description is most apt I think as an introduction to this book because by examining their needs and satisfying them we are most likely to be able to fulfil the goals put before us—to enable them to lead their lives to the fullest extent.

---

* Whilst attending the three-yearly conference of the Association for the Scientific Study of Mental Deficiency at The Hague. The next one is this year in U.S.A. Enquiries about membership for this outstanding organization should be made to the current President, Professor A. D. Clarke, Department of Psychology, University of Hull. Membership fee, £2.50.

12   INTRODUCTION

This book describes some of the attitudes, methods and activities teachers of the severely subnormal* child might find useful in arranging his education. Teachers tend to read about the sphere of education in which they are currently involved. It seems reasonable, therefore, to write especially for those teachers in special education working with severely subnormal children.

Experienced teachers knowing children will conclude that I have adapted in the main what I feel is sound from current thought about child development and progressive education generally. I hope they will see the differences and that the teachers of these children need special training (cf. Chapter 12).

Evidence is now mounting both in the popular press and professional journals that teachers, especially those being trained, are clamouring to be taught some of the skills of their profession.† As a teacher of teachers wanting the best consumer service for children I understand this need. Somehow I do not feel it has always been satisfied even in the mainstream of teacher training. This book is based upon personal teaching experience of a very wide variety of normal and severely subnormal children and adults, and reading and thinking developed over a number of years in preparing lectures. It aims to indicate some of the skills involved in teaching severely subnormal children. I make no apologies for trying to help the teachers do a competent job with these children, for they need help and support and a continuous flow of ideas. Much of the work seen in the best schools demonstrates to the educational world at large that these children are educable and benefit from an educational approach. This was discovered between 1961 and 1971 because those training the teachers believed that most* children are capable of growth and were able to evolve their own patterns of training as the needs of the teachers and the children became apparent. This training certainly included a good measure of 'how to do the job' for the benefit of the children concerned and to give the teachers some form

---

* The Education Act 1970 did not create an eleventh category of handicap. All these children despite the fact that they could have any one, two or three additional handicaps from nine of the categories were 'lumped' together, for expedient administrative purposes it appears, in the E.S.N. category. Local authorities have discriminated them by now calling them E.S.N.(S), i.e. educationally subnormal (severe).
† Cf. Chapter 12, Specially trained teachers.
* 'Most' is linguistically intentional because there are some children in this group who because of their clinical condition deteriorate.

of professional feeling and confidence. I find it very interesting that the Open University publication *Teaching at a distance*, spells out to Tutors how to do the job.

Perhaps the difficulties, inherent in teaching severely subnormal children, highlight the absolute necessity for those training the teachers to play a continuous supportive role by constantly seeking out new ideas to *share* with their students and to encourage students to share ideas with each other. By doing this in the past we felt we played a realistic and practical part in helping the children to lead richer lives. The problem of severe subnormality was never far away from us for we worked with the children alongside the teachers during their training trying to ensure that theory and practice went hand in hand. The communication engendered meant that we were all able to develop our thinking helped by the others in the group.

In developing concepts about a structured approach to individual children, we encouraged those we trained to look at the child and understand his NEEDS rather than to look at what we thought should be taught and then design methods to teach it. Herein seems to lie the greatest difference between us and those who select a task to be taught and condition a child to respond to it in the way that is considered appropriate to the particular adults concerned. We have carefully examined some of the theories of Piaget. particularly those relating to children under seven, and tried to see the implications of these theories in practical terms for teaching severely subnormal children.

The approach I have suggested (resulting from my own teaching experiences and the collective experiences of a body of very dedicated teachers and other kinds of specialists) is an attempt to marry the best of an informal approach to education to a planned systematic structured approach to the individual child. The first, i.e. an informal approach, should take into fullest account the creative, social and emotional development of the children and this demands creative teachers. The second should be designed so that each child is assessed[22] diagnostically (initially by a specialist team), taught and then tested with precise measures of development by the teachers at say six-monthly intervals using observational and other techniques. If this pattern of teaching was not only accepted theoretically but acted upon within all schools we would be more sure than we are that each child would reach his maximum potential relative to his handicap—at any stage in his development. Where what was expected was not happening the teacher would then call upon the specialist team for further assessment.

Concepts take time to develop and it seems very relevant at this point to say that all teachers on In-Service courses (Day Conferences, Weekend Courses, Week Conferences, etc.) would benefit from being shown the skills of the educational psychologist, the physiotherapist and the speech therapist with their objective measures of development; and would benefit from courses designed to encourage their own ability to develop objectively in some aspects of their work as teachers. Too much time is often spent on courses listening to lectures. Little time is spent designing sessions where lecturer and audience become actively involved on a real problem. This happens in all courses on the creative aspects of education. I see no reason at all why it could not happen too with measurement and assessment aspects of education and with other specialist aspects of the work.

In describing a particular educational approach I know that I am not stating anything new in print.

However, I must remind the reader that the impact of educational philosophy (some of it centuries old) and the increase in knowledge about child development had not made itself felt to any large extent in this country until the beginnings of the 'sixties in schools* for the severely subnormal child. It seems necessary for this to be stated lest among my critics are those claiming that others before me have taught the same lessons about children and that therefore there is little justification for me to restate them as I have in the following pages.

If indeed I need to justify the way in which I have presented the material in this book and described an approach that is largely commonsensical, the following thinking by an American academic whose theories are becoming well known in England will perhaps reinforce my reasons for doing so in the mind of some readers at any rate. My reinforcement comes from the children themselves.

> I (Jerome Bruner) shall take it as self evident that each generation must define afresh, the nature, direction and aims of education to ensure such freedom and rationality as can be attained for a future generation. For there are changes both in circumstances and in knowledge that impose constraints on and give opportunities to the teacher in each succeeding generation. It is in this sense that education is a constant process of invention.'[30]

It will immediately become obvious to the reader that I make generalizations about the needs of severely subnormal children. In doing this I am not suggesting that all these children are the same.

---

* Called at that time Junior Training Centres, for they were the responsibility of the L.H.A.'s.

Watching them and being with them over the years I know they have general needs as all other groups of children have. I have tried to formulate these needs and to be rather specific in stating some of them for I feel I have come to understand them from this personal direct contact.

In describing their needs perhaps I will structure thought about them; perhaps teachers of other kinds of children will want to teach them. Any teacher spending some time with severely subnormal children in the ways suggested in this book and then returning to teaching normal children will do so with a sharpened awareness of the needs of all children.

Most of the chapter headings are intended to remind the reader of the educational needs of these children. The first part of the book examines the needs of the children in terms of the activities they should experience, because they are children with rights to childhood. The rest of the book concerns itself with the part played by the teacher in satisfying further needs. Repetition is unavoidable. Indeed, to some extent it is intentional (as it is when I am teaching). Repetition at all levels of learning is a vital part of teaching and this book sets out to teach. I remember Mary Lindsay (an ex H.M.I. in Special Education and Honorary Adviser to the N.A.M.H. Courses 1960-65) who was excited with us as we saw together the changes that were possible for the children saying 'The aim of the good teacher is to make things clearer for the pupil'. The practical results I saw in the classroom and the high standard of provision for learning achieved by young people during training when we tried to make things clear reinforce my belief in the possible continued usefulness of this book as it is presented.

Throughout this new edition the ideas of teachers are mentioned. I have referred to these teachers by name on many occasions. This is quite intentional for in doing so I am trying 'to share on a wider scale the professional expertise that is available and successful'[31] and that is also known to me. I also wish to develop an attitude that the practical ideas of imaginative teachers are as worthy of description and recognition by others in print as is the work of the theorists and researchers. The work of each should be recognized and valued equally.

I have also added to the suggestions made regarding research topics. These are not generally speaking addressed to professional research workers in the educational, social and nursing spheres (though perhaps they might be influenced too) but (a) to future young students taking B.Ed. and Options in Mental Handicap and (b) mature teachers on advanced post-training Diploma Courses.

INTRODUCTION

These groups are always searching out possible research subjects and, as I understand my own experience, provided their Tutors are not afraid to evaluate the system from time to time alongside their students the topics suggested will repay their efforts and serve the handicapped too.

2 To be known as persons

However hard we try to fit human beings into categories and types in order to administer their affairs and plan for their daily existence we are bound to fail. When we meet children who were considered until 1971 as 'unsuitable for education in school' we can see them as distinct personalities, if we take the trouble to look. Each has his own individual needs. We cannot place them into categories and expect that, because they are mongols, microcephalics or epileptics, they will behave in a certain way. Teachers of this group of children should rid themselves of the idea of stereotypes and think in terms of children growing, however slowly, children strangely varied in their personalities, achievements, special difficulties and needs. They must be vitally concerned with such personalities and with methods of education likely to foster growth in the best possible way.

I often talk to my friends about severely subnormal people I know. Sometimes they ask me about their progress and what they are really like. I rarely mention their clinical conditions or refer to mental ages. Instead I tell them about their personalities, their lives, their families. In this way I try to arouse interest in persons who because of their special differences and difficulties need care and understanding throughout their lives.

Jane was the first young severely subnormal child I had ever met. She was tiny for her 8 years, had fair hair and a lovely smile. She sat and mechanically thumbed the pages of a picture book while I talked to her mother. During our conversation I discovered that although Jane did not like cheese, fish and eggs, she enjoyed ice-cream, apples, oranges, boiled ham, chips and toast. She did not like soft food but she would eat those which were harder and needed biting. She always pushed away boiled carrots but had liked cabbage at one time!

The parents desperately wanted to talk about their child even to a stranger. They were proud of her achievements even though some of these revealed their own difficulties in a struggle to accept a handicapped child. 'She must have things right', 'When she sits she always pulls her skirt down', 'She does not like us to talk at the table, so we don't'. The surprise I expressed on learning that a small, severely subnormal child could so dominate her parents was quickly explained to me. Jane was told at school, 'Don't talk, eat your dinner'.

It took some time for these parents to understand that Jane was imitating the words she heard her teacher using. I had to explain that they were wrong thinking that Jane had really understood the impact of her words 'Don't talk' upon the listener. They began to see that she probably remembered these words because they were heard constantly, day after day, in the school she was attending. I was truly surprised that schools existed in which handicapped children were prevented from communicating in a natural way.

Jane's parents continued to praise her behaviour. 'She has a neat way of eating', 'She will not pick up anything from the floor'. It soon became obvious that they tried to shield her from all considered sources of danger. 'We never give her water because of the germs', 'We sometimes boil it for her if she is ill', 'We never let her eat sweets because they might damage her teeth', 'The type of children we would like her to play with have left the district', 'We don't let her into the street for the children are very rough and noisy and children can be very vicious', 'She would go up the stairs on her own now but we don't allow her. We are afraid really'.

After living for eight years in such a frightened and restricting environment it was no wonder that Jane was unable to unwrap sweets, could not use the stairs to go to bed, could not play with simple toys, could not dry her hands completely and had to be dressed and undressed like a baby. Her main achievement was that she had good toileting habits and rarely had 'an accident'.

However, it was a welcoming home to a visitor and a home where the parents expressed their need for advice. It was suggested that Jane should be allowed to do more for herself. Two and a half years later the results of the parents' efforts were much in evidence. Jane's mother felt much more confident that she could cope. Jane had begun to play with dolls and was washing their faces. She was drying her own hands and trying to wash her face. She could put on her gloves and hat and had started to fasten buttons. When her mother asked her to carry crockery and cutlery to and from the table and to dust she did so. Not only was she getting fun and pleasure from these activities she was also growing in confidence.

Jane's parents were much more willing to let her 'have a go'. When Jane was eight she had been prevented from using a fork lest she hurt herself. Now she was using a fork and being encouraged to spread butter on her bread with a knife. Her knowledge of words was increasing: here, mammy, baby, shoe, drink, stop it, thank you, please, no, yes, pig, were words she could say and use correctly. 'She has picked up the word 'pig' from a big girl at camp. We don't mind really because we know that she is now taking notice', her parents told me.

It was gratifying for these parents to see that a visitor to their home noticed that their child was progressing. They had the basic need of all parents to know that their child was 'coming on'. Teachers need to discover ways and means of knowing the parents and the homes of the children in their classes personally and intimately. Only in doing this can they play the fullest part possible in the process of giving support, encouragement and practical advice (perhaps throughout life) to a family with a handicapped member in it.

When we consider education for normal children we usually have some ideas about the roles they will play in the community as adults; the jobs they might do; the kind of lives they will lead. Broadly speaking this often enables educators to see more clearly the part they have to play in the whole educational process. When we come to consider the growth from birth to maturity of those who are severely subnormal we have no such picture. Their education therefore presents us with a problem, for we are not leading them through to adulthood with any certainty that they will ever play a completely independent adult part in the community.

This does not mean that education for these children needs to lack purpose. Rather does it tend to highlight the fact that the teacher's task is to see each individual's growth as a part of a continuum of stages and sub-stages, i.e. each stage leading on to the next. She has to keep in mind that she will have initial difficulty in assessing the stage reached by each child even if she is familiar with developmental processes in normal children and adolescents; unless she understands that each stage will last much longer than in the normal child, and will begin much later.

We know that the intellectual development of the severely subnormal is limited, as is their capacity for leading a completely independent adult existence. To date we do not know the full extent of the intellectual or social potential over a lifetime if continued education becomes their right as it is for all other adults. I know that very great possibilities exist for the continued emotional and social development of severely subnormal people if learning experiences are given well into adult life. The steady growth of community services for the severely subnormal in the future might ensure that such provision for learning is made increasingly possible, particularly if attention is paid to the quality of the staff.

In connection with this I am reminded of George who had weekly sessions of teaching with me for six years (1961-7) and whom I have continued to know and visit as a friend. George is a severely subnormal man in his early forties. He is a quiet, stocky chap from a sensible, comfortable, upper working class home. He attends an Adult Training Centre where he does simple contract work and enjoys some leisure pursuits.

When I consult the detailed observational records of our work together I know that development has taken place in a variety of ways. John Dewey[32] states that the child's own instincts and powers furnish the material and give the starting point for all education: 'that interests are the signs and symptoms of growing power, that they represent dawning capacities'. Such ideas seem applicable to all education whether it be of the child or the adult. Giving George experiences of all kinds, therefore, and following up his expressed interests have been the mainstay of my educational method in addition to forming a close, friendly, counselling relationship with his parents. From 1963 onwards I spent at least 20 minutes of each 2 hour teaching session talking with George as I would with a normal friend. Some of these conversations were tape-recorded. His mother listening to them attempted to imitate the technique I used (cf. page 23). The family bought a tape recorder and many hours of mother/son conversation were the result. (Transcription of some of these will appear in my next book.)

Generally speaking George's development was seen in the following ways:
(a) a growth of relationships with an ever-increasing number of people of all ages and abilities;
(b) language—growth and relevant use of vocabulary;
(c) a growing ability to express his own ideas, desires, needs and attitudes towards events and people;
(d) improvement in his self-regarding image, i.e. in confidence in his own ability and usefulness, and role in the home;
(e) increase in interests;
(f) learning some useful skills;
(g) a growth in curiosity and initiative throughout the years;
(h) increased knowledge about the world about him;
(i) increased understanding of what he has observed.

His progress was measured by the fact that his slouch became less noticeable, his face more relaxed. He will initiate a conversation and talks 'man-to-man' with his father. He also talks in a much more give-and-take manner with any children or adults he comes into contact with when he gets to know them. His taped conversations and hundreds of dated drawings have revealed a growing interest in the world around him as well as growing knowledge about other people's jobs and hobbies. They have shown me the part played by television in his learning. Some of his conversations have displayed growing critical abilities (normal in adolescents) not only about the Centre he attends but also about members of his own family. Spontaneous questions about people we know in common have shown his personal thoughts and care for others.

Here are some other achievements which George has shown and which the teacher of severely subnormal children might find interesting. Whatever age of children we teach we cannot do our job really successfully unless we know about other ages and stages of development. When we do we can place our work with a particular group of children in the context of the whole educational process.

(1) He now has some awareness of groups of objects in a practical situation, 2, 3, 4, 5 and the symbols which represent them. He still has difficulty, in spite of practice, with the symbols 4 and 5. He could recognize written numbers up to ten but he has no grasp of their numerical value after five.

(2) He knows the days of the week in relationship to each other.* At 28 he did not know these but they were taught over a period of a year by associating the name of the day with a well-known family event.

(3) He knows some of the names of the months but not all of them. Again learning is taking into account familiar events, e.g. his birthday, when the roses bloom.

(4) The language of time concepts are beginning to be established. He cannot tell the time although by 1969 he was beginning to match spontaneously the fingers of his watch when it had stopped with the fingers of the clock in the room.

(5) He learnt to recognize all the common coins.

(6) He has been taught that money has some value in terms of buying power and from time to time he makes purchases for himself. He still needs constant encouragement to use his money though he nearly always has some money on his person now. (His mother reported to me that whilst he was on holiday with a group of other severely subnormal adults he spent nothing. They were not encouraged to spend money by those in charge. Their initiative was also discouraged by well-meaning adults who provided each member of the party with two presents to bring home.) George is able to remember at least four items of shopping and bring them

---

* In 1974 when I was checking if he knew when Tuesday came, he said 'before Wednesday'. This was when he registered for a Further Education class.

correctly.
(7) He practises year by year to tell his current age. He has to be reminded. Part of the teacher's task should be to help her pupils with this.
(8) He has learnt the language of his collar and shoe size.
(9) In spite of weekly practice and a variety of methods he has not succeeded in learning to recognize consistently his full name or to write his first name. He knows that the writing on his identity bracelet is his name. To my knowledge he has never referred to it spontaneously in order to copy his name.
(10) He has improved his ability to copy and has made use of this ability to send an ever-increasing number of Christmas cards to friends and relations. Spacing of words still needs practice. If told to 'leave some white paper' he does so. It appears that he copies the size of the words of the copy. If it is large his copy will be large, if small the writing will be small. It is interesting to know that when he recently went away for the weekend with a group of students he asked to send a postcard to his girl friend. He was helped to do so.
(11) He learnt to fill and use a simple box camera successfully with the minimum of help.
(12) He can see when a job needs doing and initiates his own part in it without being asked, e.g. moving a mound of sand from the drive to a more suitable place in the garden.
(13) He understands and can give the answer to riddles like 'Why did the chicken cross the road? Why did the fireman wear red braces?'
(14) He can use a record player and knows the records he wants.
(15) Under the able supervision of his father, whose hobbies are carpentry and gardening, he can use tools skilfully and purposefully.
(16) He arrived at the point of asking his teacher to take him to the Do-It-Yourself Exhibition (1968). At an appropriate moment during the visit he asked her if she would like a drink of tea.
(17) He has enjoyed a game of miniature golf and getting the ball into a hole. His enjoyment was in the skill involved in aiming correctly and not in competing with a partner.
(18) His 'Draw-a-man' score of spontaneous drawings was $5\frac{1}{2}$ in 1961 and $8\frac{1}{2}$ years in 1967. He was encouraged to draw throughout the six years of teaching for it was an excellent method of communicating his ideas about the world around him. At no time did he receive instruction about how to draw. He began to copy complicated drawings of machinery and the inside of car engines in 1967.
(19) During 1964 and after three years of teaching, spontaneous

copying of words from magazine headings was observed from time to time at the top of his own drawings. This indicated that he could sometimes recognize and use words from a source outside the immediate teaching situation.

(20) He now takes off his cap quite naturally when entering a house or theatre.

(21) On one occasion he missed the Centre bus, boarded a bus going in the correct direction, managed to gain the support of a passenger in paying his fare, got off at the terminus in the centre of the city and by asking a number of people finally made his way to the Centre, some two miles away from the town. It took him nearly two hours to do the journey, but he succeeded.

George finding his own way to the Adult Training Centre (1965)

George   I crossed the road, the Zebra Crossing.
Mother   Did you go on the 22 bus first?
G.   Yes.
M.   You got the bus?
G.   I got the North Western bus up to Wilmslow Road, then I saw Graham across the road, Graham—across the road, then I thought I would go back for my trunks.
M.   You decided to come back then?
G.   Yes.
M.   Speak up and tell me.
G.   I decided to come back.
M.   And yet you knew that your bus was due, that was rather silly wasn't it?
G.   Well yes but I did it in the end.
M.   What did you do then? You came back here?
G.   Yes I came back here.
M.   And where was I? Did you look for me?
G.   You were in the passage and I passed you. I went out of the front door (the what's it's name) the back door and closed the gate after me. (long pause)
M.   Carry on. Go on.
G.   Then I walked down there.
M.   Did you get the 22 bus again?
G.   No, I got a bus to Piccadilly.
M.   You got a bus to Piccadilly?
G.   Yes.
M.   Speak up and say it plainly.
G.   I got a bus to Piccadilly, where the shelter is.
M.   And what about money?
G.   I got a man to help me.
M.   You got a man to help you?
G.   Yes.
M.   And how much fare did you pay?
G.   He gave me a shilling.

M. He gave you a shilling?
G. Yes.
M. The man did?
G. Yes. He told me to get a bus. Cross the zebra crossing again and come back again and wait where that shelter is on Wilmslow Road.
M. On Wilmslow Road?
G. On Wilmslow Road, and I shown him my address on my wallet.
M. Speak up George.
G. I shown him my wallet with my address in and then I went upstairs.
M. You went on top of the bus, speak up.
G. I went on top of the bus.
M. And then when you got to Piccadilly what did you do?
G. I got off. Then crossed over.
M. Well, how did you get to the Centre from there?
G. I asked people.
M. Yes, you asked people.
G. Yes, and they directed me and I got to the Centre and went to the baths after that.
M. Did you walk to the Centre from Piccadilly?
G. Yes.
M. Why did you walk?
G. Well, to do my exercise and to enjoy my legs to do the exercise.
M. What time did you get to the Centre, were you late?
G. No I didn't go to the Centre, I went straight to the baths after that.
M. You went straight to the baths?
G. I went straight to the baths.
M. Because you knew they were there?
G. Yes. Norman told me to go on.
M. He told you to go on? Oo and what did Mr. --- say when you told him?
G. I didn't see him.
M. Well who did you tell? Did you tell anyone at the Centre what you had done?
G. Tommy told Mr. --- Tommy --- (that boy). He told Mr. --- .
M. And what did he say? What did he say?
G. He marked me in.
(This is an exactly-as-taped conversation)

(22) He has a 10 minute conversation with me on the telephone each Sunday morning (1974). He does not dial the call. A friendly neighbour does it for him.

Conversations and explanations
(We must be patient enough to explain things to them and tell them about our lives and the people we know). The following topics were suggested by him:
(a) work—making a card table, folding plastic bags, comparing and discussing the colours of bags for dustbins, gardeners and pedal bins in the home. Putting the label round 2-4 sheets of wrapping paper;
(b) gardening—weeding, greenfly (particularly appropriate this

year) and how they are born;
(c) his proposed holiday with three other 'boys' (I managed at one time to rid George of using the word boy when he was referring to the men at work. This usage of the word 'boy' by the staffs of adult centres is very common. I should imagine this is the reason for his still using the word.); what he will take with him; shopping for new clothes;
(d) making models/scrapbooks (quite spontaneously) for a young friend (aged 13 years);
(e) looking after his father (when he was 70) for a week when he sprained his ankle. George looked after the house and did the shopping;
(f) the importance of George asking questions of people if he doesn't know something. He wanted me to tell him if there were four pieces of paper in the pack he was making up at work. 'Are there four' I told him to ask the supervisor. On another occasion he wanted to know something about a film he had seen on T.V. 'I haven't grasped it,' he said, knowing I would try to explain (they need to learn who will explain things to them);
(g) machinery in a factory;
(h) money values—what I want when he comes home from his holiday. We discussed a tin of Nivea cream for 15p—the coins he would need, the place where he would find the cream, the look of the tin. He associated this conversation with something that had happened to him at least six years ago. It was when he went to the cinema alone. I had taught him the names of the old coins and told him and shown him what he would need to give to the lady in the box office. When he finally arrived at the box offie the attendant knew him and let him in FREE! He had no opportunity to use what he had learnt. He did not bring the present but a few months later (when I called for him to take him to the Christmas Fair at the Adult Training Centre) he handed me a parcel wrapped in special paper. It was a wooden stand. He had made it himself to display holiday postcards. Later on at the fair he showed me the minute wooden hut he had made himself with matchsticks, and two small boats, one started by the instructor, which he completed, the other made entirely alone by him. These were on a model designed as a game—The Treasure Hunt (meaningful activity);
(i) what he meant by the word 'traffic'. He told me it included 'cars, lorries, etc.' Eight months ago when I asked him a similar question as we were going along in my car and approaching

traffic lights, he said 'traffic lights.' I then explained to him the meaning of the word;

(j) discussing the police on their motorbikes when they go in front of wide vehicles. I asked George why he thought they were there—his answer 'Keeping guard of it all the time.' I then tried to explain the width/danger to other cars and how their presence encourages these cars to slow down;

(k) when we were talking about the friends from the centre that he is going away with, he mentioned the name of one. 'He swears a lot.' When I asked why he thought he did, he answered 'He's got no Dad,' 'Just the way he's made;'

(l) George has talked to me about those 'handicapped people on the bus.' He has not in any way indicated yet that he identifies with these. I have started talking to him about people who are handicapped and who live in a hospital because they have no families. I introduced the topic by telling him about a man I had met whilst shopping, who remembered me, and I him, from ten years ago (he was a mongol man of about 40 living in a small subnormality hospital and at the time I met him he was walking in a fairly large town looking at the shops with a friend from the hospital);

(23) He has expressed (1973-4) a desire to visit his relatives by himself and to go to church. But now he is a companion to his father.

(24) He has had to come to terms with the death of his mother and the loss of his brother to another country. Here there is an opportunity to get him to use his language, for he could send a tape/letter.

(25) He asks me how people (we know in common) are. Sometimes this is quite specific, e.g. how is Lionel's (my husband) leg?

(26) I have started talking to him about seeing clearly. He is in his forties now. It seems important that amongst the needs of the adult severely subnormal someone should ensure a regular check-up on eyes for 'ageing sight.' Normal people begin to realize that something is not quite right with their eyes in their forties. They can do something about it independently. I wonder what percentage of adults over 45 in adult training centres and hospital workshops are seen to be slowing down or not attending as much to their work and are given an eye test and spectacles. Even if they do not need glasses to read they might need them for near viewing activities—even eating a meal can be more enjoyable if it can be seen clearly. Putting on 'nail polish' by the women will certainly

need the aid of glasses when ageing sight is a feature of their physical development. It is also important for those in the adult training centres to check upon teeth. George's false teeth were 'falling' when he was eating. A check-up by a new young dentist (1975) revealed that two teeth had been left in his gums by the previous dentist! These were pushing on the false teeth. As a result of my observation and reference to this to his father he will be provided with a new set of dentures in the next month or two.

Perhaps by far the most useful skill (in addition to his increase in conversational skills) that George learnt during his weekly visits was to prepare simple food for himself and for his mother (under her instructions) when she was ill. When young people such as George have to live in a hostel it seems useful for them to become independent in making something to eat and drink for themselves and others. Perhaps one of the greatest deprivations of severely subnormal adults in hospital and even in some hostels is that they rarely have the opportunity of preparing a drink or food for themselves. Instead they have always to rely upon the services of others.

Simple preparations have been carried out with George, using graded, illustrated steps. The value of making simple dishes (e.g. tea, toast, beans on toast, bacon and egg, egg sandwiches, chips) has been in their simplicity. I feel that whatever is taught to the severely subnormal adult in cookery should be simple and practical enough for him to do it finally for himself without supervision. Cooking for fun in a group can of course be a useful learning experience and one we must not underestimate. Certainly I had a lot of fun teaching George to cook and his parents were pleased that he had had such an opportunity for becoming more independent as well as useful to his family.

These descriptions of two severely subnormal people I know give only a very limited picture of the very many interesting facets involved in teaching them and knowing them. Perhaps they illustrate that learning continues to take place over a long period of time with skilful teaching and the support and interest of parents.

Footnote. George has now (1974) registered at the local College of Further Education to attend an Art Class for the handicapped. He has paid 5p for the year. He will travel with a group from the Adult Training Centre to the class. A young man living in a Working Boys' Hostel will see he gets off the bus at the right stop on the return journey home. Thirty-five out of 200 trainees are able to attend these classes. About 50 per cent of them are in the E.S.N.(M) range of intellectual ability; the others are E.S.N.(S). The criterion for having the opportunity of attending the classes is that they can get home (a) taken by parents, (b) alone.

3 Essentials for educational development

One of the greatest joys of my life is in being a teacher. The involvement and the commitment to helping a child or an adult learn always gives me happiness. At the end of my first year from College the Primary School Head for whom I worked summoned me to her desk in the hall. After thanking me for my year's work (a delightful annual custom extended to all members of staff) she remarked that she had never known a young teacher give the children so many learning experiences in real-life situations. I did so intuitively it seems to me now and not because of any intellectualized educational philosophy. I did so because I wished children to enjoy their learning and to understand. This seemed impossible if learning was confined to listening to the teacher and sitting still in large groups. Unless one made enormous efforts one could certainly never see the members of one's class as real children or understand their individual needs.

I am indebted to this Head for she gave me the clue which I have continued to ponder upon and act upon ever since—that we must never underestimate the part played by real experiences in the learning process whether this is at the child or adult level of learning. The need for first-hand experiences and constant repetition of real experiences is greater for a child who is mentally handicapped than for any other group of children I have ever known. This belief plus the ability to search out and give a wide range of experiences to children must be part of every teacher's built-in philosophy and practice, if she is going to understand these particular children.

Whichever group of children we decide to teach there are two important factors to consider before we begin. The first is the discovery of the general needs of the particular group of children we are teaching. The second is an examination of the individual's needs. The teacher of handicapped children does not differ in this respect from all other teachers but because the job of helping handicapped children is more difficult she must do her own on-the-spot research into the needs of the individuals in her care. She cannot always afford to wait for the results of scientific enquiry which might help her to assess a child's difficulties more accurately.*

---

* The Language Imitation Test compiled by Paul Berry can be easily administered by teachers and acts as a starting point for a remediation

I am not going to spend time discussing basic essentials such as love, security and the satisfaction of material needs—food, clothing. We can read about these in any well known book on child care and development. Neither shall I be spending time describing the mistakes a teacher can make if she begins to teach a child without first establishing that his sight, his hearing, his general health is right for learning.

OUTLINE OF NEEDS

(1) To be considered as children capable of growth for the most part (cf. page 12).
(2) To have freedom of choice for natural movement and activities in a specially structured environment.
(3) To receive continued praise and approval from teachers and others under the teachers' guidance; from staff seeing behaviour in terms of communication which needs to be interpreted if it is to be understood and gain a positive adult response.
(4) To have opportunities for play that is understood by the teacher.
(5) To have an immediate purposeful response to natural interests and to language.
(6) To have a special kind of teacher.
(7) To have a varied and stimulating programme of curricula activities.
(8) To have planned systematic and sustained individual teaching by the same teacher over a long period of time.
(9) To be in an educational climate where all the adults concerned work together for the benefit of the children in their care in partnership with the Head.

Since the publication of this book in 1971 a useful, supportive book for teachers, this time from Poland,[33] is in circulation in England (1974). Prepared and printed with financial support of a research grant from the Social and Rehabilitation Service, Department of Health, Education and Welfare, Washington, D.C., it describes the needs of severely and profoundly retarded children as seen by a group of practically involved research workers over a period of three years.

---

programme. Papers describing the use of this test and some findings are also available from The Hester Adrian Centre, Manchester. John Presland, Deputy Educational Psychologist, Birmingham, has also compiled an interesting Comprehension Test (below 1 year to 5 +) for teachers to use. The test was tried out in a Language Survey (organized by me in cooperation with the inviting authority staff) and carried out in a Mental Subnormality Hospital in November 1973.

The editor sent me a copy of this book for comment. The relevance of the findings might be usefully included at this point in this present edition for there is still so little in educational literature about the mentally handicapped that is of use to promote the thinking of teachers.

'The needs of the severely retarded child do not differ from those of any other child but they do differ in THE WAY THEY ARE REALIZED.' Nothing could be nearer the truth as so many of us have discovered. These needs are described by the editor in the following terms:

'Stable, consistent and affectionate ties with persons tending the child.
Stability and predictability in the external world.
Self-sufficiency in daily life even though they will rarely become fully independent.
To steer one's own behaviour in a certain, however restricted, area.
To be cherished and to feel a sense of belonging to someone.
To understand and be understood.
To be noticed in a non-evaluative (neither injunction nor interdiction) manner from time to time throughout the day.
To be among other children.
Feeling of personal worth and possession of a social role.
Socialization of drive needs; sexual needs (cf. Chapter on Adolescence).
Achievement of psychomotor development.
To display aggressive and defensive behaviour.
To make use of all the sensory modalities—to explore.'

I was particularly happy with the emphasis on the emotional/social/personal aspects of development in examining the needs of these children. So very often it is the intellectual part of development that parents, teachers and psychologists are more concerned with, sometimes to the detriment of the happiness and mental health of the child.

To return then to my own points about the general needs of these children. Let me expand my ideas about these for you in the way that I have come to understand them.

To be considered as children
Many of you will be surprised to see that one of the severely subnormal child's needs is to be seen as a child. By this I mean that they first of all must have the same opportunities as normal children to show what they can do, how they can learn, how far they can get before we think of their difficulties (or clinical types) in any special

way. We may spend so much time giving them standardized tests revealing specific difficulties (though these are essential too from time to time), trying out our own skills relating to what we think is meant by specific techniques, and indulging in presenting the children with a watered-down version of a traditional school curriculum (reading, writing and sums), that we fail to provide them with exciting and appropriate activities and experiences with lively and understanding teachers. We may also be thinking so much about the possible limited future of the child when he reaches adulthood, and in preparing him to live this life that we deny him the possibility of living wholly through each stage of childhood.

The teachers' inability to see all of these children as children is often revealed in a number of ways:

(1) A tendency to discuss them in their presence in terms of their mental, medical, clinical conditions.

(2) Not often using the children's names to gain their attention or when talking to them.

(3) An exaggerated concern for social competence and a narrow interpretation of social education generally. No one working with handicapped children can overestimate the importance of making sure that the children become independent in a number of social skills, toileting, washing, dressing, feeding themselves as soon as possible—more surveys in progressive schools might indicate more clearly to the teacher the part played by maturity, opportunity, experience and motivaton in gaining these skills. Then she will be free to consider other aspects of a handicapped child's personality: his ideas, creations, inventiveness, curiosity, the expression of his own needs and desires, his enjoyment of people who are interested in him, his memory for people.

(4) Acceptance of observed behaviour because he is mentally handicapped rather than because he is indulged in home or school, mismanaged in either of these places, in need of an eye, dental, medical inspection, emotionally disturbed or from a socially deprived home.

(5) The tendency to give withdrawn, profoundly handicapped children less systematic planned attention (particularly if their noses are dirty) because 'they won't improve anyway, so what is the use.' Such thinking means that little thought has been given to the possibility that the quality of life for that child would be enhanced if he gained his share of attention.

Opportunities for spontaneous movement

If one considers the normal child's opportunities for spontaneous movement during the first five years of life we know that his general physical skills, his growing feelings of confidence and independence as well as much of his learning, takes place because he is allowed freedom of movement within a reasonably wide but safe radius of his home. The fortunate child not only has his own house, the garden, and perhaps a neighbour's house and garden in which to move about, but as he is approaching his fourth/fifth year he is allowed to go along to the shops nearby his home. It is precisely these years, i.e. from the early months to six or seven years in terms of global mental levels (though what this means precisely cannot really be explained) which mainly concerns us in teaching severely subnormal children.

I have decided to spend some time discussing this matter of movement for although it is most important for all children, and severely subnormal children in particular, this is the need least recognized and encouraged by the teachers of these children. A parallel in the field of the general stream of education comes to mind in the way in which the majority of teachers of children in the 7-11 year range have in the past ten to fifteen years begun to recognize that all children need to talk about their activities (sometimes, as we know, incessantly) and that at certain stages in their development they are considered deprived if they are required to listen to the teacher for long periods of time in silence.

Qualified teachers of young children and progressive teachers of first and middle year school children have always recognized the need of children to move about in school finding their own materials, carrying on naturally with their own activities and forming relationships with other children and adults in their own way. Teachers of severely subnormal children have an added difficulty. The children are often normal in their physical growth (height, weight) and so it is not always easy for their teachers to accept that because of their mental levels they must still have opportunities, often only afforded to much younger children, to move about an interesting and stimulating environment in a natural and spontaneous fashion. I can never understand this completely, for the heavy, sluggish adolescent in the school is a familiar sight. Keeping him (and more often her) on the move in purposeful activity in order to combat what appears to be a natural tendency to 'sit' at this stage needs careful consideration so that even physical development does not suffer.

Many, many handicapped children are still being deprived daily of working through even the basic stages of their gross motor and intellectual development because they are being encouraged to remain at sedentary tasks, by the provision of equipment and activities doing little else but encouraging sitting down and being quiet all day long. The severely subnormal child's desire (once motivated) to move about should not be looked upon as just a desire to play, naughtiness, lack of attention, lack of concentration and lack of desire to learn. Rather should it be seen as a sign of his natural needs, of his level of development and often as showing his curiosity, initiative and growing independence. Of course movement which is disruptive may be just as much an indication of boredom and insufficient stimulus at the right level as it is with normal children. Whilst it is well known that children exist who are hyperactive because of some pathological cause, their number in the schools at any rate is small. I often wonder when hearing teachers talk about ALL the hyperactive children they have in their class if they are in fact providing sufficient opportunity for the child's natural movement and spontaneous involvement with objects and materials within a very full but well-arranged environment of activities.

Teachers of severely subnormal children as well as others who care for them often try to prove to themselves that this need should not be met. Corridors are lifeless and a child is often not to be seen. It is rare to see children working in the corridors. Movement from one class to another is not encouraged and it is not unknown for children to be tied into chairs. I can fully understand the teachers' anxiety with some of the children I have met but I cannot understand the approach to the problem—at least a very long rein could be utilized to ensure safety of the child and the teacher's peace of mind where there were insufficient helpers. I remember reading that this idea was found useful by two parents taking their young children on a boat journey. In talking about this problem a friend suggested an extra large play-pen with a built-in floor for use from time to time. The danger here of course might lie in the teacher not providing enough for the child to do in a restricted area and forgetting that the child needs to be in the larger part of the classroom or school for some part of the day at least. As I write I am reminded of a child in a special care unit where the teacher (M. Baker) contains a particular child in a small play-pen for some periods of time each day. The child is surrounded by toys and interesting objects dangling on string. He certainly is well provided with opportunities for sensory motor development, particularly in view of the fact that this teacher has paid some attention to positioning the child to give him maximum opportunities to learn. Sometimes teachers claim that if the children are moving around they might hurt themselves or other children. They say that the children are not working and that they are wasting time unless doing something at their tables. The teachers themselves so very often have the need to imitate the image of the teacher of their own school days or the 'real' teacher of normal or older children. They feel that a teacher is one who stands at the front of the class and teaches from that position; that a teacher is only teaching when she is talking to the children as a group and commanding their attention by promises, threats, rewards, punishments or even by interesting visual aids; that the children will only learn to be members of a group if they are taught as a group.

Clearly there is a time when the children should come together as a group for a common purpose—singing together, playing instruments experimentally, making a boat or performing a story, for these experiences in the hands of the understanding, skilled teacher will foster feelings of belonging. A great deal of the teacher's work will still nevertheless concern itself with the individual child and specially selected groups of two/three. In order to provide herself with the opportunity to carry out this part of her work she must provide a wide variety of activities and encourage the children to move amongst them to get something for themselves to do. I have seen some excellent very large group work in drama where children 4-16 years old have worked together. It has concerned itself with movement and doing rather than listening to a teacher.[34]

Apathy, rigidity, restless behaviour, lack of curiosity and initiative are qualities often attributed to these children. As their teachers we need to take care that they are not features WE force upon them by our particular needs and forms of management.

It is more interesting to see handicapped children busily employed in individual, representative and dramatic play and in creative pursuits than to see a teacher trying to 'force' what she thinks they need to learn often using formal group methods. How interesting and exciting to be with them on their journeys if one is curious and thinking about the responses they show one and how to use these to encourage the child's learning process. One is never in doubt about their desire to be involved in something interesting if one reminds oneself that it is the emotional and social development of the children which should interest the teacher and please her as much as their intellectual development. Happiness for both teacher and child is then the keynote. One is never in doubt about their interest and liking for people, fleeting or sustained, according to their age and individual levels of development.

Enforced restriction of movement is no longer a feature of present-day progressive schools or in adequately-staffed Hospital schools. Restriction of movement in a variety of other ways is still sufficiently common to warrant some time being spent on spontaneous movement. I have heard quite recently of 'teaching methods' being used where the child is firmly directed all the time to the activities available in the classroom. In such a situation one can only presume that the teacher has a mistaken view that these children cannot become self-motivated or self-directed; that they have not the same need for interaction with other children and adults as part of their education. There is a small minority of severely subnormal children who perhaps might need more direction than the rest, but the evidence as I have seen it suggests that the majority have the urge to do like all other children.

If a teacher lacks the confidence to allow a severely subnormal child to move about freely she has not understood the theory underlying the statement that children learn through their own actions upon objects. When children explore their environment they are discovering the kind and properties of objects from a variety of positions in space.* They will also be discovering the kinds of activities going on around them and the activities of the people within that environment. They will learn that the ladies in that room are making the dinner; that if you take the tarts made in the classroom to them they will put them in an oven/stove; that that man is responsible for keeping the school warm. Other children will be seen busily engaged on their activities and will be imitated later when the opportunity is ripe and the stage for doing whatever they have assimilated has arrived.

Perhaps the work of Woodward in which she applied some of Piaget's theories to severely subnormal children and found that the sequence of their intellectual development was the same as that of normal children is still the best reinforcer for experienced teachers—this being so I see little reason for methods which can only be depriving the children of necessary learning experiences in a normalized environment, i.e. like other young children.

---

* We need to remember to change the position of children who cannot move themselves from time to time during a day so that they can see objects and people from a variety of angles. When working with young blind children especially we need to help them to become aware of their bodies and the bodies of those around them by letting them sit on our bodies in a lying position. Consider the novelty to such a child when she stretches out her hand and finds hair, a mouth in another place. If the teacher turns over and lets the child sit on her back yet another kind of experience will be the result, including different vibrations from the body when she speaks.

Janice Sinson[35] in the Leeds Mencap Nursery (cf. page 45) found in measuring a number of developmental areas of pre-school children 'superior results in mobility and agility. It seemed to be a direct result of the opportunity for free play all morning with a wide variety of toys, climbing and pedalling apparatus.'

Perhaps teachers have difficulty in giving the children what they need for they often assume that the body and the mind develop at the same rate. What they have to keep on reminding themselves is that this is not so. They have to realize (and learning about child development is not easy for young teachers unless practice and theory are programmed to make sense during training)* that although the sequence of intellectual development in some respects is perhaps the same as for normal children the limit reached will be different and the children will remain at each stage or substage for a longer period of time. This tendency to remain at a particular intellectual level for a long time without anything appearing to happen as a result of constant and continuous intervention constitutes a major job hazard for the teacher of these children and this is why they need continual positive support. Some may become anxious and worry about their ability to teach. The brighter the children appear the more anxious might the teacher become because it would seem that that child should be doing more. Realistic more than idealistic short-term objectives need to catch the teacher's attention if she is to gain full job satisfaction. As I see it all workers in special education need constant support and reinforcement. *They* need to be noticed. *They* need praise for what has been achieved and only when children's needs are being denied, criticism for what still needs to be done. Those working with the most profoundly handicapped children perhaps need the most support because of the degree of involvement and commitment it entails if the job is to be carried out with the minimum of frustration and fatigue. A feature of frustration that might appear in the lives of teachers in the future is that some administrator/organizer will say that after a given period of time a teacher working with these children should teach other kinds of children for their own 'good'. I should like to add that where these ideas exist there seems to be a complete implied lack of sensitivity about the problems inherent in mental subnormality and negative non-accepting attitudes towards those who are mentally handicapped. Of course I should also like to add that some teachers finding an easy niche might be eased out of the work

---

* If as much attention were given to programming and structuring the information given to young teachers in training as is given by academics to learning in children, the children would indeed be better served.

not for their benefit but for the children's. Perhaps teachers in all spheres of education need a change from time to time. However, I hope that no one will begin to lay down 'what is good' for the individual teacher—her own needs and interests should always dictate the situation unless the learners are suffering.

To return then to Piaget—constant reference to the original observations in his books rather than to the theory will give teachers a wealth of material to adapt to their needs to devise the content of an educational approach. Teachers working with pre-school children and older profoundly handicapped children will find his *The Origins of Intelligence in the Child*[36] particularly useful. My original list of activities given from 1967 onwards to students working on teaching practice with these particular groups of children was compiled from careful examination of the records in the first 150 pages. In writing out the list of activities and materials my own ideas for other activities were inserted. A paper[37] by Carrol, a psychologist, in 1972 to a group of teachers in a Conference in Swansea indicated that this approach, i.e. referring to Piaget and improvising might be useful for psychologists in terms of assessment.

Teachers working with children in the so-termed intuitive and pre-operational stages of intellectual development (and this might mean with the severely subnormal all their lives in view of the absence of longitudinal studies and therefore of collected knowledge to the contrary) will not find as much help as for the earlier stages, for as Gillham says[38] in the first number of *Special Education/Forward Trends*, 'Piaget's theories give little insight into the processes of change in language development during the intuitive stage'. As I see it, teachers have to do an enormous amount of discovering for themselves if they are to feel the continuity, the gaps in knowledge about the contents of learning at this stage. I should like to suggest that they make a serious observational study of the associations the children make between objects, between objects and events, and objects and people. There is also a strong case for them to develop sufficient confidence to share their observed knowledge with colleagues in writing in view of the usual time lag between the discoveries of the research workers and the publication/interpretation of their work.

The teacher's part in promoting sound development is to ensure that the experiences planned for the children increase in number, quality, complexity—experiences that 'do not depend upon reward that lies outside the activity it impels.'[30]

Another trend I fear might increase as more qualified teachers without special training (or even well-programmed compulsory In-Service training) enter this field of education is a tendency to spend too much time on sedentary pre-reading and reading activities (sometimes using teaching machines) and activities designed to enable children to count by rote and learn their colours (features of past curriculum work that some of us have been striving to change attitudes about for a long time). The provision of such activities seems to suggest that the teacher is more concerned with her own ability to teach (sometimes tricks) rather than querying the value of what she is teaching the child or what he needs. Susan Isaacs ideas in the 'thirties are as fresh and apt in their message now as they were then, particularly when we think of education and severely subnormal children today, for she wrote: 'We have been content to apply our new psychological knowledge of how the child learns to the ways of getting him to learn old things. We have not used it to enrich our understanding of what he needs to learn nor of what experiences the school should bring to him.[39]

Lest teachers and others gain the impression that I am contending these activities, or activities with the child sitting quietly at his table with the teacher teaching should not be part of the curriculum content for some of the children, I must quickly add that if they are appropriate, enjoyable, planned for the potential stage of the child, this is not so (or where the findings of research workers in the future indicate that neither the time of the child nor the teacher is being wasted). I fear only that the proportion of time spent on such activities by some teachers, because they are easier and less trouble, might militate against the acquisition of expressive language. It is my contention that responsive people and planned situations enabling the child to move around in his environment as he needs are more likely to stimulate language and the growth of vocabulary and, what is perhaps even more important, the use of language in his contacts with others.*

This will be particularly so if equipment (sometimes improvised) is readily available and designed to motivate purposeful movement. As Kephart[40] states 'information develops only from an active engagement of the WHOLE organism in response to impingements of the environment and not through the sense organs alone. Any such engagement is dependent upon movement by the organism, overt in the early stages, covert in the more advanced stages.'

---

* One young student working in a Special Care Unit one day gave a child an egg whisk, a bowl, water and soap powder. She encouraged him and helped him to whisk up the water. 'Ice-cream' was the child's response. The same piece of equipment in a class of older children brought forth the response 'machine gun' as it was being used in play.

Reasons for spontaneous movement

When children move about the classroom, corridors and other classrooms in the school generally they will discover objects of all kinds. When they handle and touch these objects they are helped to focus attention upon their outstanding features for, as Piaget[41] tells us, 'It is not until they (children of normal intelligence) are about six years or over that they can explore systematically with eyes alone.'

One method of telling stories to the mentally handicapped is described[42] by my colleague Joan Fitch in her booklet *Story Telling for Slow Learners*. It was a method arising out of the need to help young teachers understand in as many ways as possible the importance of providing three-dimensional objects for the children. Whenever a story was to be told we suggested that the child should have the real object or a representation of it (a toy/picture) to accompany the story. Sometimes the students would let the children pass round the object whilst the story was in progress. Others would let the children pass the object round the group as it were and then place it in a position easily seen by all the children whilst the story was being told.* If the findings of research workers are to be taken notice of we certainly need to examine this particular combination of sensory modalities more thoroughly. I was interested to note that twenty minutes or so after telling Susan (a blind mentally handicapped child of $3\frac{1}{2}$ years) that what she was holding was a cup, she said 'tup' when she held it again in exploratory play. Ball play over a six months' period to encourage Susan to move about (on her bottom) was accompanied by the words ball, bowl, case (because we played with the balls in these items and Susan was put in them as well) and was followed by Susan saying her first word attached to an object 'ball' when presented with an orange—further to this she discovered the bowl on the floor and said 'bowl.' This is an interesting example to set us thinking about the number of modalities we can present material to be learnt in at any one time to a mentally retarded child (cf. page 59).

---

* Students on courses of teacher training are often asked to compile their own story books—sometimes creating the stories themselves—sometimes just collecting them from a wide variety of sources. Students training to be teachers of the mentally handicapped in Northern Ireland (now in the Ulster Polytechnic) have been most fortunate. Not only have they made up their own stories but their Principal lecturer, Mr. G. Begley, has edited some of them and had them duplicated in a bound cover. The book is called *An Anthology of Poems, Playlets and Stories for the Special Care Classroom*. Special Care is a term covering all the mentally handicapped in Northern Ireland.

Enquire about these so that your children can continue to enjoy story time.

To a sighted child, two modalities (hearing and sight) are there whether the child wills it or not unless we engineer a situation where one is cut out, i.e. we blindfold the child.

Another reason which completely justifies movement as far as I can see is that the child can get really close to a teacher who is talking. If she then remembers to face the child and position herself so that she is at his eye level and with her face towards the light the child can then more easily see and consequently imitate the lip, mouth and facial movements she makes. He can also touch his teacher's face and throat and feel the muscles and the mechanisms which are used in speech.

When one visits a school where the children have had daily opportunities for spontaneous activity on large physical education apparatus over a period of 4/5 years in addition to opportunities for natural purposeful movement throughout the day, one is impressed by the ease of movement, the grace, the confidence and pride in physical achievement that is present. One forgets for the moment that the children are so handicapped. One is almost certain too that the use of their language skills and their ability to represent their experiences graphically are in fact in advance of those children who do not have such opportunities. Research by specialists in physical education interested in language development is needed to reinforce the research confirming this impression.

When the children are allowed to move about the classrooms and the school they can find something/someone which interests them and captures their attention. They become confident in finding materials for themselves. They are also able to display their own initiative and show what ideas they have. At the same time the teacher has an opportunity to give purposeful instructions which she has thought about for a particular child in order to enrich his understanding of words and vocabulary. 'Put the paper on the top shelf' might have to be repeated many, many times with speech and the action going together before the child learns where the top shelf is situated. 'The paint brushes go in the cupboard' might bring no immediate response from some children. Many of our instructions might indeed not be understood until opportunities occur for hearing these words repeatedly in association with the use of the objects and the actions. If the handicapped child is never given such instructions but has the materials, the games and the 'sense' training apparatus placed before him as he sits obediently and passively at his table, a wealth of opportunity for learning has been lost. At the best he is not being a trouble and this is ver easy; at the worst he is not learning.

When children explore their environment they are discovering the kind and look of objects from a variety of positions in space.* They are also discovering the kind of activities going on around them and the activities of the people within this environment.

It will be many years before most severely subnormal children will be going alone into the roads and streets. For some this will be never. Consider therefore the interesting things they can let their minds dwell upon within an interesting but **safe** environment; that cupboard doors and doors open and close in different ways and make different noises, that pipes are hot, that taps turn on and off, that water overflows from a bowl if the tap is left running.

As previously stated they will learn that the ladies in that room are making the dinner; that if you take the tarts made in the classroom to them they will put them in the oven; that that man is responsible for keeping the school warm; that the light goes on and off if a switch is pressed; that something made of pottery breaks if we drop it; that one side of a knife is sharp and cuts. Other children will be seen busily engaged with their activities and will be copied by the viewers when the stage and opportunity is ripe.

To the careful observer 'looking' seems to play an important part in the learning of normal children. It is the same with severely subnormal children. One has only to notice what an apparently aimless child is looking at and remember this later to see how he uses what he has seen. This of course really should suggest the importance of always having something interesting to look at; something going on around the children all the time.

Social development with all its implications for language and adaptability to others is an aspect of the education of severely subnormal children which will be discussed later. Nevertheless in emphasizing that teachers need to allow and indeed to stimulate movement they must take into account the part this can play in affording the children plenty of opportunities to interact with all the

---

* It must be emphasized that we need to remember to change the position of children who cannot move themselves from time to time during the day so that they see objects and people from a variety of angles. However handicapped the child there should be a continuous attempt by the teacher to motivate movement.

Leacroft School S.C.U., Manchester has a (120 cm, 4 ft.) high platform in one corner of the room. (The idea of having it belonged to Janet Taylor.) It was made by a father. It is cushioned with foam and an appropriate seat for the individual child. It is fenced all round. Children placed at this height have yet another view of the world around them.

other children and adults in their own group and later with all the other groups in the school.

Lunzer and Hulme[43] discovered that the play of severely subnormal children resembled the play of younger normal children of like mental age. Their research certainly needs to be repeated for there is much more understanding of the meaning of play in learning by the teachers of these children in the past decade. Consequently the children have appeared to play more imaginatively, more concentratedly. I have seen solitary play, parallel play, play in two's and small groups, role play, representational play (when a piece of wood becomes a gun, when a stick becomes first a golf club hitting imaginary balls and then a billiard cue). Such activity wherever I saw it had not happened by chance I am sure, but because the children had had freedom to move about in a planned environment over a number of years and were taught by teachers understanding this basic need.

4 *Pre-school education*

THE VERY YOUNG SEVERELY SUBNORMAL CHILD

If we consider young mentally handicapped children as a group we shall be thinking of them from the first year of life up to about seven or eight years of age. At least this is how I think of them for so many of them in the upper age ranges mentioned are like little nursery school children to look at. Physically some of them will be like babies when we first meet them whatever their chronological age. Some of them develop through the toddler stage to the 'Oh yes, he's a real boy/real young lady' stage of physical development. Some in the first school years will look like normal 5–6-year-olds and will grow as normal children.* Others will remain physically young throughout their lives. I am reminded here of Raymond, 18 years of age, who was just over 60 cm (2 ft) and walked in a baby-like fashion, and Yvonne, 25, who was long and thin but only about 105 cm (3.5 ft) in height. Both of them lived in a mental subnormality hospital.

We shall have children in this group:

(1) who will die before they are five; children who might die before they reach ten. I have headed my list with this group because by and large the training we give to teachers rarely prepares them for this phenomenon. Preparation needs to help the teacher (a) to consider the effect upon the mother and father when they know they have a dying child; (b) to examine how to plan to help the mother TO BE and TO DO with her child (however handicapped) so that the memories of herself with her child when he dies will be positive for her; (c) to ensure that as far as can be judged the quality of the child's present life is maintained. Consideration of the role of FEELING in education must be uppermost in the teacher's mind in this situation.

(2) who are ambulant or non-ambulant, those who are identified at birth as mentally retarded such as mongols; children who are normal until 18 months/2 years and then because of certain viral or bacterial infections become mentally retarded. I am thinking here of conditions such as encephalitis and meningitis and very rare central nervous conditions. Children with rare conditions such as

---

* To my knowledge there is no study comparable to TANNER's in *Physical Growth and Education* in the field of the mentally handicapped.[45] A useful survey might be made.

tuberous sclerosis may very well be diagnosed by six, and whilst a third of them may remain normal in intelligence,⁴⁴ the rest as far as I can ascertain from doctors will follow a steady path of deterioration with incumbent family sadness; the implications for the educational programme, where what is prepared by the teacher has to take into consideration growth in reverse as it were, are indicated in terms of the kind of counselling such a family needs whilst they have the child at home, for he will very likely go into permanent residential care as the condition worsens.

(3) with serious sensory defects such as blindness, deafness and those handicapped to one degree or another by cerebral palsy. Many of the latter will certainly be profoundly handicapped. In the past few years there seems to be a growing number in some parts of the world with spina bifida/hydrocephaly. When spina bifida is accompanied by hydrocephaly the child is usually mentally retarded.

(4) who are disturbed sick children with bizarre behaviour patterns—the object twiddlers, the vomiters, the head bangers, the hyperkinetics. Research on how to help these particular children seems to be very fragmented. No agreement amongst workers has yet emerged. From the standpoint of the teacher this may be a comfort because it means that as she is not forced into any one approach she has an equal chance of finding successful channels of treatment as anyone. From the U.S.A. and beginning now in England opinion seems to be directed towards more scientifically oriented behaviour modification techniques of handling these children.⁴⁶ In other countries, notably Holland, some research workers seem to favour the results of a more natural normalized approach, i.e. extra attention, cuddling, family counselling, a continuous one-to-one relationship in large proportions. Teachers and other adults having contact with these children on a day-to-day basis need to keep detailed notes on the things that help them to be positive or to communicate (however distortedly) and send them (irrespective of the standard of expression in them) to share with research workers. What a fund of knowledge we would gain perhaps to the benefit of the children concerned and also to the poor, often distracted, teachers who have to cope with them. Research seems almost devoid of any longitudinal study carried out in this area by an educationally oriented research worker with the intention of helping teachers to cope more successfully. Research so often lasts for a year, perhaps two at the most, and little involvement or commitment by the worker to a problem in

practical terms seems to be the outcome. The time seems right for teachers to demand that the large amounts of money spent on research has its spin-off for them, particularly as without their involvement so many research projects could not be carried out.

When we consider such a wide variety of children, we are left in no doubt at all that we must look at each child individually. In working with them we must always be aware of the concept of profiling (as indeed with all children). It is not a new academic concept* but it is taking a long time to filter into the practical professional know-how of teachers. In assessing each child we shall find very wide discrepancies in his achievements. Janice Sinson, perhaps the first research worker to measure and describe† the progress of individual pre-school mentally handicapped children attending a progressive Mencap Nursery in Leeds, shows how by using the Mary Sheridan Scale carefully we 'might find that we are teaching a pre-school child ball games at the level of a 4-year-old in posture and large movement control whilst concentrating on a pre-language programme with that same child at a one-year-old level.'

Susan, a blind mongol child of $3\frac{1}{2}$ years with whom I am working, when assessed six months ago by the psychologist was said to have a language age of 23 months, a hand-eye coordination age of ten months and a motor age of well under a year for she is not yet walking—in fact we may have an example of specific disability in the walking area over and above the other handicaps, although within nine months of teaching she was moving around on her bottom and discovering space in the home.

Jamie assessed at the same time (a mongol child of 5 years) had a social age of about three years, language age of two and a physical age of four years.

Mary, a microcephalic child of eight living in a mental subnormality hospital, looks like a child of 6-7 years in height. She has a comprehension age of about one year. Her expressive language achievements consist of ten words and several phrases, imitations of the phrases she hears from the adults around her in the particular

---

* Professor F. Schonell was advocating it in the late 'forties. [47]

† *Assessment and Social Education of Severely Subnormal Children* in a Pre-school Unit; Paper submitted to an international Conference, Denmark, 1973, and now published in the 'Seminar Report' 1973 obtainable from Mogen Lunge Andssvageforsorgens LAERERFORENING, Kompagnistradae 32, DK 1208 Copenhagen, K.[35] Written in clear, simple English, because it was prepared for an international audience, this is a paper that should be read by all working with the mentally handicapped. Other papers in the publication are equally worthy of attention.

institution in which she happens to live.

Generally speaking these very young children need opportunities through play and simple games (often made up spontaneously by the adults concerned) to experience a wide variety of planned activities with interesting objects and materials. As far as I can see these do not always need to be special but they *do* need to be introduced relevantly.

An interesting developmental scale discovered in Stirling University by my friend and colleague Olwen Gregory* during the course of her work[19] in Glasgow (where she used it to examine the characteristics of 120 mentally handicapped children in Day Centres) seems to suggest the kind of play curriculum the teacher and the parent might be experimenting with. Two American research workers Uzgiriz and Hunt devised the scale. Based on Piagetian theory it gives the skilled imaginative and observant teacher ample structured material on which to base her teaching. It certainly formed an immediate link in my mind when I saw it, with my own list of activities (p 85) and with the way in which we had been thinking about structure in play for a long time. Its main difference lay in the presentation and of course the scientific quality of the work.[19, 48]

With Mrs. Gregory's permission I have extracted material from the scale and from her adaptation of it and interpreted masses of information in précis form to be more readily available for use by teachers and others.

---

* She is the first person in the U.K. (to my knowledge) to have used this scale for the purpose of assessing profoundly handicapped children.

ASSESSMENT OF EARLY DEVELOPMENT 0-18 months[27, 48]

UZGIRIZ AND HUNT, UNIVERSITY ILLINOIS 1966. ADAPTED OLWEN GREGORY[19]

	Extracted and Interpreted for Teachers[25]	*Toys used in each section: Gregory*
1. Looking and Permanence of objects		*8 items*
(1) Watches object through 180°	(1) –(3) Self explanatory. Vary colours, size, introduce noise in some	Red car
(2) Reaction to disappearing object		Link of pearls on gilt
(3) Finding partially hidden object	(4) Hide under 1 beaker, bowl, container, piece of cloth	Striped plastic beaker
(4) Following completely hidden object		Polystyrene beaker
(5) Finding object under superimposed objects	(5)(a) Hide under 1 of 2 beakers, bowls, etc.	Plastic margarine carton
	(a) Hide under 3 objects one on top of the other	Inside of matchbox
(6) Following object through invisible displacements (i.d.)	(b) Wrap up an item in cloth/paper and put 3 objects as in 5(a)	White cloth serviette
(7) Following object through series of i.d.	(6) Item in inside of matchbox poured out under 1 container; under 1 of 2 containers; under 1 of 3 containers	Smarties (if no reaction to toys)
	(7)(a) Sweet hidden in hand under beakers 1/2/3 left under 3; then under 3/2/1 left under 1	
	(b) Sweet left under 1 though hand goes under 1/2/3; systematic search from 3 to 1	

2. *Providing for movement with a purpose* 10 items

(1) Appearance of handwatching
(2) Achievement of visually directed grasp

Present bell in cage 6in./12in./18in. from face; to the left; to the right.

(3) Repetition of action for interesting result

Present rocking clown

(4)(a) Overcoming obstacle to reach for object

Present cart on table with transparent sheet between it and child. Show child how to fit rods on cart. Take off. Give rods to child. Remove cart out of reach to test 4(c)

(b) Letting go to get another object

(c) Using locomotion to gain object

(5) Using objects to gain object

Put ring/smartie on scarf. Note if child pulls scarf to get ring. Return scarf, lift ring up 4in. Note if child still pulls scarf.

(6) Development of representation of means.

Put cart on floor in sight of child. Pull it up vertically by string on to table. Lower but leave string without reach of child. Present necklace in plastic container (bottle). Take out. Can child put back. Present bottle knee level, floor level if necessary. Give ring without hole to stack.

Bell in wooden case
Brightly coloured cart with string and rod
Coloured rings with hole for rod
Plain wooden ring no hole
Scarf necklace, long
Plastic beaker
Transparent sheet of plastic
Rocking clown
Smarties

3. *Development of a sequence of motor/mental actions in relation to objects* *16 items*

(1) Development of mouthing
(2) Visual attention to object
(3) Simple movements towards
(4) Interest in
(5) Development of complex movements towards
(6) Development of letting go
(7) Development of ideas based on social learning and
(8) Development of social interaction
(9) Recognition and naming

(1) (2) Holds. Mouths. Brings before eyes to look at
(3) Hits, hits objects on surface, shakes, waves, hits 2 objects together
(4) Examines object
(5) Slides objects on surface, crumples stretches out towards object, tries to tear
(6) Drops objects systematically, throws objects, puts another object in it, builds with blocks, drives car on surface, makes doll walk
(7) Demonstrates drinking from a cup, wearing a necklace, hugs doll or animal, listens to musical toy
(8) Shows object to a person; points to another object in association
(9) Names object

Bell in case
Striped beaker
Six 1 inch bricks (2 yellow, 2 white, 1 red, 1 blue)
Shopping basket
Velvet mouse with sequin eyes
Transparent egg box
String
Foil
Pearl and gilt necklace
Squeaky rubber lamb
Red car
Doll, doll's hat, doll's shoes
Tambourine
Large wooden/plastic spoon

4. Development of Causality

(1)	Repetition of actions producing interesting result	Give each toy listed in turn and demonstrate. Leave toy to see response of child. Repeat action. Observe. Note down the quality of the response. Set off clown and train out of sight. Children need a great deal of experience with these causality toys. It will usually be given *with* the adult present.	Rocking musical clown Humming top Policeman on wheels (press down on hat to activate) Jointed dog on stand (press base to move dog) A train which moves when button at side pressed A jolly clown with cymbals (plunging action to set going) *Stevens* Live and learn toys, Lipstick, Pedal bin, Torch, Pull down musical box, Weebles at the Park on the swing, the roundabout
(a)	Shows interest		
(b)	Moves arms vigorously		
(c)	Repeats actions to keep objects going		
(d)	Grasps objects		
(2)	Uses the gesture of the activated object		
(3)	Starts movements involved, touches, looks for way to activate object		
(4)	Recognizes person is causing action Recognizes reason for action Searches for independent causes		
(5)	Gives to person. Explores way. Tries to activate object any way. Tries to copy.		

5. *The object in space*

(1) Development of alternate glancing at objects — Present any two of the first four toys — Large yellow rubber cube
Development of localization of a sound in an object — Present sound toys out of sight to right, left, above — Multi-coloured plastic ball
Understanding the path of a moving object/of a rapidly moving object — Roll a ball slowly behind a screen — Pearl and gilt necklace
Recognizing the reverse side of objects. — Drop plastic cubes, ball, for child — Glove puppet
 — — Squeaky toy
 — — Bell in cage
 — — Soft shaker

(2) Relationships between objects — Activate jointed dog. Hand to child upside-down with head in palm — Clown with cymbals
Container and contained (a) — Car and sloping plank, cf. Weebles walking bean — Mechanical toy
Equilibrium. Building towers — Use plastic cubes and tall containers 2(a) — Dog on stand
Understanding gravity, the fall, the detour of objects — Use cubes for building towers — Car and sloping piece of wood
Absence of familiar person — Push toy car under a long low table to emerge other end — Plastic cubes

Ask where's mummy, daddy (other familiar person).

6. *Development of imitation*

Vocal	Gestural		
Differentiation vocal from crying	Imitate familiar gesture	To gain a picture of a child's level of imitation	
Response to familiar vocal productions	Imitation of complex actions of familiar gesture	(1) immediate (2) deferred	
Imitation of familiar sound patterns (babbling)	Imitation of unfamiliar visible gestures	you need to observe	
		(a) your own movements/expressions/activities	
Imitation of unfamiliar sound patterns		(b) the movements/expressions, etc., of others	
Imitation of (a) familiar words (b) new words		(c) the life around the child (past and present)	Car up arm Face cloth Waving/banging objects Shaking a box filled with blocks Opening and closing fists Patting cheeks Walking with very large/tiny steps
Extensive imitation of words			

N.B. It is not necessary to have the same toys as listed in the third column. Presenting them in this way reminds us of the *kind of* toy to use for specific reasons.

Evaluation of usefulness of the Uzgiriz and Hunt Scale as presented

(1) It can be used as an observation scale.
(2) It helps the teacher/mother/play-helper to fix in her mind six important areas of development in the first eighteen months of life and the kind of responses to objects she might expect in the spontaneous play of the child; the kind of activities she might introduce to the child;
(3) The description of the toys used by Mrs. Gregory is given in order to focus attention on the possible function of a toy in terms of thinking about a child's intellectual development. The lists set off our own thinking and encourage us to add to the materials collected by Olwen Gregory. If as adults we copy what other skilled workers do we will create other possibilities for ourselves.
(4) One is continually hearing from teachers and others that 'they don't know where to begin with a child in terms of stimulating him.' As I see it, acquaintance with this scale negates this claim for most of the children.
(5) Teachers observing the behaviour described that is possible or stimulated by them will more easily see that the behaviour is positive. Doctors advising mothers about their children's play will certainly see that play even at this level has meaning. Teachers might formulate their own progress charts to profile the child's behaviour in each of the six series. Mrs. Gregory's own observation charts seem rather too complicated for me to use as a teacher but psychologists would find them useful.
(6) The toys in the development of causality section reminded me that it is far too common to see toys that do not move in the classrooms/play groups for young mentally handicapped children. Admittedly the toys listed are expensive and need the adult available to use them WITH the children but then it seems to me that that is what education for the young child who is handicapped is all about.
(7) The scale enables the adult to see the importance of helping the child to attend to objects—to learn to concentrate on the nature and the functions of objects. It is my impression that it might take months of working with a child using the toys as suggested allowing him to become familiar with one's voice before he spontaneously becomes interested in the face of an unfamiliar (not Mummy or Daddy) adult, over varying lengths of time. When this happens the adult needs to play little games like passing a toy between two or more adults and each giving it to the child when he looks in the face of the giving adult. Each time the child's attention should be

caught by the adult saying his name—pausing—giving a smile at the merest glance.

Adrian (3 years) took thirteen months before becoming really interested in the movements of my face. One day I observed him glance at me very quickly on four separate occasions and then turn away. On the same day he came and curled up on my knee as if to go to sleep. In that position he was able to look into my face quite easily. We played pulling faces games and a nice anticipation game. I rocked him and sang, 'Sleep, sleep sleep today, sleep sleep sleep today·' long pause, then I shouted, 'WAKE UP, WAKE UP,' and helped him up in the air. On the first occasion he was startled because it was a new game. One could feel later the anticipation as he waited to be thrown up. Adults working with these young children need to use a wide variety of anticipation games. 'Round and round the garden like a teddy bear' and 'This little piggy went to market' are good examples of the concept, but perhaps we have to make up more of our own spontaneous games of anticipation as the appropriate moment arrives. All the mechanical toys in Series 4 can be made to run along a table or low bench—the falling off (carpet necessary) provides another anticipation situation (as does a ball rolled to a child).

(8) In considering the section on the development of a sequence of motor/mental actions in relation to objects (the development of new schemas) we need to observe with a great deal of attention the number of actions in a sequence. The list of 16 items is an interesting one—a bowl, a towel and a small piece of soap added to it would enable the adult to see other levels of association in the way these were used. To quote again from Adrian—he took the man doll (Action Man) put him in the bowl and using the towel only washed and dried him (sequence of two activities). He washed different parts of the doll including his feet. Later he dried his own feet (sequence of one action). In the real situation of washing his hands after the toilet he could wash his hands himself, turning on the tap and placing the stool on which to stand near the bowl (learned sequence of activities). He could not dry his own hands. I have mentioned this addition to the equipment in order to stimulate more thinking about how we can encourage the child to extend the number of actions in a non-verbal sequence; about how, by what we provide, we can help him to form associations (cf. page 6). I should like to draw your attention to the fact that perhaps in promoting and later, evaluating holding, we should note the shape, size, texture of the object held as well as the way in which it is held and the length of time. If a toy/object is constantly thrown by the child we need to concern ourselves with the possibility of it being thrown with a different hand grasp than on a previous occasion; being thrown in a different position in space relative to the child, the furniture, the adults in the room. What I am trying to say here

is that until the child has saturated his experience in possibly thousands of permutations, holding will not be fully established. Susan has had to be encouraged over a long period to hold anything. Her response to a touched object was to reject. Balls she immediately throws away and small hard cuboid objects. Long dolls and the doll with the noisy eyes she holds for longer periods of time and bangs them against other objects in space. Paper is held also for longer periods of time and she not only shakes and waves this but she smooths parts of her body (legs) with it. Putting jam/marmite/meat paste on the edge of a cup explored by her tongue might encourage her to hold it longer and thus prepare her for holding to drink a discontinuous material by herself. The object she has held for the longest period is a torch. We think she can see light.

(9) In watching the development of looking at objects, we might have to consider that a particular child will pay attention first of all over a long period of time only to red moving objects before he is ready to move on to pay any attention to other coloured objects. We shall certainly have to experiment with some children, as Olwen Gregory did, in presenting objects at different distances away from different positions of the face.

(10) Such a scale might promote even further thinking regarding play in the early years of life by those organizing Toy Libraries* for the mentally handicapped.

One of the important aspects of development in these early years is to help the child to imitate through carefully chosen play activities. The children will need opportunities to learn how to listen to sounds of varying intensities, sound patterns of varying lengths, speeds and voice inflections, and to imitate familiar as well as unfamiliar gestures. Teachers of these young children need to be thinking of the importance of imitation in the learning process both in its immediate and deferred forms. They need to understand that imitation has to be acquired and for this to be so to realize the importance of relationship formation with a child. Pierre Janet in Piaget's book *The Child's conception of the World*[49] writes that 'imitation is due to a sort of confusion between the self and others. The sound a child hears stimulates him to make the necessary movement to continue it without the child seeing any difference between the sound that is independent of him and the sound he has produced.'

Some psychologists say that when a child imitates actions he is

---

* *Toy Library Association Address:* The Secretary, Toy Libraries Association, Sunley House, 10 Gunthorpe Street, London E1 7RW.

helping himself to reconstruct the life around him. It is also helping his emotional security for he can do what others do. Broadly speaking, the child at first imitates by chance without meaning to. Then he begins to imitate immediately what he sees and makes approximations of what he hears. Later he seems to imitate something he has seen and understood a long time afterwards—in other words the imitation is deferred. The intervals of time between the seeing/hearing and the imitating of the action(s), sounds/words should be noted carefully by the adults around the child.

When therefore we observe a mentally handicapped child beginning to imitate activities that we know he has seen (because we have performed the activities or seen them performed ourselves or have heard about them from his parents or other adults) we know that learning by imitation can begin to take place. Learning by imitation cannot take place until imitation is present. Imitation has to be learned. We therefore have to try and consider how imitation can be promoted and give the child a host of experiences to copy.

Playing a wide variety of hiding games seems to enable a child to form relationships with objects as well as with the adults concerned. They will encourage a step forward in the direction of imitation development:

(a) hiding different parts of the body (feet in shoes), covering parts of the arm, hiding the feet, the hands under bowls, boxes, cloths (opaque, lacy), covering the whole body, the child's body, the body of large toys with a blanket, taking a child's fingers, thumbs, hands, toes in your hands, letting him do the same to you;

(b) peek-a-boo games using doors, cloths, furniture, very large hats, nylon scarves. Peek-a-boo involving a number of adults and the child;

(c) hiding wound-up noisy mechanical toys under bowls. A. at $3\frac{1}{2}$ years is able to wind up the car himself. He put it under a white plastic margarine container. His look of surprise when that 'ran' across the floor was fun indeed; hiding objects (completely, partially) under cloths that are plain, patterned;

(d) passing objects through long tubes of cardboard (some having one end open only).

In, out, on, off, up, down, behind, under, over, round seem to be the words that adults have to be considering when they play with young mentally handicapped children. They need to be helping them to form the concepts of these words long before they will be speaking them themselves in imitation of our use of the word. How difficult to measure the extent of the child's real understanding of the word UP

even when he can say it.
A. said 'up' when he was lifted off the high stool and when the boot cover of my car was released and went upwards.
A. at 3 years 10 months says 'down' relevantly when stepping off the pavement.
S. (3½) says 'up' when she is on her back and comes up to a sitting position.

We need to write out all the possibilities of the use of the word 'up' (and the other spatial words); all the situations in which the word can be used; all the activities we can carry out with the toys we have, to demonstrate UP. We need to understand the importance of presenting as many experiences to the child containing the concept of 'up' in a myriad ways.

In considering how to focus the attention of nursery helpers on to using these basic spatial words on every possible occasion, particularly at a time when the child is discovering his own body in space and learning to control it, I suggested to one Headteacher that she pinned up the words written separately and boldly in black paint round the walls of the cloakroom, toilets and washrooms. In these everyday social situations there is ample opportunity in every self-help activity to help the child gain motorically some of the concepts involved in these particular words:

(Name of child) pull your pants *up&down*.
Sit *on* the toilet. Get *off* the toilet.
Press the lever *down* (to flush).
Put the seat *down*.
Pull your sock *up*. Take your sock *off*.
Put your foot *in* (the sock, the shoe).
Put your arm *in/up*.
Put your head *through* (the neck of a jumper).
The dress goes *over* your head.
Put the plug *in*. Take the plug *out*.
Turn the tap *on/off*.
Put the light *on*.

The child's name should be spoken loudly and clearly to catch his attention before the sentences are used with EMPHASIS on the important spatial word. If I heard all adults talking with this amount of awareness of the opportunity I should know that these essentials in helping a child gain concepts in motoric situations had been communicated.

To return then to the discussion about imitation, we have to observe what *we* are doing/have done with the child; what is happening around the child so that we understand and can interpret the behaviour, particularly to the family. Unless we train ourselves to think in this way we shall misinterpret much of the child's behaviour. We shall certainly not be able to build positively and structurally on what he gives.

Adrian was helping me to wash the dishes playing alongside me. He took a saucer from the rack and dropped it. The noise, the pieces on the floor were sources of interest to him. He made as if to drop another but was prevented. Several weeks later his mother found him in the kitchen very early in the morning, opening the cupboard getting the dog bowl and dropping it. Playing in the water he had been shown how to pour and scoop water. Weeks later he was observed 'pouring toy animals' and using the scooping movement to collect up the bricks. After nine months of structured play (play which built on activity to what the child gave in response to the items played with) Adrian began to hide objects himself—ball under bowl. He did this several times. I gave him the language 'Ball gone.' In the same session after playing with sunglasses he came over to me and put the glasses on to me.

Adrian at nearly 4 years is beginning to imitate more words.

Jamie at six years three months is copying (echoic) relevant words almost on demand.

Adrian at 3½ when we were playing with the dolls going to bed (reconstructing his living experiences) put the dolls on their stomachs. His mother sleeps like this. He took the doll to the 'toilet,' I held out the doll over the toilet. We did this twice. On the second occasion he bent his head to look at the doll's bottom. One day he went into the kitchen with the toy Sooty and taking the dog's towel from its hook, wiped Sooty's paws. (he had seen his mother wiping the dog's wet paws after walks in the garden.)

Jamie saw the tape recorder on the table. The switch was up. He took the tape recorder where he had seen it before, on the carpet, and put the switch down. It would only 'work' when it was on the carpet—that is to say in the same position where Jamie had always seen it work. Much more experience of the tape recorder playing in a variety of places and positions would be needed by Jamie before he would appreciate that wherever it was, if he put the switch down, it would start playing.

When we see these young children imitating activities going on around them spontaneously we shall know that they are ready for learning other behaviour through imitation. This is particularly important in learning:
    social behaviour;
    self-help skills;
    to talk.

One of the nine skills in language described in *The Illinois Test of Psycholinguistic Abilities*[50] is motor encoding. This is the ability to understand what is seen (in the test the child is presented first with a series of objects and then a series of pictures, among them a variety of musical instruments) and then to respond to the information presented in movement—pretend to drink from the cup, turn the drill handle, play the guitar, dial the telephone. As teachers of these young children we shall be concerned with all those behaviours which lead on to this more complex behavioural skill in the acquisition of language.

When we play putting on/taking off hats, glasses, scarves, necklets on the child, on ourselves, on other adults, on large dolls and teddy bears, we are creating situations where the child can see an innumerable number of actions and, when he is ready, encouraged to perform them for himself. When we pretend to eat, drink, cut food with tiny toy knives and forks (from behind a child so that he sees the action as he himself will perform it); when we pull faces in front of a mirror again from behind the child; when we play 'This is the way we clap our hands, stamp our feet, wash our face, clean our teeth, etc.,' we are building up behaviours that should result in the child's ability to encode (understand) motorically (i.e. through a motor action) in ever-increasing complexity. As I think about such play behaviour I am forced to ponder about all the various directions of movement patterns made in space by an adult with the arms and upper extremities of the body that the child will see performed in front of him and also think about the possibilities of and/or necessity for programming these in our personal preparation instead of moving in random fashion. What I am trying to say here is that in the same way that teachers have been encouraged during training to think about the complexities of their own language structure and vocabulary when talking with the mentally handicapped, perhaps they need to become more aware of what children are seeing of the body movements and gestures of the adults.

When Adrian's mother wanted him to learn to say 'down' (he could say 'up') she was surprised when lifting him up from the high stool to help him down he said 'up' as he went down.* I had noted how her shoulders and body had to go in an upward direction so that as she was saying 'down' Adrian saw 'up' in body gesture movement.

An interesting experiment carried out by Oudenhoven and Haspers[51] in Leiden University, Holland, indicates the importance of the adults thinking about the gestures they use when they talk to children. My own observations leading to the suggestion to my colleagues (when they were playing with young handicapped babies in front of students) that they might introduce new sounds to the

---

* Jamie his mentally handicapped brother says 'down' at five years when we play the game of Up/Down. We 'climb' our hands up over our head, wait and then suddenly drop them down with a big DOWN shouted out. We also play Thumbs UP thumbs DOWN. The child has to imitate the gesture of thumbs UP or DOWN and then anticipate the next move. It might be the same or is changed. To encourage pointing we played 'Where's Jamie,' 'Where's Mildred,' 'Where's Adrian.' Much laughing accompanied this game—particularly when anticipating Where's... pause... 'M' (shouted).

children deliberately with no visual stimulus present (cf. Structured Environment 1971) were made because my impressions were that children often displayed searching attention behaviour to the adult's eyes, hair, lipstick, etc., rather than to the sounds she wanted them to listen to. The research is timely and relevant. I will describe it briefly

Much information given to children is through language. This is usually accompanied by other characteristics—intonation, pitch, tempo, tone differences and sometimes gesture. The speaker himself has characteristics; he is dressed in a particular way, is standing in a specific spot. These incidental features might influence young children more than the actual content of what is being said.

Normal and mentally handicapped children were used in the following experiment. A tape giving instructions was played and randomly the children were given the instruction 'Pick up the box' or 'Press the button' in a high pitch or low pitch respectively. After ten trials the order was reversed. 'Pick up the box' was said in a low pitch and 'Press the button' in a high pitch voice. Ten trials later the pitch of the instruction was as in the initial trials. The reversals were regarded as criterion trials; if the child responded mainly to pitch he could make a mistake. If he paid attention to the actual content of what was said he would not make a mistake.

Additionally a series of test instructions were included accompanied by a gesture of the right arm; in the one case a forward gesture like an offering motion and the other a backward gesture, like an invitation, were included. Also a series in which instructions were given on tape in a friendly/harsh tone. The designs of these last two series were the same as those of pitch. By unexpected shifts in order of presentation these research workers were able to determine to what modality the child was paying most attention. For each part they had two parallel series and therefore the children could make four mistakes.

NUMBER OF ERRORS IN THE TWO GROUPS

	Pitch	Gesture	Mood
Retarded children	3	10	2
Normal children	1	9	2

The groups do not differ significantly from each other. Both groups make significantly more errors under the GESTURE condition.

Whilst the question of gesture is uppermost in our thinking at the moment I should like to add something of possible importance from my own teaching experience with Jamie (when he was 5 years). One day on his return from school I observed him for the first time since knowing him, beckoning with the index finger of his right hand to his little brother to invite him to the kitchen. I responded, for his brother did not understand the meaning of this gesture. As I took Jamie's hand I said 'Come.' I suggested to his mother that whenever Jamie used this particular gesture she should tell him 'Come' and carry out the request. This stage seemed to herald the beginning of his understanding that words stand for something. Within the last six months he has begun (a) to use words to regulate the adult's behaviour, e.g. 'Me, me' when he wants a turn at something; (b) to copy a word clearly if he is told to say it, e.g. 'Pop' when the pop-gun popped, 'Plug' when we were playing with the toy sink, 'Nenna' the name of his friend when he saw her; (c) to use two-word phrases.

We so very often hear that these children talk to each other through gestures and use gesture to communicate with adults. I am led to think that perhaps the adults have not always interpreted the meaning of a child's gesture and *immediately* linked the gesture up to a word for the child. Linking a word to an object is a great step forward in language comprehension—perhaps we ought to be giving much more attention to the possible sources of this behaviour and to how we can help the child to link his gestures to a word and then phase out the gestures. It does mean that our observation and response has to be skilled for many judgments have to be made.

To return to the conclusions of Oudenhoven and Haspers—as the gesture has an important stimulus value it behoves mothers and teachers not to use gesture as *the* most important means of expression. If each time you speak to a child you can be simultaneously aware of what your body is doing you will realize how difficult it is to inhibit your natural speaking accempaniments.

Teachers of these young mentally handicapped children have to be extremely interested in the ways in which communication techniques develop. One possible way will certainly be through association. In the early stages the adults will have to be observing carefully, for the associations will be non-verbal and not as with a normal little girl of two years who, on seeing my large amber brooch and touching it, said 'marble' followed by 'Manda.' She wanted to tell me that her sister had a marble game. The whole family (four older children and the mother) helped me to make the connections for they knew the whole situation. If only as much effort was made in the pre-school years to help adults see the meaning of a mentally handicapped child's communications and respond to them we should see more clearly that their behaviour nearly always makes sense but that we are often too slow to understand it and often ignore its meaning.

Some examples of association
A., 3 years, found a white card in my bag. He knew where my pen was and got it, then sat at the little table to scribble.

J. thought the string on the threading ball was for pulling the toy along, by 5½ years.
H. profoundly handicapped (18 years). When doll seen, 'combed' doll's hair. When she saw basket, put it on her arm.
Anjali, age 3 years, put fingers in bowl of spoon, took 'food.' Gave food on spoon to Mrs. O.B. Put fingers in weeble seesaw as she would in a spoon—both the seesaw and spoon were concave objects.
A. After emptying the tine box of its contents, he put into it a toy train and then went to where the lid was lying and tried to fix on the lid. When I moved the coffee table to another part of the room, A. went for his chair to sit at it. A. tried to get into the upturned doll's table which we had been using as a bed. Daddy made a doll's bed for the 'doll going to bed' play. A. tried to lie on it. When A. saw green ink on his hands he looked at me and wrung his hands together in a washing action. When A. found a comb in the handbag he put it on his hair.
J. (5½). When I was winding the key of the mechanical toy for him I said, 'wind.' 'Wind,' he answered, 'pull, pull.' His mother reminded me of this link. We had played the little dance altogether—'Wind the bobbin up, Wind the bobbin up, Pull, Pull, Clap, Clap, Clap.'
A. When A. found the musical box (pull down string action, when string disappears tune stops) playing, he put it to his ear. He stood on the spot and started to sway from left to right in time to the music.
A. saw the toy egg on the table. He had just had an egg for his dinner. I had placed the toy egg in an egg cup on the doll's table ready to help him reconstruct his experience. He took up a plastic knife and tapped the toy egg with the knife using the handle to make the hitting movement.
S. When she was given a piece of apple she put it to her mouth. This was not the development of mouthing behaviour but association with eating. It is interesting to note that Susan started mouthing behaviour towards objects 18 months after the commencement of my lessons with her and after a month of dental treatment (the dentist extracted a tooth and filed her very pointed front teeth) and also after she had started to imitate words and name one or two objects appropriately, e.g. ball, jar, bowl, 'cords on', cup. One might have expected this behaviour very much earlier in her play development. What I am suggesting here is that the condition of her teeth may have prevented her from going through the stage of mouthing objects at the right time in her development of approaching objects; on the other hand the blindness may have upset the developmental sequence in any case. A further possibility may have been that she had gone through the normal mouthing stage before I met her (before 2½ years of age) and so therefore had no further desire to return to an earlier level of development (cf. Reference 19, pp. 47–52).
David. age 2½ years. Used handkerchief to dust with.
Gaynor. age 10 years. When presented with string looked for beads to thread (gestured). Put necklace round her neck. When she saw doll she said 'comb' and combed doll's hair. She put the basket on her arm.
A. age 3 years. When he saw *me* smoking he went for an ash tray. He had been taught this when the Home Help had a cigarette, but on this occasion he got the tray spontaneously with no telling.

If young mentally handicapped children have had the opportunity during their early years to learn through movement experiences to interact with people and to have well structured play sessions with an adult who comprehends play as an important part in their development and comprehends its meaning, then by the time they arrive at school at five years (I think I can safely say that most L.E.A's are not yet providing education for these children below this age) many of them will be able to indulge in solitary play over ever-increasing lengths of time, for their play with an adult will have increased their ability to attend to objects and have given them a store of images. In terms of motoric acts some of them will be at Bruner's ICONIC level of representational development, that is to say they will need precise demonstration before they attempt some activities; others will be at the earlier level the ENACTIVE where they need physically guiding through motor activity in order to start off the movement. A few will be able to follow up with a simple activity after being given verbal instructions and will therefore be at the SYMBOLIC level.

Most of these children will have occasional temper tantrums. Sheila Hewett in *The Family and the Handicapped Child* [52] found that 69 per cent of her handicapped children between 5 and 8 and 69 per cent of the Newsom's normal 4-year-olds had temper tantrums. The difference, however, lay in the frequency reported. 'Daily' and 'almost daily' was reported twice as often for the handicapped group. The 8-year-olds in the handicapped group had many tantrums daily. Two factors seemed responsible for this:

(1) Serious difficulties in communicating so that the children were deprived of expressing feelings of anger and frustration and therefore of a means of avoiding frustration.
(2) The child could not tell his mother when he was afraid, bored, hungry, in pain.

I should like to add that the child because of his communication difficulties cannot indicate that he sometimes wants to help the adult. In thinking about temper tantrums we need to devise techniques to modify adults' behaviour so that their management of the child will not force the child into this form of communication. Wherever parent counselling groups have to deal with this particular difficulty they need to watch the parents' behaviour with the child (this applies also to the behaviour of teachers and to those in charge of children in hospital). They will undoubtedly discover that many of the temper tantrum outbursts are a direct result of the adults' behaviour. We do need to develop the habit of always looking at what is happenning around the child as well as at the child himself.

Those receiving the 5-year-old handicapped child into a school situation perhaps need to surmise that however positive a home he has lived in he will have lived his first five years in homes where the emotional climate of the parents is bound to be one where they are constantly wishing that their child was normal. As Sheila Hewett says 'they (the parents) will be in a state of continually trying 'to accept the unacceptable." Unless planned efforts have been made by those helping the families in the first five years of life to introduce the family to the school the child might be attending well before the first day at school, the mother will suffer a further shock when she sees the other handicapped children in the school.* This means that the home climate will contain added difficulties—and this at an important time for the child.

A high proportion of the mothers in Hewett's sample claimed to have feelings of depression even though they were in good general physical health. The teachers receiving these young children need to be continually aware of this factor and make school as relaxed a place as possible with an element of fun and enjoyment pervading the day—smiling, laughing and sometimes outright giggling with a child should be very much part of the teachers' style, with a good proportion of positive bodily contact.

Music, relaxation and bodily contact

Perhaps it is relevant to say here that adults working with these very young children whether at home, at school, or in a play group, need to thoroughly enjoy the rhythmic/speed aspect of music. They also need to understand the enjoyment of noise. When working with a mother and her handicapped baby, music with strong rhythms such as one finds in most children's quality records enables a relaxing fun atmosphere to be provided for all. It suggests activities like bouncing the child up and down on the knee, bouncing the children for so many bars in the music—pausing . . . then:

(a) going on for another measured phrase/bar;
(b) instead of pausing, lifting the child on to the floor, repeating the bouncing, etc.;
(c) keeping still for so many more bars;

---

* With the present forms of general teacher training I cannot see attitudes being produced that will enable the mentally handicapped to be fully integrated into normal schools nor the educational climates being conducive for integrated staff relationships. I suspect that in considering the question of integration those responsible for policy making will have their eyes on the practices of the U.S.A. and Scandinavia. What one has to bear in mind is the possibility that the reasons underlying their practices will have stemmed from different economic and geographical sources. Whatever decisions are made regarding integration in Britain we must be sure that the children and their parents get the teachers they need.

swaying/rocking him vigorously as well as smoothly to the music, swinging him to the music with both adults holding the arms and legs, walking him round in one's arms (according to his age/stage, handicap), on one's back so that the rhythm in the body acts as a form of movement communication. These are very simple obvious activities but I do not think that the majority of these young children are getting this kind of rhythmic stimulation accompanied by music and planned bodily contact with the adults for say half to one hour each day. To me this is as much a necessary relaxation fun period for the adults as for the child.

Sometimes in my work with families we have all sat on the floor with small musical instruments and accompanied a record with bells (wide variety), kazoos, tambourines for little children, specially made shakers, animal noise sounds, any other kind of safe blowing instrument that can be found . . . what a noise . . . what fun . . . how lovely when it is all over. In such an activity (— noise — silence) it would seem that the foundations of the growth of comparisons are laid.

Making up songs about the child using his name, and singing them to him loudly/softly with varying rhythmic patterns, speeds, pitch changes, will give him a wide variety of experiences probably useful to him in the listening aspects of acquiring language; perhaps too in acquiring the expressive aspects of sound patterns.

Perhaps by indulging in such regular, pleasant activities, important relationships will be formed. Dr. Hannah Olechnowicz says[53] that 'the teacher (it can be all the other important workers in the child's life too) must understand that she has to be the child's SOCIAL PARTNER and in establishing a relationship with him will encourage all those factors leading to non-verbal communications (e.g. smile exchanges helping the interest and gradual comprehension of facial expressions).'

She needs to know that, only as non-verbal communication expands, does the need arise in the child to use a richer form of communication, language—the younger or more profoundly handicapped the child the longer will it take that child to get to know her as a special person in his life.

All education rests upon a psychological knowledge of the needs of the learner. As Dr. Olechnowicz from Poland says (cf. page 30) the needs of handicapped children are no different in essence from those of the normal child but 'the way in which these needs are realized might be different.' It is these ways with special reference to the young handicapped child that I wish to discuss in the next few paragraphs.

Since the new Education Act of 1971, more concern and provision for the pre-school child and his parent has been promoted in some areas of England. An interesting feature in about a dozen L.E.A.'s has been the appointment of peripatetic (visiting) teacher/advisers. These teachers visit the homes of all the known pre-school mentally handicapped children from the age of two years. They work with the children using early learning stimulation techniques, advise the parents, leave toys with them to use with their child, build up catalogue collections of toys and prepare their own cards for parents about the value of certain equipment. Two such teachers in Derbyshire, Joanne Webster and Susan Mounsey, provided me with some useful notes on the way in which they had gone about setting up such a service. They found that the parents needed most of all PRACTICAL help on a REGULAR basis. They wanted to know what to expect of the child as it grew up and what would happen when school age was reached. Their comment to me that, if a child has no assessment of his abilities and disabilities before he is five, valuable years have been lost, was full of meaning for me. Particularly was this so after my experience teaching the pre-school handicapped children in three families.

These teachers evaluated their experience after three months. They found the parents so receptive because they were there to do something *visibly positive*. They also discovered that the parents themselves were doing valuable work with their children using intuition but needing reassurance and support to encourage them.

As I read their experiences I was immediately reminded of the Middlesex Home Teaching Scheme of the 1930s described so well in a little book entitled *Serving the Mentally Handicapped*[54.] A staff of six were responsible for fortnightly visits to 200 defectives unable to attend an occupation centre and whose ages ranged from 7 to 54. The organizer of this scheme (Frances M. Dean) commented that 'Initial opposition is frequently met with on the part of the parents . . . not because of lack of interest in the handicapped person but to the fact that in many instances both home and school have failed to teach him anything useful and everyone therefore has grown accustomed to the idea that any further attempt to do so is a waste of time.' 'BUT,' she continues, 'after a few visits both parent and pupil are tidied up for the lesson—the table is cleared for the Handwork and perhaps even a fire is lighted in the bedroom to make more comfortable conditions for the teacher.' What a lot of progress has been made over the years in parents' attitudes. The visiting of homes of all new admissions by the old supervisors (Heads of Occupational Centres pre 1959;

Training Centres pre 1971), the formation and activities of the National Society for Mentally Handicapped Children, the researches of Tizard and Grad[5] in the mid-fifties, laid the foundations of thought regarding teacher-parent involvement in families having a mentally handicapped child.

In 1966 a group of mothers with very young normal children and a young handicapped child met together with Dr. Roy Faulkner in Stevenage New Town. Together they discussed the possibility of the setting up of a play group containing normal and handicapped children; a play group that mothers could organize/attend if they wished; a place where they could talk informally to an interested doctor. This group initiated what have come to be called Opportunity Play Groups. At the moment there are over 50 such groups where handicapped and normal young children come together in the care of mostly voluntary untrained workers. The aims of these groups enumerated by Dr. Faulkner are as follows:

(a) to provide nursery classes for any handicapped child one month to 5 years;
(b) to enable normal and handicapped children to play together;
(c) to provide simultaneous meeting for mothers.[55]

If one thinks in terms of young handicapped children needing to have well-structured early stimulation programmes from highly skilled workers, these play groups cannot at the present time be said to be fulfilling such a function for few skilled workers exist in the ranks of the volunteers and teachers involved.

If one thinks in terms of 'troubles shared' having a catharctic effect/temporary relief for the family and the possible isolation of many of the handicapped children if no such group existed, then I should say they are performing a highly effective community action service the results of which might be measured one day in preventive mental health terms.

Integration and the young handicapped child

If one is thinking of the principles underlying integration one has not only to consider the handicapped child but also the young normal children amongst whom these children will be.

My opening paragraphs to this chapter attempted to describe the wide variety of children included in this group. Those responsible for planning the placing of mentally handicapped children and voluntary bodies campaigning for integration need to take this into account and look at individual possibilities. Bowley and Gardener[56] writing about the young blind handicapped child say, 'Blind children usually learn to play with other children rather later than sighted children but by four they will be enjoying imaginative play. There are certain difficulties in regard to play companionship. Sighted children tend to treat the blind child too greatly as a baby, or as a passive partner, or ignore him altogether because he cannot keep up with the pace of their games. Herein lies one sound argument for letting a blind child attend nursery school where there are children with a similar handicap and similar problems to solve.'

An interesting provocative paper of its time (1960) was that written by a doctor in the Department of Social and Preventive Medicine, Manchester University—Dr. Joyce Leeson.[20] The paper describes the visits she made to the homes of six young mentally handicapped children. The recommendations she made for the community care of these children on the basis of these visits are as valid today, in spite of the advances we have made, for they are certainly not implemented in all parts of the country. Indeed I have even come across feelings of hostility when close parent/teacher involvement has been suggested to teacher groups. It occurs to me that those training the teachers both in colleges and on In-Service training courses have a great responsibility here in bringing their students/teachers into planned contact with parents (cf. page 70) over the period of their training and developing the concept that parent/teacher involvement is a very special part of Special Education.

Briefly then the recommendations Dr. Leeson made were as follows:

(1) Daily training for children over 2 with free transport provided.
(2) Staff to study nursery techniques (Tizard).
(3) Careful psychological assessment so that attention is given to the individual needs of each child.
(4) In rehousing families (Salford) care should be taken not to remove the family with the handicapped member far away from relatives.
(5) A special clinic might be established, staffed by a multidisciplinary team consisting of paediatrician, psychologist and social worker. Such a team would assess young children suspected of mental handicap and form an integrated plan for the care and training of the child, and the guidance of the parents.
(6) Parent counselling should have an important place in the clinic's activities and a close relationship between parents and the training centre (now of course special schools) should be fostered.

Fourteen years later the majority of very young handicapped children are still not having the educational help they need in spite of the growth of Opportunity Classes, of peripatetic services,* of parent involvement, workshop groups[15] and more L.E.A.'s admitting children to school before 5 years.

Family crises
Hostels for the mentally handicapped (both Local Authority and privately run) have been mushrooming up all over the country (no figures are available as to the numbers of these or about the quality of the staff working in them). Such accommodation to ease family crises may be necessary but society (including the parents of these children) should demand that the hostels are homes not small institutions; that the staff should have continuous In-Service training and community support; that the hostels are regularly inspected by people *knowing* the mentally handicapped. Whilst in Sweden I was taken by a colleague to an Authority home for the mentally handicapped. It was a normal large bungalow with an extra building in the garden for play and a very large garden. Six children varying in age lived with a 'Mother' and 'Father.' Dr. Barnado's Society appears to be attempting recently to introduce such schemes in this country with its fostering methods of accommodating children.

Assessment units
Whilst assessment units have increased since 1960 these certainly are not in sufficient numbers and by and large do not seem to satisfy the needs of the parents or the children. Perhaps our aim should be an assessment unit in every Local Authority with staff specially trained to write out practical suggestions for the parents of each child. Perhaps it should be statutory for all general practitioners to refer immediately a child to such a unit if the milestones of development are IN ANY WAY abnormal; where a skilled team of workers might discover the child's potential at any point in time and give constructive help until he joins the school system. Perhaps the mass media could be persuaded to use some of its finance in advertising the whereabouts of Assessment Units. The present red tape of the family doctor having first to refer a child could perhaps be scrapped, so that parents could use the services of the multidisciplinary team in the Assessment Unit. Hasten the day when there is a direct line of approach for parents. What kind of pressures can be brought to make this a reality?. I have mentioned the general practitioner because only quite recently I have met a child of three years who is handicapped in a number of ways. It

---

* One L.E.A. informed me that even a scale 4 post had not attracted applicants wanting to work with young mentally handicapped children and their parents.

would appear that no one yet has been able to observe her in a test situation or in a structured play situation sufficiently to assess her potential or to pinpoint the nature of her handicap. The North West Assessment Unit at the Royal Manchester Children's Hospital is known, yet the attitude seems to be there is time yet for her to be fully assessed. Such an attitude suggests that assessment categorizes and is therefore not to be undertaken too soon. As I see it a teacher can waste a lot of time finding the child's level, however skilled she is in observation, unless she has additionally a more scientific diagnosis to work from. Why does everything take so long to be implemented? Perhaps it is because there are too few descriptions of personal professional methods in the literature and too much emphasis, in the past at any rate, on research designed to repeat over and over again what every right-thinking person knows. Models of good practice everywhere should be discovered, described and evaluated.

Developing positive attitudes towards parent/teacher involvement
Dr. Leeson's recommendation about parent counselling and close parent/teacher involvement is steadily increasing with a certain amount of momentum in certain areas. In thinking about the development of concepts, including parent education involvement, one has to remember that those educationists training the teachers to gain this concept from 1960-71 were doing so often against a background of opposition from persons (many of them untrained) calling themselves Mental Welfare Officers whose job was to liaise with the school and home. They in turn were in a dilemma because so many of the teachers at that time had had in fact no training. This meant that confidential information was not to be available to non-professionals.

Students on one- and later two-year specialized courses for teachers of the mentally handicapped were however brought continuously into contact with parents in a number of ways:
(1) A family link system was evolved in Bristol so that a baby-sitting service was provided from the student group. In such a depth experience students would learn how to talk with parents.
(2) Children attending a play group 1963-5, in which students discovered that the mentally handicapped could make a choice of activity and could play without adult interference providing the numbers of activities were sufficient (pp. 127-129), were taken home by the students on a rota basis.
(3) Parents willing to be questioned by the students on any aspect of their child's arrival or progress were brought into college annually

to spend a morning with the group. One of the most important needs of many parents in coping with their own emotional attitudes towards their problem is to talk and talk and talk. Any opportunity where they can share their problem with a variety of involved people can be seen as a positive step for them.

(4) Tape recordings of conversations with parents of James and Karen (with the permission of those involved) were later analysed by the student groups.

(5) Perhaps present course Tutors could extend this particular technique to include those *in loco parentis*, e.g. hostel housemothers, nurses in mental subnormality hospitals. They seem to need interest from outside in the community almost as much as the parents themselves.

(6) Students on the new two-year courses (1964 onwards) began to write their long essays around the problems they found in the homes of the handicapped. This meant that they had to visit the homes regularly and thus gained in experience with such parents.

(7) By the late 'sixties more teachers had received training to work with the mentally handicapped and most Local Authorities (though not all by any means) had relaxed their attitudes about teachers visiting the homes of the handicapped and they were willing to afford *bona fide* students opportunities to go into the homes without restriction. Consequently in the second year of training students had to make 8-10 evening visits to the homes of a handicapped person and keep a detailed diary of their experiences. Many students maintained the relationship long after their required visits were completed.

(8) Not all teachers are able to begin a conversation with parents from the range of social classes. It seems to be a skill that might be developed during training. As with all skills it needs practising. In order to focus the attention of students on the development of normal children under two, so that they would understand pre-school handicapped children, an experience was arranged for them enabling them to understand child development in action. They were attached to a family having a child of two months and were expected to make fortnightly visits throughout their training. Originally this plan was introduced into the course by my colleague Joan Fitch and extended by Olwen Gregory. Its purpose was to help students understand the concept of child development. Its spin-off in other terms alongside all the other experiences gained during training was to enable some growth of confidence in dealing with parents. When students evaluated the course, growth of

confidence was mentioned by a large proportion of those qualifying.

(9) One of the most useful experiences that teachers in training can have is to have contact not only with children who are mentally handicapped but also the adults. An optional experience was for students to organize a social club for mentally handicapped adults one evening a week. Most of the adults attending this club were in fact brought by their parents who were encouraged either to have a couple of hours off from their offspring or to sit in a room away from their sons or daughters and talk to the other attending parents. Thus parents on the premises gave students yet another chance to absorb this communication concept.

(10) Keeping up a written dialogue between a teacher and parents is an idea that was re-introduced into our thinking through a Headteacher hearing about the home/school diaries of Dale* and trying out the idea in her own school. The essence of such an approach was for the teacher and the parent to exchange weekly notes on the child's experiences, progress, knowledge of new words, appearance of new behaviour. One interested student (Ann Southren) spontaneously followed out this technique on her next teaching practice and was thought by the parents in that school 'to be the best student the school had ever had.' The technique was incorporated into the next teaching practice for all students—as was the suggestion that all students should visit the homes of at least two of the children in their teaching practice class during their five final weeks. Many teachers in the North West are now using this home/school diary method as part of their professional method. One of the dangers in this unless the exercise is carefully supervised by the Headteachers might be that young inexperienced teachers might give information that is not really helpful; they might discontinue a habit looked forward to by families when personal pressures intervene. One way round this difficulty is that a special time is set aside each Friday afternoon for the writing up of these little booklets. One or two well chosen sentences not a long essay is what is needed. Ideally the teacher should retain a copy so that important information of a continuous nature is not lost. A précis could be added to a special column in the suggested notebook kept by each teacher (Appendix 2).

---

* *The Deaf Child at Home and at School.*[57] I have written 're-introduced' because in teaching Sybil (1952-7) (page 168) I described for her mother all that I wanted her to do with her during the week, in a little notebook kept especially for the purpose.

(11) Contact with the officers of the National Society in formal lectures and informal discussions is yet another way in which the importance of the teacher and parent working together can be emphasized DURING training. They are usually interested in lecturing to students and bring to such sessions the reality of mental subnormality. Through their welfare services they come into first-hand contact with the problems of a family with a handicapped child.

Research and parent/teacher involvement

My colleagues and I were always seeking out new situations for training students to become skilled observers of children and at the same time affording them opportunities to assimilate the practice of skilled teachers' work. We were introduced to the interesting work of a parent of a mongol baby, Rex Brinkworth[58] (Birmingham) by Professor Mittler, a regular visitor to our course, and helped by him to find cooperating parents we decided to bring in one or two families and work with their babies in front of the mothers and the students. Lists of play activities compiled by me for students two years previously were used and extended by my colleagues in this experience and later in the Hester Adrian Workshop for Parents. The students observed and recorded in detail the activities of the teachers/my colleagues and the responses of the children. Discussion of their notes with the parents and their tutors was yet another useful way it seemed of interesting students in the possibilities inherent in gaining the cooperation of parents in the education of their children, without encouraging them to become introspective. Several of the students on qualifying incorporated the concept in their own situation and worked with parents in their classroom on a rota basis.

The Hester Adrian Research Centre has been busy in the last four years extending the concept of parent/teacher involvement and parent/child involvement. The well documented experience of the first Parents Workshop[15] in which parents as well as teachers[22] were encouraged to:
(a) observe objectively and record systematically;
(b) select a task to be taught;
(c) carry out the task with maximum efficiency;
(d) evaluate the results
is a must in reading for all those working in the field of mental handicap and particularly with young children, for the new concept it gives of sharing accurate knowledge about a child's developmental level and progress with his parents is so important.

Many schools have now set up their own version of these parents' workshops, helped to do so by research workers from the Research Centre. Two further research projects involving parents in the education of their handicapped children are planned over the next three/four years, for as Cliff Cunningham writes, 'Professionals can no longer afford to ignore that education must be seen as a life-long process beginning at birth and not at school; the importance of parents must be recognized and they must be used in the education process. We cannot afford to wait until the child is of school age or even of nursery age.' In thinking about this question of parent involvement we need to be aware that these parents will come from all social classes. Those in social class iii, iv and v may need *demonstration* of what to do over varying lengths of time before they can become fully involved; if feelings of depression are in fact one of the important features of many of the mothers' personalities,[52] the lack of positive affection in some mothers of severely subnormal children suggested by Cashdan and Jeffree[59] may indeed have become 'distorted' (a useful word given to me by David Norris during a conversation I had with him in 1974), for overt displays of affection in those feeling depressed may very well have to be well suppressed lest the sadness becomes too overwhelming.

The methods used to involve parents will perhaps need to take into account this emotional aspect perhaps rather more than applying an intellectual approach to their problems.

In 1966 I wrote that 'if we believe that teachers need to help parents to encourage their children it follows that the teachers need to come to know the parents in almost as many ways as they know the children. They might also begin to see their role in a wider sense; a role embracing not only work in the classroom but in the home too.' I would add now on the basis of further teaching experience that teachers need extra training or special support systems to do this successfully.

At that time this idea of teacher home/school involvement seemed rather revolutionary even if a necessary professional concept in this sphere of education. Now almost ten years later the idea is becoming much more established and incorporated into the educational practice of those concerned with the mentally handicapped.

The next decade might see an increase in this practice and in research evaluating the long-term results in terms of the mental health of the parents, the child and the commitment of the other adults concerned.

5 Choosing their own activities

Activities which we choose to do unaided and in which we are successful are very often those learnt sufficiently to warrant no further help and direction. They are often at our level of ability. They are certainly those which we enjoy and are interested in because of the pleasure they afford us. Sometimes the choice of spontaneous activities in a relaxed and encouraging atmosphere reveals difficulties.

Similarly when children embark upon activities of their own choice and are successful they develop confidence and are eager to progress. If one applies this idea to severely subnormal children one can appreciate their need to have some freedom of choice in their activities. The confidence gained will help them to learn many other things. If we let the children choose their own activities we shall see what they can do for themselves, what interests them most, what their levels of achievement are (measured against what they might be) how they organize their time, whether they display initiative or not, what makes them curious, and what kind of teaching and extra experiences we should give them to develop further.

When severely subnormal children are encouraged to choose their own activities, to work on them, and become self-activated we are helping them to concentrate.* Useful experiences will be gained possibly at the right time for a particular child. They will help him to build up a mass of ideas about the environment and the people in it.

In watching the children's activities we might discover that they are trying to communicate something about themselves or about their knowledge of the world, which because of a lack of language facility, they are unable to indicate in any other way. We might learn also that some children learn best by spending large amounts of time daily (for weeks or even for months) on the same activity whilst others learn best by choosing a variety of activities.

---

* If one observes carefully one can see this concentration to a task in hand growing longer and longer as their interest is caught by structured activity and as they develop. I was glad to see at last one psychologist challenging the 'conventional wisdom about the poor attention and concentration of the mentally handicapped' for as GILLHAM says 'it may be a function not of the child but of the kind of learning situation in which he is placed.' I do agree. It has never been my practice as a teacher to concentrate on lack of attention, only to discover how to catch and sustain it.

Skilled and imaginative teachers will certainly see how to develop the interests which the children display in free choice sessions. Sometimes this will be in a one-to-one planned situation; sometimes in a group.

Examples
Sylvia noticed the real cups and saucers and plates on the table of the 'Home Corner' as well as a circular-shaped tray. After arranging them as for a meal she decided to collect them and put them on the tray. Her problem was how to fit them all so that none were left on the table. After several trials with various arrangements she managed to do this. Her choice of activity had involved her in a useful social as well as a valuable spatial experience.

Bobby played in the shop. He filled a string bag with purchases. 'Tell me what you have bought' I asked him. He took all the purchases from the bag and put them in front of me naming them as he did so. All the names of the tins and boxes were correct except that of the Ovaltine tin. This he called coffee. He named the matches cigarettes. He continued his play. When his teacher asked him where he was going (entering into the play) he said, 'To the shop.' 'What will you buy?' she enquired. 'Ovaltine,' he informed her. He was practising his newly learnt word in the play situation. Later, with help from the teacher, he began to recognize the label on the tin and to associate the taste of the drink which was made with the substance contained within it. He also learnt to make different kinds of drinks with his teacher and the other children in the group as part of the cookery lesson.

Graham wanted to practise sawing a piece of wood. He opened the vice on the woodwork bench as far as it would go and chose his piece of wood. He discovered that a particular piece of wood would only fit in if he placed it in a certain way. He had been comparing the size of the wood and the space into which it would fit. A freely chosen activity was giving Graham the chance to use materials and gain the feeling of the wood as well as to gain some increased skill in using the saw.

The following very brief records of a little boy's activities during a month of free choice sessions will show once more how much the teacher can learn about the children at such times, particularly if she keeps short daily notes.

Monday. Played tea parties using the water for about half an hour.
Tuesday. Very naughty for the last part of the afternoon. Tore a paper shape of a house.
Wednesday. Played tea parties and pretended to make pancakes.
Thursday. Played Punch and Judy with the puppets and gave a little show for me.
Friday. Spent some time drawing on the big blackboard. Chalked some big squares and said it was Criss Cross Quiz.
Monday. Absent.
Tuesday. Played in the sand making sand pies. Turned them out on to a 'plate' (tin lid).
Wednesday. Pretended he was the bread man and drove round the room with

a basket 'selling bread' to everyone.
Thursday. Made a house with two tables and a large piece of material.
Friday. Absent.
Monday. Played with the dough for a long time.
Tuesday. Made me some tarts out of dough to be baked for a cake shop.
Wednesday. Played with other puppets and put them to bed in a box. Brought the puppets to the story of 'Sooty's Party'.
Friday. Played in the shop both buying and selling. Drew some snowflakes and wrote 'snow' underneath with my help.
Monday. Played in the shop again.
Tuesday. Played with three other boys jumping over cardboard boxes for half an hour.
Wednesday. Painted a gas lamp for the model and the Punch and Judy show. Told me he had gas lamps in the street. Was the shopkeeper for some time. Then said he had to go on with his washing and get the clothes in the spin-dryer.
Thursday. Drew a boat and coloured it in very well. Wrote his name without copying it.
Friday. Made a van out of six chairs with another boy and pretended to take eggs round to people's houses.

What do such brief records kept by a busy teacher with ten or twelve other severely subnormal children in her class tell us about Ian? We can see that although severely subnormal he is able to choose his own activity; he can play on his own and sometimes he plays with small groups of boys. The records indicate the kind of experiences he had in the environment provided and how he experimented with the materials he found. He enjoyed playing a variety of roles—being the man selling bread/eggs. He has learnt from observation, for he imitated his mother washing the clothes. Using a pencil to write with and crayons to fill in a drawing showed his teacher that he had achieved a fair amount of skill.

The new teacher began to take different objects to interest the children in her class. One day she put a cow's horn on the interest table. John found it. Finding a piece of paper he used the horn as a template and drew round it. He repeated the process and coloured in both horns. When he showed them to his teacher she asked him where he would see horns. He responded by drawing a large picture of a bull above the two horns.

Dr. Hannah Olechnowicz in her published research findings for teachers* reinforces my own findings that teachers need 'to recognize the fundamental value of non-verbal learning; need to give the children opportunities for communication through free choice.' To quote from her work 'a group of severely retarded children (I.Q.

---

* *Studies in the Socialization of the Severely and Profoundly Retarded.* [53] A book (195 pages) for teachers.

below 20) though displaying a lack of interest in almost every type of nursery school occupation were given the opportunity to explore *at will* objects new to them (flashlights, boxes of all sizes and shapes, machinery parts and so on). Given full freedom to examine these with hand and eye with no effort by the staff to teach them names or issue verbal instructions, these children showed a normal exploratory behaviour at the level corresponding to their mental age, that is comparable to that of children aged 15 to 24 months. When we analyse the ways that cognitive needs are shown in the mentally retarded we should always bear in mind that the fullest manifestations of these needs will be found in the child's own spontaneous activity and not in response to verbal explanations from the teacher.' Her book describes in the simplest terms possible a three-year research project carried out by seven university women in a day centre in Warsaw with severely and profoundly handicapped children. Her comments that 'many retarded children withdraw from play because they are often presented with toys inappropriate to their individual mental levels, e.g. dolls instead of sand, books instead of dolls, and thus fail to become interested and appear unable to learn' caused me to reflect upon so much inappropriate activity seen in some of the schools I have visited in different parts of the country; upon the insistence by a number of writers that this group of children has to be taught to play. Some of the children indeed do conform to this idea about their inability to play spontaneously or purposefully. The majority of mentally handicapped children in my experience do not. I must stress however that those observing them do need to understand the sequence of development in play behaviour and this sequence will inevitably be delayed in this group of children. They also need to understand the meaning for the child of his spontaneous handling of toys and other objects. Most adults looking at children's play are beginning in *their* thinking at too advanced a level of play, e.g. that of a normal 4- or 5-year-old (cf. Play Workshops, page 99 footnote).

Praise and approval
Praise and approval and a good deal of appreciation of their spontaneous activities are amongst the important needs of these children. Teachers might fail however to give them strongly enough, or at the right times, because the actions which should be praised are often so fleeting and perhaps appear so unimportant to us as adults that we miss seeing them or fail to understand why approval is so vital to the child.

Failure on the part of the teacher to give effective praise may be due to a number of factors:

(1) She may not have trained her observation skills sufficiently.
(2) She might consider that progress is acknowledgely so slow that it is not worth her while to 'make a fuss' about tiny insignificant actions.
(3) She might genuinely not know what to look for to praise.
(4) She might give praise (using tones/words) for a successful action when the action is no longer taking place. Thus Paul Berry (a part-time colleague on my course in Manchester 1971–2) was supervising a small group of students in a ward teaching situation. Together they had been observing the progress of walking (number of steps taken) in one particular child. On the morning in question the child had taken more steps than ever before. As the child reached the adults he fell down. Immediately the student said 'Good boy.' She had 'rewarded' the inappropriate action because in *her* thinking she was rewarding what had gone before! Of course we do not know what facial/bodily expressions of encouragement were being given naturally.
(5) She might be underestimating the importance of stable emotional development and her part in fostering this.

It is important for me to emphasize that observing, understanding and following up the insignificant details of a severely subnormal child's behaviour are of major importance for the teacher if she is really going to help him to progress. Her approach should be encouraging and positive at all times. It should build on what the child gives.[22] She should be constantly asking herself 'What is the purpose of a particular action *to the child?*' In seeking an answer to this the ability to be aware of the child's purpose will grow.

Examples
Janet picked up two large nails from the woodwork bench. She banged them gently together. She realized that a pleasant sound resulted. Great was her pleasure when her teacher noticed and promptly invited her to repeat her action and later with other nails to make new sounds. In other words the teacher was recognizing that Janet was experimenting with sound and that she had made her own discovery.
Cecil was knocking some tiny nails in the wood. He was making a guitar from the wooden shapes cut out for him beforehand by his teacher. Repeatedly he hit his fingers with the hammer and the nail fell out. His persistence was rewarded however and suddenly he shouted, 'I've done it.' It was the sign for his teacher to praise him highly for effort and to encourage him to finish the task of knocking in all the other nails to complete the job.
Rosie discovered the flour and salt 'cakes', sausage rolls, and tarts in the shop. She took some to the table and put them on plates. She set the table for four. Noticing her teacher's interest, Rosie persuaded her to sit down at the table with two children from the group. She announced that they were going to have a tea party. 'How lovely,' exclaimed her approving teacher. Rosie found

the waste materials box and taking some sheets of coloured paper from it twisted them into conical-shaped party hats.

Linked to this desire for approval is their need for teachers who become aware of signs of initiative and creativeness *at whatever level* it occurs and in recognizing it give approval; who observe so closely that they can see for themselves that many of these children do learn spontaneously from life around them as do normal children and do not have to be taught everything.

Adrian (3 years) applied the index finger of his right hand to the button on the torch and pressed. He saw that there was no light. Then he brought the index finger of his other hand on to the button. With both fingers he applied pressure and put on the light. In his play Adrian took the doll to the 'toilet.' Several weeks later whilst Adrian was sitting on his Daddy's knee I told him how Adrian had taken the doll to the toilet (our play activities had included those aspects of life to do with eating, going to bed),spontaneously during one of our hour-and-a-half sessions. Ten minutes later Adrian slid off his Daddy's knee and took the doll to the toilet. Not wanting him to get it wet I followed him and held out the doll as I had done with him on several occasions. He bent his head to examine the doll's bottom.

Adrian (3 years 11 months). Jamie his brother was sitting in a box waiting to be pulled round the room by Adrian and me. Adrian had previously gestured to a hole in the side when I brought out string to make a harness for pulling. Adrian pulled. The box was heavy. He immediately went to the other end of the box and pushed.

Alan named the boat he had made from wood with the help of his teacher 'Misty'.

Vanda suggested that the doll she was making in the house corner needed a nightdress. When it was finished she asked where its nappies were.

Jimmy who rarely left his table spontaneously, got up from his seat one day and helped himself to a piece of paper from the cupboard. He wanted it to draw round his hands. He had seen someone else doing this days beforehand. It was the first self-initiated action seen by his teacher.

Ian was hitting a large nail into some wood with a small light hammer. After several attempts he looked round the bench and found a heavier hammer.

Barry was working in the sand. He was emptying the sand from one of the beakers into the pan of the scale. Some of the sand remained at the bottom of the beaker. Barry tapped the beaker with a spoon to loosen the sand. It remained. After several attempts he put the spoon inside and scooped out the sand with it. He was learning that when one method of doing something fails he must try another. Praising his action reinforced his feelings of success and gave him confidence to attempt other things.

Philip saw the box of balls. He emptied the box and put the balls in a row. He found a wheelbarrow and made up the game of throwing the balls into the box and the wheelbarrow. He was using initiative.

John. A long piece of string and some canes were put into the tent. John proudly showed us much later the bow he had made by himself from the materials we had provided.

Billy was in his wheelchair. He could only use one hand. The other lay twisted and useless against his body. His teacher wanted him to experience tapping out a rhythm. She had brought a specially made castanet without a handle for him. It rested on the palm of her hand and Billy used the fingers of his strong hand to tap the lips of the castanet together. He noticed that he could vary the sound by moving his fingers to different positions. Great was his joy at this simple achievement. A smile spread across his face when he was praised for moving his fingers and thus making this discovery by himself. His fingers had moved so slowly that an unobservant teacher might have missed this action and the opportunity to give the praise so much needed by him.

Approval and praise which is sincerely expressed by the teacher's tone of voice, a hand or body gesture or merely the shine in her eyes can mean much to a child who is achieving. Sometimes these should be expressed overtly, that is to say, by a warm hug, a friendly pat or a squeeze of the hand. On rare occasions a kiss on the cheek might be given. Mature teachers do not need to fear this type of bodily contact with their pupils, whatever their physical size for it might be the only means of communicating approval, joy and interest at a child's effort at some stage in his development.

Immediate response to facial expressions, gestures, language, activities, interests

Experienced teachers know that there is a very strong case for giving an immediate positive and structured response to a child in order to help him learn and in some cases to motivate him to begin. The timing of the response is very important as is the QUALITY of the response itself. This can take many forms:

(1) Mirroring a child's expressions, gestures to communicate that you have noticed and are willing to do something about it.
(2) Providing a new piece of equipment or new play materials (sometimes quite novel ones) to further a child's experience. Showing the child another possibility with the toy to give him other images to assimilate.
(3) Speaking to the child, sometimes copying his sounds, his sound 'strings' (cf. letter strings in reading), sometimes using carefully chosen words, sometimes helping him to hear a new word formed from sounds that he already has in his repertoire. Thus Adrian says 'car' and 'up' appropriately. In our doll table play the word 'cup' is much used.
(4) Taking a child/children to see something near the school because of expressed interest in language or in play.
(5) Helping the children to make a model/collage/picture as a direct consequence of expressed interest through language or behaviour. I was very interested when an excellent experienced teacher of the handicapped said to me that whilst she was training and going into

other schools and classes for the mentally handicapped she was very surprised to see that the pictures and collages on the walls of the classrooms did not reflect to her that the teacher had been thinking about how to use children's interests. It seemed to indicate that teachers had not thought about linking up the children's interests with the look of the classroom. Classrooms communicate to an informed visitor what the children are doing, how they are thinking about their world, how effectively the teacher uses what she is observing.

(6) Giving a model of correct language forms relative to the needs of the particular child. By this I do not mean that the teacher spends time trying to get the child to say something more correctly, but that in immediate further conversation with the child she brings in something new in terms of the thought but uses the incorrect words/syntax in the correct context for the child to hear.

(7) Explaining misunderstandings of one kind or another.

(8) Making or obtaining special apparatus to help a particular child; if he is old enough to understand, helping him to know that it is especially for him.

Examples

When the children were listening to a record Robert decided to take a stick from the music table and pretend it was a guitar. I asked him if he would like to make one. We shall make one in the individual session.

Sharon played with the doll's furniture and arranged the bedroom furniture. She picked up the small boy doll saying, 'Ah, ah, bo, bos.' 'Put the baby to bed,' I said. She picked up the man doll and stood him on a chair. When I pointed out her mistake she laughed. To extend Sharon's play with the dolls I shall bring her a large cardboard cut-out of a doll and clothes for her to colour and dress the doll with. We shall then have more to talk about.

Kenneth and Shaun dressed up today as an Indian and a cowboy. Kenneth kept coming to me and, pointing to Shaun, said 'Dead.' Shaun chased Kenneth saying, 'I'm going to shoot him with this knife.' I corrected the mistake. Tomorrow I shall take a toy gun and a knife to reinforce the knowledge and the correct use of the words.

Shaun and Jackie played with the doll's furniture. I shall make a large plan of a house showing the various rooms and pictures of the furniture for matching. Some might then like to match the furniture as a game. I can work with a child in an individual session with this teaching aid.

John (blind and attending a hospital school) used the typewriter on my table. He felt it all over. When I asked him what kind of noises he could hear from a typewriter he said, 'tapping, ringing, scraping, beating.' Later I guided him to the music table and encouraged him to use and listen to all the instruments on it.

Rita (attending a hospital school) seemed heavily drugged. As a student I had not been given any information about this. She seemed hardly aware of what was going on in the room. She made loud 'ah, ah' sounds, turned her head from side to side, and knocked her head with her fist. She made no response to any of the tests I gave her, except that she put some pictures mounted on card into her mouth. One day whilst the other children in the class were out walking with the nurses I had Rita alone. I put a number of small dolls, a brush, a compact and several pieces of material in front of her. She fingered the cotton. She then pulled at her dress, fingered the doll's hair and pushed them away. I opened the compact and placing it at the side of her said, 'Put some powder on your face.' She lifted up the puff and dabbed it on her face. She pulled the puff across her face and smiled, looked in the mirror, closed her eyes and went to sleep. Later when I was blowing up balloons for the other children she looked in my direction. I took her a balloon. She held it, patted it and pushed it to her face. She laughed, threw back her head and when I asked her to throw it to me she did. I kept on placing it in her hands. She threw it to me again and again. I then tied it to her chair and she waved it from side to side until it burst. She was startled at first but then laughed and walked over for another one which I tied on a string. She watched the other children playing with them. I tied them on a string and hung them to make a mobile. She looked at them.

Johnny was in the book corner. He was looking at the books I had made. Every now and then he would say the name of the object he saw. I made a chart that night with his name on and smaller drawings of the objects in the book. The following day we fixed up the chart in the book corner together and stuck on pictures of the objects he knew alongside the pictures on the chart. As he learns more names of objects and the associated pictures of them I shall add his progress on the chart.

The children were playing in the home corner. When I asked them what they were pouring into the cups they said, 'coffee'. I made them a coffee pot that night to add to the cups and tea pots already available.

Susan has had to learn to reach out and grasp strange objects without fear and then keep hold of them. Nine months after beginning a structured play approach with her, her mother observed that she was banging two objects together (cf. Uzgiriz and Hunt, page 46). For part of each following session I introduced her to a wide variety of objects designed to give different sound experiences; to give different experiences of texture. One day she banged a dressed plastic doll and an undressed doll on a toy table and chairs (she imitated the word 'chair') and on a small plastic bowl. Imagine the sounds she was hearing. Tissue paper was waved, shaken and 'banged' by Susan on a variety of available objects including her own legs. A new movement effort appeared—she *smoothed* the paper on her legs, on the formica-topped table and on her record player.

So I could continue example after example of ways a teacher could respond immediately to a child's observed needs. When she is responding meaningfully she is teaching. Such a strategy demands a great deal of concentration and awareness on the teacher's part and trained skilled observation. It also demands a willingness to add to the child's present experience by providing *extra* relevant materials/experiences. It also means that the teacher has to have feelings about the value and meaning to the child of the countless activities he *spontaneously* performs in the complex path he has to tread in order to develop and be able to interpret them and see their significance.[60]

6 *Structure in learning*

WITHIN THE CLASSROOM

The next important need we must examine is a specially arranged environment. If teachers do not plan the environment and the daily programme to fully engage the attention and interest of all the children, whatever their capabilities, difficulties will arise. A major difficulty will be that the teacher will not be able to give enough attention to systematic work with individual children. Not all teachers realize that they should make a great deal of equipment for themselves. Neither do they use enough voluntary help (including parents) in the classroom. If they gained this extra help many more of the children could be having the individualized programmes they so badly need with their teachers.

Although I have already described elsewhere[22] the basic requirements for classroom equipment many of us know will stimulate the children to become self-motivated, there will be constant reference throughout this chapter to the activities, the materials and the arrangement of the learning areas. A suitable learning environment can be provided by any teacher if she has access to equipment, an urge for constant hard work and an eye for the liveliness, beauty, brightness and arrangement of a classroom. She needs too to appreciate the meaning of a child's creative efforts. If she does she will take the trouble to mount and name the art work of all the children in order to display it well. Collage and simple models made by the children will also be displayed in such a way to make them attractive and to encourage the children to talk about them.

The phrases 'structuring learning' and 'structuring the environment' for learning are currently part of our educational jargon. Different teachers invited to explain these terms would probably give a variety of explanations. For practical purposes I have mainly interpreted the meaning in ways I will now discuss. Throughout, the reader will note that 'structure is never synonymous with regimentation.'[61] It can exist within an informal approach.

Order and sequence in learning
The teacher needs to look carefully at the order of the activities she systematically introduces to the child. This then will ensure that the children are given opportunities to work methodically through all the

activities with her as well as to experience and reconstruct them both in play and planned school experience. Constant observation of the spontaneous behaviour of children generally will suggest other ideas so that the teacher can introduce an ever-widening variety of ordered activities. The order in which activities are introduced by the adult to the child is perhaps one of the most important factors in all learning. Experiment, experience and research should incease the teacher's understanding of this principle so that she will apply it to severely subnormal children. The practice of collecting and keeping alongside of her in school developmental scales of all kinds will enable her to assess the meaning of the activity and the relationships in age terms.

Structured play activities (mental levels—1 year to 6 years)
Looking
(a) *Looking at moving objects*, e.g. shapes, mechanical toys, toys made to swing, some kinds of mobiles placed where children can touch them too when they are ready,* flying paper darts, torch beam on wall or ceiling, the teacher's hands clapping and feet shuffling and stamping in rhythmic fashion forwards and backwards away from the child.

(b) *Looking at stationary objects.* e.g. familiar household objects/toys/hanging toys. Looking at and handling toys one at a time. Teacher should place item in the palm of her hand (and on other parts of her body and the body of the child) for child to look at/push off/handle/take/give back and to do the same with. Brightly coloured, very large and novel (as well as familiar) items should be presented.

(c) *Making toys and objects appear and disappear.* e.g. (i) Push-up clown. (ii) The Mothercare pop-up doll; this idea was extended by

---

* Cf. GREGORY.[19] I am reminded here of a hospital ward where at least fifteen flying fishes on coiled springy wire had been purchased (£10-£15). These were placed well out of reach of the children and were not placed where wind could make them move. Olwen Gregory working on a week's course with nurses encouraged them to make 'The Jungle.' This was a six-foot-high cube-shaped frame where all manner of objects could be hung and where a number of profoundly handicapped patients could sit in a group within the cube shape amongst the dangling items and have a variety of experiences. Another teacher (Derbyshire) seeing a slide of 'The Jungle' made her own version for 'little' children in a Special Care Unit. A 3ft. × 4ft. cube frame was made with slats of wood placed across the top. From these slats she hung brightly painted tins of all sizes and sounds. Together we found the position the child had to be placed in (a) to be sure he could see the objects; (b) be motivated to stretch out his hand to touch and bring about a 'happening.'

Dianne Charlton in 1972 when she made the characters of the three bears' story in pop-up—a new kind of puppet form. (iii) Jack-in-the-box. (iv) Sweet or button hidden in hand. Both hands held out. Child has to find item. (v) 'I've got your hand' game. Take child's hand in both of yours. When he withdraws it repeat. Continue whilst he enjoys it. (vi) Adult puts her hand on the table. Child places one hand on top. Adult puts other hand on top of child's. Then child. Adult pulls hand away, then child and so on. (vii) Making games with different parts of the body disappearing, e.g. feet into socks or into sandals (partial disappearance) or into shoes, legs into wellingtons, arms into sleeves, head into jumper, hat on to head. If we have tears when mentally young children are being dressed we need to heed the possibility that to a child seeing his 'foot gone' will cause him anxieties. Adults should hide parts of their body from the child and let him see them appearing again.

(d) *Playing games of peep with people.* Adult hides behind paper/under large hat/under scarves over head/behind door or item of furniture then reappears. Encourage child to do the same with teacher/other child. Roll child in the blanket. Unroll and play 'Now he's here, now he's gone.' Let child get into large cardboard box and put down lid: 'Now he's here, now he's gone.' Use a large case with catches taken off.

   (i) Taking off hat in front of mirror for child to see. Putting hat on in front of mirror. Encourage child to do same by helping him in this action. Repeat on doll, large teddy.

  (ii) Playing hiding games with food, sweets or objects behind/under/inside transparent/opaque container(s), e.g. box(es) or tumbler(s).*

Hiding beads and toys in sand to look for.

Hiding beads and toys in sand and marking spot with coloured flag/other toys (Margaret Baker).

(iii) Uncovering, e.g. taking objects, toys, etc., off paper, card, table, etc.

(iv) Covering differing shapes and sizes of paper, card, tables, trays with objects, paste, paint, crayon, cards.

---

* I extended this idea (1973) to include noise-making moving items hidden under transparent/opaque bowls, cartons. The child is attracted by the sound, will listen and then enjoy finding the item making the noise. Mrs. Mary Lamb, one of my mothers in the Eccles (Lancashire) Self Help Group, after reading this list of activities made up another original useful game for her 7-year-old handicapped child. A tower of graded cups was made and a piece of paper hidden in between the flat surfaces of two cups. The game was to guess where the paper was hidden.

(e) *Playing peep games*† with specially made/bought equipment.
(f) *Posting objects*, e.g. balls, bricks, three-dimensional shapes, through very large specially made posting boxes. Posting items through varying sizes and shapes of aperture. Jill O'Brien (1974) extended this idea by putting children inside large boxes, cardboard houses, along with the items to 'post' outwards. She named this technique the 'In-Stimulus'. Clearly, such a method demands an adult to cooperate to post back from time to time. The apertures cut in the boxes should be so considered that some objects will not go through; some objects (e.g. paper, cloth) will only go through if their shape is changed.
(g) *Matching* objects, shapes, colours, textures. Matching with one, two, three differences.
(h) Looking for the missing object, e.g.
   (i) Child has two pictures before him, say a goldfish bowl complete with fish and plants. One of the pictures has movable cut-outs of the items it contains. Child has to complete picture by comparing with the model.
   (ii) Teacher builds up a scene of a room with toy furniture. Child copies. When complete, child looks away and teacher removes one/two/three items. Child has to find them, tell teacher which items are missing.
   (iii) Teacher places three/four/five items in front of child and tells him to look at them. Child then turns away. Teacher places removed item amongst other items in a different place on the table and tells child to find what is missing. This game can be played with/without language.
(i) *Looking at specially made films and slides.**

Touching, grasping, giving, dropping
(a) *Touching* and mothing everything (safety to be considered here). Feeling objects with feet and other parts of the body.
(b) *Grasping* (cloth, paper). Cover child's face with tissue paper, cloth. Cover one's own face with cloth for child to pull off. Cover doll in pram/bed for child to pull off cover.
(c) *Giving* objects:
   (i) to a person at the side of him who in turn gives it to the teacher

---

† Ann Southren (1970) pasted together half-a-dozen cube-like boxes to make a peep box. Each of the boxes had a hole pierced into its side. Games of peep and see what is there (toys, sweets, objects of all kinds) were very popular indeed.

* The lives of the children themselves at home, in school. Slides showing sequences of familiar activities (cf. page 92).

who in turn gives it to the child;
(ii) to a person directly in front of him (someone might have to help him from behind).

Giving and taking objects which are small/larger/very big, objects making a noise/objects making no noise, objects of different textures.

(d) *Dropping* soft/hard objects from varying heights, objects which do/do not roll when dropped, objects which roll and make a noise.

Carrying, emptying, pouring, filling

(a) *Carrying* toys/objects about the environment, e.g. paper on floor to paper basket, cutlery from drawer to table, toy from table to cupboard, plate from table to shelf.

(b) *Emptying* bags/baskets/boxes of various-shaped objects, e.g. soft toys, balls, bricks. Jill O'Brien (1974) (discussing with a mother the problem of toys all over the place when her handicapped child had finished emptying them out of the box) suggested a substantial wooden box with holes drilled in the sides. Toys and objects could then be tied on long/short string or elastic. Any thrown out would then be easily retrievable. (Barry was a triplegic man of 26 years functioning at a profoundly subnormal level when I first met him in 1963. In order to give him a game to play alone whilst I worked with other profoundly handicapped men in the group I tied bean bags to his wrists with elastic. A box/bucket/bag in front of him gave him plenty of aiming practice. He could retrieve the bean bags for himself and so was independent in this.) A large transparent plastic toy box with/without holes drilled in the sides would enable the handicapped child to know toys were there (O. Gregory, 1972).

Emptying liquids/other materials from containers.

(c) *Filling* bags/boxes/baskets with a variety of items

Filling containers of various-shaped openings, e.g. bottles, jars, boxes, with straws/pebbles/buttons/beans/liquids.

(d) *Pouring* liquids from bottles and other transparent vessels

Pouring liquids from opaque jugs/bottles/teapots.

Pouring some liquid from and leaving some in a transparent bottle/jug/bowl, opaque jug/bottle/teapot/bowl.

Pouring liquids, e.g. jelly mixture into transparent bowls (M. McKay, 1968)

I should like to suggest that a dozen liquid-soap containers each with a hole/holes arranged in various places (on the side, in the bottom) will provide a host of learning experiences for the children

during bath time and water play.
(e) *Carrying* objects from a bag/box/basket to scales. Returning objects from scales to container.
Transferring objects from a container to scales, taking them from scales, putting them into a bag and 'selling.'

Manipulation
Pulling own socks off. Adult puts them on again (on and off).
Pushing things down. Pulling things up. Twirling objects round.
Putting fingers in hollow objects. Making holes in soft substances with fingers/sticks of various thicknesses.
Scribbling with pencils/crayons/chalk/felt-tip pens, etc.
Rolling cars up and down/forwards and backwards.
Rolling cars down an incline.
Taking cars up an incline.
Handling and manipulating varied objects and continuous (e.g. water, sand, flour) materials.
Taking lids off boxes, tops off jars/bottles. Putting lids on boxes/jars/bottles, etc.
Playing with opening and shutting toys.
Opening/closing doors and cupboards with various kinds of handles.
Nesting objects, e.g. towers, dolls, cubes.

Reconstructing life activities. Play with the adult.
Reconstruction of real life activities using strong sets of toys (kept especially for individual work with boys and girls in language development), e.g.:
(1) Going to bed and getting up. Family figures/a bed with mattress, pillows, sheets, blanket, cover. A chest of drawers, a chair, a wardrobe, etc.
(2) Kitchen furniture and activities items, e.g. two plastic washing-up bowls plus dishes plus tea towels and dishcloths (small for intimacy with a young child). Two sets provided so that if the child is at the imitation stage he can imitate the teacher's actions. Other kitchen items for setting a table, cooking, etc.
(3) To date I have never seen a good-sized toy replica of a bathroom including the toilet. Perhaps some toy firm would make good the omission for in using these with fair-sized dolls the teacher would have many opportunities for giving important words in the reconstruction situation (cf. Chapter on the young mentally handicapped child), e.g. up, down, on, off. Adrian plays washing the man, lady, baby doll using a tiny plastic bowl, soap, nailbrush, toothbrush and towels.

(4) Other toys to reconstruct the life situation, e.g. if a particular child lives with a family having a car, a caravan, a tent.
(5) A model of a playground complete with slide, roundabout, swings and a seesaw. Oval shaped toys represent the people.
(6) A stainless steel sink with taps that turn on real water. Complete with draining rack and tiny dishes.
(7) Two baskets (one big, one small) shaped the same, complete with plastic representations of fruit and paper bags.
(8) A stove complete with light in oven and pans for cooking, plasticine meat, peas, bacon, etc.

Much of the play might take place with the adult (a) on the floor with the child, (b) on high stools using a long shelf, or (c) on a table where both can sit alongside each other comfortably. I have found in my play with Adrian that his interest for this kind of play has increased from 15-minute sessions to those lasting up to 40 minutes. By this I mean that he will go away from the task after 40 minutes quite spontaneously—and find another one. This does not happen every time we play but on many occasions it does.

One of the disturbing features of the teaching of the young mentally handicapped child under eight is that one rarely sees the class teacher (even when she has an assistant) involved and engrossed with an individual child in this kind of imaginative symbolic reconstructive activity designed to enable the child's comprehension of his world and language to develop. Neither does one see the kind of appropriate equipment I have described for the play that is needed. Table activities of the inset jigsaw type are still too much a feature of the school's activities—'minding' education not SPECIAL. Joan Reynell[62] in a paper presented to a Study Group attended by 28 academics in 1972 asserts that from a preliminary investigation where 'graded symbolic play material (large dolls and tea-sets, small model village play) was used there is evidence that the ability for symbolic processing, as indicated by the use of symbolic play material, is a necessary basis for adequate verbal language development.' This links up logically with the work of Lunzer and Hulme (cf. Chapter 8 Understood play.), where Lunzer says that 'representation is the precursor of language.' Reynell's paper should be compulsory reading for all those concerned with the mentally handicapped.

*Doll play linked to reconstructing daily activity of child**
Handling homemade rag dolls of different sizes and weights, e.g. very

---

* I have used a large number of shop-bought dolls representing babies, a man, a woman, a girl, etc. Arms, legs, eyes and a foot have detached

large ones, fat ones, long thin ones.
Undressing/dressing dolls; pretend feeding/washing the dolls.
Putting dolls' clothes on hangers.
Taking dolls out of beds—different sizes of beds to fit dolls.
Dressing dolls for bed/for winter/for wet weather/for the beach, etc.
(from Kindergarten, Zagreb, Yugoslavia).
Dressing boy dolls, girl dolls.
Comparing sizes of doll's clothes with own/other children's.
Helping to make a doll. Making dolls (large).
Making dolls' clothes.

Simple construction
(a) *Building* 'towers' and 'bridges' with bricks of all sizes and textures. Building with large cardboard boxes, some covered in materials, e.g. fur, wallpaper, foam, plastic, etc. Building up towers with large, thick, oblong cards.
(b) *Simple form boards,* i.e. shapes of familiar objects, familiar objects placed to build up a picture. (i) Child takes out pieces of the inset. Adult puts them in. (ii) Child puts in inset. (iii) Child puts in and takes out insets.
(c) *Jigsaws*
  (i) 2/3/4/5 pieces in the first instance.
  (ii) Heads and tails games. Vertical and horizontal cuts, e.g. rabbit sitting up cut horizontally and elephant/dog cut vertically into 2/3 pieces. Other animals, fish, people.
  (iii) Find the face. Cut-outs of faces from magazines. Fit together 2/3/4 pieces to make the face.
  (iv) Find the smiling face, the sad face, the man's/woman's/child's/baby's face.
(d) *Geoboards.* Supply children with a variety of nail boards with different numbers of nails (2, 3, 4, etc.) and different arrangements on them (e.g. a circle, an oblong, a circle with a nail in the centre) and some rubber bands (limited number or unlimited number, same colour or variety of colours). Recently I have seen a giant geoboard 6′ × 4′. Elastic was used instead of rubber bands. The creative effect was attractive.

Sorting, arranging, associating, sequencing
(a) *Sorting in the general environment,* e.g. crayons, scissors, leaves,

---

themselves. I found this useful in testing the comprehension of a normal little girl of 3½ years without expressive language. 'Show me the doll without an arm, with no eyes,' etc.

dolls' clothes, pebbles, musical instruments.
Piling up objects/papers/magazines.
(b) *Arranging* objects in line, e.g. cubes, oblongs, toy animals, cars, etc. Same cars/different cars, same colour/different colours.
Ball mosaics. Obtain apple container trays and several coloured balls to fit/match. Obtain egg trays and pot eggs.
Make patterns with child.
Pegboard patterns. (Large size pegboards)
Arranging items in the shop, e.g. big/little tube of smarties.
Arranging the sets of dolls' clothes in colours/sizes/by use.
Setting the table for 1/2/3/4 people (i) with pictorial plans for matching; (ii) with diagrammatic plan for matching; (iii) with no plan.
(c) *Ordering*.
  (i) Giving one-to-one relationships (several boxes of apparatus). Use up to five objects/pictures of each example. Examples:

soap—towel	toothbrush—paste	bed—pillow
gun—soldier	cup—saucer	car—garage
pipe—man	knife—fork	hat—man/lady/boy/girl
tie—man	wrist watch—lady	straw—bottle
egg—egg cup	basket—lady	beads—lady
collar—dog	dog—dog basket	bird—bird cage
chair—doll		

 (ii) Matching seriation of shapes/objects; (a) real objects; (b) pictures
 (iii) Simple classification. Lotto cards to include dress, food, people, pets, men's/women's/children's clothing; using mail order catalogues (two) one can devise useful classification. The children are often familiar with these catalogues and so are interested in the pictures.

(d) *Sets of sequences* depicting actions from life. Seven cards would depict many activities from beginning to the end.
Examples:
  put on vest (plus bra if an older child)—vest
  put on knickers—pants
  put on underskirt—trousers
  put on dress—T-shirt
  put on socks—socks
  put on shoes—shoes

take toothpaste tube	put plug in bowl
unscrew cap	turn on taps

take toothbrush	feel water
squeeze paste on brush	turn off taps
brush teeth	soaping hands
drink water	rinsing hands
spit out into bowl	drying
fill the kettle	cup, saucer, spoon
boil water (stove or plug)	pour in milk
put tea in teapot	pour in tea
steam from kettle	put in some sugar
pour in water	stir with spoon
stir	return spoon to saucer
put on teapot lid	drink tea

Whilst six, seven actions would be necessary, in each complete sequence the six or seven cards could be duplicated to make a pack of cards. Games like Happy Families could be played or two children with the same pack each could see who was first to find all the sets in his own pack. Table games are enjoyed by many mentally handicapped adolescents.[63]

Planned deliberate periods of listening, pre-verbal and verbal stage
It is now an established fact that talking is not instinctive but has to be acquired. Listening skills are probably also acquired in a varied environment of random and planned noise and specific sound experience. The rhythmic elements in speech patterns cannot be ignored and it would seem to be logical therefore, in helping a mentally handicapped child to listen with fun and enjoyment, to exaggerate the intuitive practice of the mother of a normal baby and expose the child to long periods of listening:
(i) to a wide variety of records with a good rhythm whilst in close bodily contact with an adult who can move rhythmically to the particular tune being played—this might mean bouncing the child up and down vigorously, rocking the child to and fro using his hands, swaying from side to side to a gentle tune;
(ii) to sung nursery rhyme tunes and other songs enjoyed by the adult using the vowels and consonants as the words. Each vowel and consonant over a period of time would then be introduced to the child, e.g. ttt/t-t/t-t/t-t/ttt/ttt/t—/t— for Little Bo-Peep, and so on. All the speech sounds could be presented in this way over and over again to the child, preferably before he comes to school but at school if he has had no planned education before coming to school. Sometimes this could be done with the adult's facial expression

controlled, sometimes with the eyes covered up and with nothing else going on (e.g. play). We cannot assume that the severely subnormal (when he is ready) will have heard all the speech sounds around him sufficiently clearly to imitate them correctly;

(iii) when we 'walk' our fingers over a child's body in playful tickling we can use rhythmic patterns of sound, e.g. la la la la la la looooooooooooooooooow ending up with a lovely 'w' sound. Whilst holding on to the looooooo sound we can make a cresendo and diminuendo. Whilst saying la la we can go very slowly/quickly. Many many variations of sound play can be utilized by the adult in the one-to-one situation with a child in this way to stimulate listening and develop attention;

(iv) when we walk dolly, teddy on a surface we can say or sing whatever sounds come into our head—dum dum dum dum dum daaaaaaaaaaaa (jump the toy into the air and make him fall) —here the child will be hearing the stress of the rhythms and the sounds; he will also be anticipating the daaaaaaaaaaaa when the doll falls down. We cannot expect a young mentally handicapped child to listen without something motoric/visual going on at the same time. John, a profoundly handicapped, undersized boy of 13 years was having music with his class. Two children, Linda and Paul, were sitting on the floor in the middle of the ring. All the adults and children present were told to whisper 'Lin-*da*,' over and over again until I clapped my hands, when they had to shout 'Paul'. John's anticipation of my clapping was evidenced by his imitation of my open hands at the ready;

(v) stopping and starting a record/your own song/your own beating/blowing on an instrument can be good fun, and will encourage a child to listen and watch if, when the sound(s) stop, a toy on a string is held up and is *still* (whilst noise is going on toy is being jigged about on a string);

(vi) stopping and starting clapping, beating a drum, ringing a bell when a signal of some kind is given;

(vii) hiding a wound-up mechanical toy under a box, bowl, cloth for child to find; hiding it under the child's dress; up the boy's jumper.

Using these particular little games I have worked for at least 40 minutes/hour with the pre-school children I am concerned with during the first twelve months of my relationship with them. Music and rhythmic work is relaxing for the adults and child and there seems to be a possibility that the closeness, the fun, the pleasure might be part of positive early socialization patterns as well as the beginnings of listening. Joan Ryan, in an article on the development of language in the *New Scientist*, May 1974, writes 'we know something about how children master the more formal aspects of language particularly the grammar. We know only a little about how such skills grow out of social interaction with others and how these skills are used to further this interaction.'

I should just like to add a word of warning here regarding the smallest bell as a result of a very interesting observation I made when working with Adrian and Jamie. Their mother and I and the two children had all been having fun with kazoos—low, loud, crude sounds. To give them a sound comparison I handed out the bells. I played the smallest, tinkliest bell. Jamie (age $4\frac{1}{2}$) wanted it so, as I thought I knew he was past the mouthing of objects stage, I handed it to him without fear. He immediately put it into his mouth. In other words he was making an adaptation to the little bell from what he had assimilated through his experience with the kazoo. The little bell is now removed from my sounds when I play with little children.

Listening toys
An old tin lid. An old tin tray.
Toothbrush holders containing three grains of rice/two silver cake balls (very soft, gentle sounds).
Musical toothbrush/hairbrush (Boots the Chemists).
Pull-out-the-string toy. As it returns into box a nursery rhyme is played.
Tea towel marble holder (makes a terrific din).
Plastic hammer containing tiny beads.
Two wooden cages with bells inside. Two tubular cages with bells inside.
Poppet beads (child has to really listen to hear the 'pop').
Two wooden pop guns.
Two wooden trumpets.
Two kazoos.
Two small tambourines.
Rocking musical rabbit, clown, Mickey Mouse.
Rattles of various kinds—different sound qualities.
Tiny xylophone.
Several bells with heavy/light quality sounds.
Small accordion.
Peas/stones in typewriter ribbon and Selotape tins.
Plastic hand puppet that rustles.
Turn-over-and-return toy cow sound. Shake-up-and-down bird sound.

Wind-up ladybird, toy car, butterfly with moving wings, crocodile, robot.
Whistle, pan pipes, recorder.
Live 'n Learn wind-up toys—five little figures walk round a revolving platform, climb up a ladder and slide down the slide back on to the platform again—music plays as the toy is wound or the child winds for himself (Jamie had mastered this by $5\frac{1}{2}$ years after months of trying and watching me and his mother activating the toy.)

Other ideas for daily listening sessions (5-10 minutes according to age/stage

A few of these ideas have been taken directly from the notebooks of student teachers. Others have been inserted spontaneously as I recalled the ideas. Further ideas have been introduced to teachers during In-Service music workshops.

Listening to:
  zips on boots, anoraks;
  door opening and closing;
  knocks on a door;
  the bell on a door, the knocker on a door;
  the wind rattling windows;
  knocks on a wall, table, chair, floor;
  sounds of leaves, twigs (rustling, cracking, snapping of these);
  plates being put in a pile, cups being put on saucers;
  sounds in the woodwork room (Crossland Ward taped these sounds);
  milk/water being poured into a bottle;
  peas in a pan, a tin box, a plastic container;
  hands clapping, tapping, banging;
  different kinds of paper—combine the experience after listening to each one separately;
  variety of clocks ticking (rapidly, slowly, loudly, softly);
  anticipating the chime of a clock, the alarm, the ping of a kitchen timer;
  one child playing an instrument in accompaniment to a record or tune played by the teacher on a piano, guitar, recorder (each child to have a turn);
  elastic stretched over cardboard;
  all the sounds that can be made with the mouth, with the mouth and fingers, mouth and hands;
  all the sounds that can be made with the hands, fingers;
  an adult blowing up a paper bag and popping it;

a scale on the piano;
children walking up a plank of wood in slippers, shoes, boots, wellingtons, slippers;
musicians playing their own special instrument—violin, flute;
everyday sounds in the school;
the teeth of a comb—rub thumb across them;
the fingers over corrugated cardboard;
the sounds made with flat palm, fingers, fist applied to various objects from the home;
man singing, woman singing, children singing, etc.

As the children get older and more experienced in having their attention brought to the interest of sound in the world around them, representations of these sounds can be made by the teacher on tape. The teacher and the children can have lots of fun together collecting sounds on their walks. One student collected sounds with the children from a building site just alongside the school; another, the bird sounds in the park; another, sounds in the railway station. The possibilities seem limitless but we have to give ourselves time during the day to work in sound with the children. Their enjoyment of sound has never been in doubt in my mind. Continual inattention might indicate hearing difficulties in some children, of course.

One of the greatest difficulties the teacher of these children will experience is the tendency within herself to abandon thinking about sequence in the activities. This might be because the handicapped, as far as I can say, do not seem to proceed from (a) to (b) in the steps we want them to pass through. In fact it seems that if we follow them faithfully in the cues they give us there seems to be little order initially. What I am trying to suggest in discussing structure in learning is that the teacher must become acquainted as far as this is possible with the order of some of the activities she wishes the child to have. The teacher of severely subnormal children should *always* be ready to abandon her own preconceived plan and follow the response of the child if the activity she presents does not gain the response she wants. If she is flexible enough to do this she is more likely to maximize upon what the child gives. If she is inflexible and persists in her own plans she might find lack of attention, lack of concentration, lack of interest, disturbed behaviour and temper tantrums. In this way the session will be wasted. She will certainly not experience how the child can teach her something about learning. In following the child she will be surprised at what he knows and about the things which interest *him*. She will also see a considerable amount of attention and concentration (cf. Gillham, page 75).*

The activities I have suggested should form a small part of the curriculum for each child.† All the children should have the experiences involved in the activites described. Sometimes these will be in play and will arise naturally; often they will be because the teacher has introduced them in a systematic way to the child. The activities presented here for the teacher's consideration should be examined frequently and added to. Fine gradations in the learning will be discovered by a teacher who is observing and recording the reactions of the children. She should not be afraid of repetition. Her part is to discover activities and how to present them to the child so as to bring forth the best responses. The child's attention will generally be a pointer to his readiness and interest. If a child is not responding she must turn to another activity where a positive response is gained and shown by attention and interest. Sometimes she will need to change the position of the child[48] or the object.[23] Each group of activities has been arranged into some kind of order as also the separate items within the groups. Some teachers have found it useful to keep a chart displaying these activities up on the classroom wall. They have then been able to record each child's involvement in the experience. If they consult these charts they will rarely be at a loss about what to do in some of the very difficult situations found in working with this group of children. The list of activities will certainly be useful. Whilst work with individual children might always be along the lines suggested by the previously described activities, creative work of all kinds (storytelling, singing, painting) and the teaching of skills should also be part of the teacher's individual approach. Sometimes the follow-up of a child's interest will be the major part of the session.

Example
Michael's interest in the pictures of aeroplanes led the teacher to supply some small pictures for Michael to make his own picture book of aeroplanes; talking to him about them; helping him to make models of large and small aeroplanes in soft wood were the mainstay of the individual sessions with Michael over a short period of time. Later on the teacher made a game for Michael which involved number matching to five, viz. a large picture of an aeroplane was presented and each part was given a number, 1–5. Numbered, cut-out parts of the plane were also part of the game. A dice was thrown and the number appearing matched with the numbered cut-out which was then placed on the relevant part of the picture.

---

* At last we have a psychologist talking about interest not distraction.
† Clearly, this presupposes the teacher is continually searching for, making and collecting a wide variety of materials, specially-chosen toys and well-designed aids.

One of my reasons for describing such simple activities is in fact because of their simplicity. Playing with children (particularly those whose physical development is so much ahead of their intellectual development) at such a simple level does not seem to be intuitive in most adults.* Unless playing with very young children has been part of the teacher's experience she is likely to think that letting the child feel her shoes, helping him to empty toys from a box and so on is largely a waste of time. In presenting this list I want to suggest that this is not so. The skilful teacher will be able to see where the activities fit into the pattern of learning. We have found many of the activities useful in working with older physically handicapped children, and also children in their teens who have come to a standstill, as it were, in their development, and of whom one often hears it said, 'He will never get anywhere. It is not worth doing anything with him.'

The knowledgeable teacher will always remember that the results of any systematic teaching that is carried out will not be stable unless the child has reached the appropriate stage necessary for such teaching to take place.

Purposeful arrangement in the classroom
The way in which the teacher arranges the areas of activity in order that the children can make sense from what is presented is another aspect of structure in my thinking about a structured environment. Classrooms should not look like junk rooms.† Neither should they contain only one or two areas of activity. The following pages contain descriptions of a number of learning areas. I should like to feel confident that teachers aimed at providing most of them in one way or another. A few examples might serve to illustrate what I mean by purposeful arrangement.

Home play areas
Home play areas need to continue to represent for the children the

---

* Whenever I have organized teachers' workshops on play, materials and toys have been produced for them to explore. On occasions when they were not presented with a task card, they have started to play at an imaginative dramatic play level. The fun of manipulating objects and exploring their properties was nearly always omitted and yet it is often at this more basic level that the adults need to be thinking in the early years of the mentally handicapped child.

† A name given to some of them by a research worker in the late 'sixties. Some classrooms have indeed warranted the term; others do nothing still but deprive.

various major activities of the home—sleeping, cooking, washing up and eating, so that in parallel or associative play they can reconstruct once more with appropriately-sized equipment the representations of life play they have had or are currently having with smaller equipment with an adult. The bookshelf could also be incorporated in this area as well as a carpet, and curtains up at the window. If the positioning allows, this might very well be a real window. I am often concerned when I see some home corners (sometimes in schools for normal little children too); they are certainly not always cared for and replenished with relevant items. One of the planned tasks of the classroom assistants could very well be to replenish and check that this area is always in a state of beauty and interest for the child. This means that, once established, additions can be made as the children's needs in their play are seen.

An arrangement within the home play area
The teacher had set the table for two before the children entered the room. On one of the plates there was a small portion of dough and a plastic knife and fork as a place setting. What a lovely idea to encourage all kinds of experiences. Wayne pulled the plate towards him and poked several holes in it with the handle of the plastic knife. He touched a piece which had broken away. He picked this up on the end of his knife. He went on poking holes in the dough.

Half a dozen 'eggs' (made in clay) in an egg container and a small frying pan on the 'stove' stimulated plenty of imaginative play.

One child had told his teacher that they drank coffee in his home. The following day she provided (in addition to the usual cups, saucers and teapot found in home corners) a coffee pot imaginatively shaped from stiff card.

Home areas
Not all schools for the mentally handicapped are fortunate enough to have a home-making area in a separate place. The adolescent handicapped child needs such a place in which to practise home skills in as natural a way as possible (by this I do not mean in well-equipped home economics rooms but in specially prepared areas where the real items of home are present). Ideally such areas will also give the children opportunities to:
(a) represent their experiences in spontaneous dramatic play;
(b) use the area to practise social skills under the guidance of their teachers.

Within a month one formal home economics room had been transformed into the kind of area I am referring to. A mock fireplace had been constructed by the teacher and the children, and the children had brought ornaments and photographs of their families. A worn carpet, two old fireside chairs, a table and dining room chairs motivated the teacher to help the children make simple cushions and mats for the table. A room divider separated this area from the bedroom, which contained a chest of drawers (a most useful piece of learning equipment) and a bed (no money had been immediately available to construct this home area so an old hospital-type bed had been obtained and painted). The set of bedclothes enabled the children to practise, sometimes in play, sometimes under guidance, the skills in bedmaking and the sequence of the activity.

The home economics part of the room then took on more meaning—bedclothes needed washing, food made in the room could be eaten in the dining area. If such an area as described is available, it is possible for the teacher to work with small groups of children in 'cookery' whilst the others play in the rest of the home.

Another school I visited in Barrow-in-Furness had a spare room at the top of the large house which was their school. This had been comfortably furnished (not with newly bought modern furniture) with a sideboard, a carpet, curtains, table, chairs, settee, TV, a record player and a selection of records. There was even a tape recorder for use by the children.* Each group of children in the school had their turn in this home-like learning environment.

Water play
Water play, so often frowned upon for the adolescents, should, nevertheless, be available so that the children can learn useful skills and gain ideas about liquids other than in a purely sensory way.† How it is available will depend upon the teacher's imagination and upon her awareness to preserve the dignity of an older child. One way in which I saw this being carried out was most successful. The following items were put into the environment during a free choice of activities session: a dish rack, four plastic cups and saucers, knives and forks and plates, a wooden spoon, an enamel jug, a dish mop, a tea towel, a

---

* In my book on Language (in preparation), I shall be discussing more fully creative talking and the mentally handicapped.

† Imitating the action of pouring milk or lemonade into a cup, tea into cup from a teapot is most difficult for many severely subnormal children. They need opportunities in their play to help them with this activity as well as with their teacher in a more planned session.

large plastic bowl, a bucket in which to carry the water, washing-up liquid.

It does not take much imagination to see the many learning experiences which could be gained not only in manipulative skills but in social behaviour. I do not really need to say that the real experiences of washing up should be ever present at school as it might too at home. In the pretend situation, skills and the associated language could be practised with the teacher or a friend on as many occasions as was wanted by any children who wished to play in this way.

Dressing-up area

Dressing-up clothes that are presented to the children are often placed in a box and dumped in a corner. Clothes in the home are found either in the wardrobe on hangers, or in drawers. In structuring the children's learning in this play situation we perhaps need to simulate this practice more (at least in part) and hang up the clothes on a bar if no cupboard is available.

In a hospital school class the dressing-up corner not only contained clothes and hats all arranged on hangers and hooks, but a bed made by standing three tea chests in a row. A fat, five-foot-long woman doll and a long, thin doll of similar height reclining in the bed gave several of the children (15+) plenty of opportunity to practise making the bed, talking to the dolls, comparing them with their own heights. A dressing table with dressing stool (improvised again from two tea chests) and containing perfume bottles, powders, talcs, lipsticks, deodorants, again gave the children opportunities to experience materials which would not be part of their normal hospital life. 'Some of the boys came up to me to tell me to smell them after using the talcs,' 'Angela spent a lot of her time looking at herself in the mirror, poking her nose, rubbing her hair and touching a mirror.' Plenty of 'hairdresser' play took place. In an opposite corner of the classroom small beds and dolls with complete sets of clothing and a small wardrobe were available. What a host of learning experiences were possible in these two stimulating and engineered situations (Jill O'Brien, 1967).

If amongst the dressing-up clothes the teacher places a couple of cases (big and little), the children will have plenty of opportunity to fold, pack (a qualitative extension of filling) and hang. A case packed with a child's own clothes was used by me to make an initial relationship with a young lady of 13 years during an observation workshop session. A long golden dance dress had been put in the case when she was doing something else. A useful conversation about her clothes ensued and great was her surprise (novelty) when she found the dance dress. She put it on and then told us all about her boy friend (creative talking).

AN ENVIRONMENT STRUCTURED FOR LEARNING

Shops and shopping

Shops are becoming a well-known feature of many of the classrooms. Few of them yet are giving the children the daily opportunity of spending small amounts of money. However the classroom shop or simulated supermarket (to be even more up to date), if it is well thought out and not just a collection of boxes and tins, can be instrumental in giving the children a very wide range of learning experiences.

In setting up the shop the teacher needs to consider carefully what it is the children are likely to be learning from her provision. If she thinks only in terms of imaginative shopkeeper-and-customer play she will be frustrated especially with the younger children for they will not use it in this way at first. She needs to see shop play in a much wider context. Solitary play in the shop will be carried out by the children over a long period of time. During this time they will be filling and emptying all the objects provided, transferring objects from the carrier bags to the scales, unwrapping parcels put there for the purpose. Later on they will be 'weighing,' 'selling,' 'ordering and arranging the 'goods.' The provision needs to be imaginative. It should also help the child become acquainted with familiar items purchased in real shops. Perhaps the teacher can make the learning even more purposeful by making sure that there are large tins/boxes, small tins/boxes, of items to 'weigh,' e.g. dog biscuits, dried beans and peas, *papier mâché* fruit and vegetables, flour and salt 'bread', sausage rolls, bread rolls, cakes, meat pies, etc. Real fruit and vegetables can be available for a change; these certainly stimulate the children's shop play.

Shop play of course should not remain in the classroom. At all ages it should be reinforced by real shopping in nearby shops and supermarkets. Teachers should be constantly seeking reasons to take the children to the shops for necessary purchases. As the children get older, and with the parents' consent, the teacher could perhaps help the children to buy small personal items, e.g. tie, pair of socks, hankerchiefs, etc. The experience must never be underestimated even if only one item is purchased. At all times the children's abilities should be used: to ask for the items, to offer the money, to carry the purchases back to school. Parents could be asked to cooperate by letting their child buy something small for the home—either alone or in the company of his class and teacher. As the children develop this could become a regular feature of their weekly programme. A pictorial record of the experience could be made for the children by the teacher. Some children might be able to keep their own record of purchases.

With regard to shops and shopping it is very encouraging to see an increasing number of schools having a shop where the children can spend their own money. It is a useful method of teaching for severely subnormal children need reality in this practical experience to encourage them to carry small amounts of money themselves, to learn that money has purchasing power, to learn to recognize the coins and to learn the names of the coins. Janice Sinson,[35] describing the afternoon programme for the little children in the Mencap Nursery, Leeds, shows how a structured scheme relating to:

(a) the ability to choose the correct coin from two different kinds in a box;
(b) keeping money safely in a pocket;
(c) handing the coin to the shopkeeper for sweets (no sweets if coin not handed) after removing it from pocket;

can be a useful learning experience even with little pre-school handicapped children.

Equipment encouraging learning (provided by a student, Jo Needham during one of her teaching practices)

An inflatable 'Diddy Man.' Kevin gave him a drink and then gave the 'doggy' on wheels a 'drink'. Later he fed him using a spoon he had discovered on the table. Hanging objects gave the children much scope for looking at them, pushing, pulling, dodging in and out of them, shaking and moving them aside. Examples:

an oblong pillow with a face on it;
plastic ducks in three sizes;
necklet which rattled when a child pulled it;
a small red and blue knitted doll;
a triangular-shaped bean-bag;
two beakers joined together containing one pea which rattled when moved;
a man made from threaded milk bottle tops (one little boy was completely fascinated by the gentle sound which issued forth when he shook it).

Arrangement of music table
All children, including the severely subnormal, should be given

opportunities for making spontaneous music of their own by free access to a music table. So often one finds that the teacher has not given any thought as to how she can arrange it to help the child to discriminate between the various sounds coming from different instruments. In addition to having a table on which the children may find a range of sounds and instruments, there should be a table on which different-looking instruments (and these will be homemade as well as bought) produce a similar quality of sound. Similarly on another occasion she could provide a separate table for instruments which need to be shaken/struck. Helping the children to rearrange the instruments at the end of the day in some sort of ordered way might be something which will repay our attention, e.g. the shapes of the instruments could be drawn in outline on a chart lying flat on the table so that the children can match them (Louise Knight). Pictures of the instruments could be drawn alongside a row of hooks on which some of the instruments could be hung. In order to build up visual concepts of a series, similar-looking shakers of various sizes (heights, thicknesses) could be provided and arranged by the teacher. The matching of the shapes in the rearrangement by the children will provide them with the experience of a special kind of order. Few teachers are seriously considering the part that could be played in building concepts through attention to the points I have tried to make in this section. Some do not yet have a music area of learning.

Arrangement of nature table
This should illustrate shape, the colour, size and language of number. The points I have just made about the music table could also apply in some ways to nature tables. A random collection of items (collected when the children are out with their teacher, brought from home or supplied by the teacher) is useful and interesting as a talking point. They can be set out by the children in a random way over and over again with great interest. However the teacher should be constantly thinking about how she can build up the children's ideas about the world by the way in which she arranges the experience. She has also to remember that her task is not finished when the arrangement is made. She must bring the children's attention to it by talking and getting the children talking and making the arrangement for themselves. Those whose level of development suggests that they are able to represent graphically, should record the experience in clay, paint, crayon, etc.

An interesting example of arrangement springs to mind. The table was covered—half of it with yellow paper, half with orange. On the yellow half there was a bowl of daffodils. On the orange side there was a goldfish in a bowl. If the reader ponders for a while on this, the implications of the arrangement will become clear. Using basically the same items other possibilities might present themselves:

(i) The bowl in which the daffodils were placed could be the same kind as the one in which the goldfish lived.
(ii) The vase for the daffodils could be opaque and painted yellow. The bowl for the goldfish could be opaque and orange.
(iii) The bowl for the daffodils could be tall, the bowl for the goldfish squat—transparent, opaque, etc.

Special arrangements which help the child to link up ideas, e.g. about a hedgerow, the sea shore, a croft (a waste piece of land), will easily spring to mind.

ENVIRONMENT ARRANGED TO CATER FOR SPECIAL NEEDS

It would appear that there are some children who find particular difficulty in attending to specific tasks in a stimulating environment such as one would hope to find existing for the majority of severely subnormal children. I do not want to name categories of children who fall into this group. If the teacher considers each child individually she will soon know which children need this kind of help. There will not be too many in any one group. It would seem that her responsibility here is to provide the kind of environment he needs for some part of each day, i.e. a place limited to the barest essentials—always remembering that he must spend the greater part of his life in an environment full of attractive and distracting influences, and ultimately he has to learn to cope with these.

Perhaps the schools of the future will have a number of 'individual teaching' rooms in which a teacher and child can work alone in surroundings which have minimal stimuli. These children are always with us whatever school we teach in.* In thinking about an environment for them we cannot ignore the fact that it should be different from that of other children if they are to achieve some measure of success in learning. If there are no spare rooms in the school at least the teacher could devise a three-walled screen around one of the tables so that the child, or she and the child, could work

---

* I can remember Brian (age 13 years, secondary modern school) who would only begin to do his sums if I covered up all the sums on a page except the one he was doing.

STRUCTURE IN LEARNING

undisturbed.† In such a way the teacher shows her flexibility in thinking and providing for special needs. In discussing this point with a Matron of a nearby residential unit‡ she told me how one severely hyperactive child became perfectly calm and still at the cinema. Perhaps this suggests that school should have its own dark room and film/colour projector for work with such children.

DIFFERENT ENVIRONMENTS AS CHILDREN DEVELOP

The keen observer should see differences in terms of provision, activities carried out, and attitudes of the teacher in the various classrooms of a school for severely subnormal children. I am reminded that this is an important point to mention after hearing the criticisms of a group of teachers who visited a lively and progressive school as part of the refresher course they were attending. 'You cannot see any progression of work as you go from one classroom to another to the next.' It was a useful comment and it made me think about the broad differences one would expect to see in the environment for children at varying levels of development.

COMPARISON OF ENVIRONMENTS

Less mature children	*More mature children*
Environment would cater for gross motor development.	Gross motor development catered for in Physical Education.
Opportunities for simple creative work, results of which teacher would display—scribbles, squirls, daubs, lines and circular shapes. Collage with varied materials.	Wider selection of simple constructional toys, table games using dice or pictorial instructions (cf. page 134) and creative materials. The use of these will reveal the child's growing ability to represent graphically the world about him.
Teacher would be approaching each child in turn at his chosen activity. She would then be working with him using the activity he was carrying out as a starting point for systematic teaching (Ch. 11).	Child would be seen working on some occasions with teacher at her table (away from group) for relatively longer periods of time (10–15 min.). The teacher would be able to continue work started with the child in a previous individual session.
The attractiveness of the room will depend upon the teacher's skill in providing large suitable pictures,* relevant collages in a variety	

---

† I did this too with Brian
‡ Laski House, Manchester.

* She will ensure that her pictures are bold and simple in outline; that attention had been paid to their size and position in the classroom, i.e. not too large, for the young child perhaps finds difficulty in seeing too large a shape as a whole; at a level which suits the heights of the children.

Less mature children

of textures; in her ability to keep the equipment fresh-looking and clean.

Teachers' charts might include:
1. A record of toilet 'accidents.'
2. A record of the children's progress in self help.
3. A list of the children's birthdays with photograph at side of each. With little mentally handicapped children, it is so easy to forget their life age. Photographs will be useful for visitors and general helpers.
4. Dated individual work charts, using 'tick' or shading method.
5. Charts indicating pictorially activities carried out with each child.
6. Photographs showing the best positions for each individual child to be placed in whilst being dressed or fed (Development Units).

Other considerations:
Hanging objects (Appendix 1).

More mature children

The attractiveness of the room will depend upon the teacher's willingness to mount the children's work for display, to arrange the models made from wood, clay, card by the children, to have a group model or two made after a visit.

Teachers' charts might include:
1. Story Aid pictures—large, bold, simple and uncluttered backgrounds.
2. Cookery charts indicating pictorially the breakdown of steps in making something to eat or drink.
3. Discovering ourselves charts, e.g. hand and feet prints arranged in a variety of ways to help children build up concepts—height, standing, sitting, kneeling, eye colours, boys/girls, socks, tights, stockings, etc.†
4. Dated individual work charts. Pictorial methods so that both teacher and child will know when it is 'his turn.'
5. Pictorial records of the children's activities at the nature table and the music table.*
6. Charts to link up the children's experience of the music table and nature table with pictorial representation.

---

† One teacher had a long branch of a tree placed against the wall. The children in turn stood against this and with their teacher's help placed their photograph and name in position of their 'measured' height. Whilst I was there I saw many children going up to this simple teaching aid and talking to their friends and pointing out their names.

* Chrystelle Browne had a chart containing the names of the children in her group and pictures of the instruments on the music table along the top. As she saw a child spontaneously use an instrument she indicated this by sticking cut-outs of the instruments against the child's name. Such a method indicated the children's interest as well as their need to be encouraged to use the music table much more or to explore a particular sound.

Less mature children	More mature children
	Puppets and puppet theatre.† A corner of the room containing a real stove, sink unit, kitchen wall units, etc., for cooking and washing activities.

DEVELOPING ENVIRONMENT

The teacher must remember that the environment should develop as the children's interests emerge and are understood. In other words the environment should be dynamic not static. The arrangement of the learning areas and the pictorial work of the teachers and the children should be changed from time to time, for novelty is an important feature of learning. Sameness can only bring about boredom and lack of interest and concentration. The appearance of the school will always indicate to me the way in which the teachers are basing work on the children's interests and how new experiences are introduced to enable them to build up concepts. It should indicate how teachers are helping the children to relive their experiences through representation of all kinds.

BEHAVIOUR OF TEACHER IN CLASSROOM

Although I shall be dealing in a later chapter with the attitudes and qualities which I believe teachers of severely subnormal children should have, I think that some mention of these might be made here too for the teacher is all too clearly very much part of the environment I have tried to describe.

Gardener and Cass[64] have described the way in which the skilled observer looked at the behaviour of the teachers in the classroom and not just that of the children.* From the collected observations, qualities emerged in those teachers considered to be successful teachers which could well be amongst those present in successful teachers of severely subnormal children.

For a complete list of these qualities I must refer you to the book itself. They are well worth considering. I should like to quote from a section entitled 'Actions of the teacher which show concern with promoting social attitudes by direct example.'

---

† Sometimes these are seen displayed on the wall. They should be used to illustrate stories, songs, incidents.

* Some research workers in the field of mental subnormality have now started to pay more attention to adult/child interaction.

'Requests the child's help or cooperation.
Enlists cooperation between child and herself.
Promotes social attitudes between children or considerate behaviour.
Arbitrates. Provides an audience by suggesting that other children shall watch. Thanks a child. Asks a child's permission. Assents by words or gestures. Praises child's performance, work or action.
Stimulates by encouragement. Helps by doing part of a child's work for him. Praises a child's gift, possessions, help or appearance.'

To achieve the qualities listed above means that the teacher has to be continuously aware of her own *active* role in the learning situation. There is no place for the teacher who leaves the children 'to get on by themselves' or who chatters to other adults, unless in the case of the latter activity it is for the purpose of letting the children hear a conversation between two adults—a possible technique of encouraging listening or in the case of very young handicapped children stimulating speech sounds/patterns of sounds.

ROLE OF THE HEADTEACHER IN ARRANGING AN ENVIRONMENT FOR LEARNING

The Headteacher interested in the children and the teachers in her care, rather more than in administration, has also a part to play. It is her responsibility to see that each classroom has the equipment needed and to ensure the teacher's part in making her own equipment. She also has to see that the corridors and hall contain interesting pictures and children's work from all classes as well as extra interesting areas of activity for the children, e.g. pets, birds, her own ideas for creative work. The Head might be constantly looking for sources of useful waste materials, for a creative approach demands a constant flow of materials into the school.

Supporting the teacher's efforts and valuing their work with the children can perhaps best be done if she regularly visits the classrooms to see the developments taking place, to talk to the children and to make suggestions on the basis of her own observation and wide experience. On some occasions she might even take over the group for the teacher to have the opportunity of standing back and looking at the children in a new relationship.

There can be no doubt that the Headteacher who invites her teachers to keep a dated weekly record of their work with each individual child (as well as with groups) is playing a most important part in helping the teacher to think about the developing environment she is providing for learning. If the teacher follows some of the principles I have suggested in this book and in *Observing Children who are Severely Subnormal*, i.e. follows the principles of systematic observing and recording and following the child's interests, she will certainly need a notebook that allows her to write out her plans briefly yet adequately so that she can see progression in her work. If the notebook is passed on to other colleagues when the child goes from her, some kind of continuity will be preserved.*

A useful plan for a possible working notebook may be found in Appendix 2. Many of the ideas are an extension of those in my first book. Others were suggested by a student's work (Miss Kathleen Firth) and further extended in discussion with students and colleagues.

---

* Teachers wanting such a notebook should contact the publishers or the author.

7 Visits into the community

Severely subnormal children, as I have said before, need more sensory experiences and real first-hand experiences than perhaps do normal children though one cannot overestimate the value of experience at *all* levels of learning.* The environment outside school is full of exciting possibilities. One should keep in mind the experience of the natural elements here—the wind, the rain, the snow, the sun—and not overprotect the children from them. The experiences which follow have been given by countless progressive teachers in the past few years to hundreds of severely subnormal children. I should like to point out that such experiences will be utterly wasted if the teacher does not use every situation to use relevant language to the children and elicit language from them. A piece of information teachers could strive to ascertain is how much greater is the children's motivation to speak when they experience the real outside world. School Council Projects might help teachers to measure this hypothesis.

The teacher needs to plan her programme in order to take the children out individually, in small groups or as a class (with plenty of voluntary help) at least once a week and preferably many, many more times. Where she is fortunate enough to have voluntary helpers she needs to ensure that they are alerted to the value of talking to the children both in a spontaneous way as well as with some planned intention of helping the children to learn particular words or have a specially planned experience, e.g. see how many round shapes they can find in a certain road. Written permission from the parents should be obtained for an agreed period of time, say a term. The teacher must keep in her mind that what the child gains from the experience is not necessarily what she has in mind for him to experience.

Roads and streets
To see and use the traffic lights.
To see and use the zebra crossing.
To look at the lorries, cars, and workmen on the road.
To a nearby railway line.
To a level crossing.

---

* Student teachers during training need a very wide variety of experiences (cf. Chapter 13) too.

Work activities

To see the postman taking letters from the box. To post a letter.
To a building site.
To a launderette to watch (young children). To use later on.
To a fire station.
To a garage.

Sports

Skating rink.
Swimming baths to watch as well as to swim.
To meet members of a football club.
To see a football match/other kinds of matches.
To play putting.
To watch tennis in the park.
Ten pin bowling.

Buildings

Museum.
Church and cemetery.
Cinema.
Youth Hostel to stay.
Greenhouse.
Café, consider different kinds, e.g. cafeteria, waitress service, those where there are cloths on the tables, those where the tables are formica-topped.
Railway Station.
Bus Station.
Airport.
To another school to watch a puppet play, to give a puppet play, to sing/dance.
To a school concert.
Shops of all kinds, Supermarkets. Indoor and outdoor markets. Pet shops.
Library.
High buildings with a lift/moving staircase.

Transport

On buses.
On a train.
In a motor car.
On a boat.

Other outdoor activities

Look at the garden/playground of the school
Go to the park to feed the ducks, see the flowers.
Zoo.
Play on the large equipment.
See squirrels or deer, kick the leaves or shuffle in them.
See a nearby pond or canal.
Visit a farm.
Climb a hill (a group of children I took on such a journey spent three times as long as normal children of the same age but they succeeded. Allow plenty of time).
A picnic.

To a wood to pick a few flowers to arrange later.
To see a nest in a hedge.
To an interesting grass verge (shapes in weeds, etc.).
To an interesting piece of waste land.
To see a beautiful garden near school.

Repetition of these experiences over the years should not be considered a waste of time. Teachers should think of the number of times they themselves have to go on a particular journey before they know all the features and the various aspects of it before their interest is truly saturated. They can then compare this with the possible number of visits a severely subnormal child will need and provide for this. The visits will have a different meaning and purpose for the children at various levels of their development.

All attempts on the part of the general public to indicate pity, either in their conversation or in a desire to 'let them in/on free' (if money is involved), should be kindly but firmly discouraged. Instead the teacher might encourage the interested passer-by to talk to the children.

The visits need to be carefully prepared. Ideally the teacher should go over the experience herself at least once to analyse the possibilities in terms of language experience for the children, the snags in terms of distance, whether places are open or closed at intended times of visiting, times of buses, etc.

On returning to school (according to the stage of development reached by each child in the group) some kind of follow-up should be carried out. It might mean that the children talk as individuals (and later in a group) with their teacher about their experiences. Another form of following-up might be through storytelling. One of the loveliest experiences I had when visiting a student was when I heard that five small children (under eleven) had been taken in a teacher's car to the garage just round the corner from school. The aim of the visit was to see the car being filled with petrol. On their return Miss Firth had arranged a small white car (the same colour and make as the teacher's), a box representing the garage and in front of this three oblong boxes with black tape fixed to their sides representing the petrol pumps.

The story she told was the real story of the five children visiting the garage with their teacher. She told them all about the driver and 'how she held the steering wheel' and bought the petrol. The children were interested in the story and listened attentively; they used language when the story aids were referred to and touched them imitatively, i.e. 'filled the car with petrol.'

VISITS INTO THE COMMUNITY

Jamie's story (sitting on my knee near my face). Jamie's mother had been for a walk with the family dog Brutus. When she returned, Jamie was giving instructions to Brutus, 'Sit,' 'Go away,' I told Jamie the following story:

Jamie, his mother and Brutus went for a walk down the road. Brutus was a big brown and white dog. As Jamie, his mother and Brutus the big brown dog were walking down the road, Jamie saw a big red ball. Jamie's mother said to Jamie and Brutus the big brown and white dog, 'I wonder who has lost this big red ball.' She said, 'We shall go to that house and see if anyone has lost this big red ball.' Jamie, his mother and Brutus went up to the door of the house and Jamie knocked on the door (gesture knock). Jamie's mother said to the lady who opened the door, 'Jamie and Brutus our big brown and white dog and I were walking down the road when Jamie saw a big red ball. Has anyone in this house lost a big red ball.' 'No,' said the lady, 'No one in this house has lost a big red ball.'

Jamie, his mother and Brutus the big brown dog went to the next house. Jamie knocked on the door. Jamie's mother said to the lady who opened the door, 'Jamie and Brutus our big brown and white dog and I were walking down the road when we saw a big red ball. Has anyone in this house lost a big red ball?' The lady smiled and said, 'Oh, yes, my little girl has lost her big red ball. You are very kind. She WILL be happy to get it back. Will you come in and have a cup of tea?' So Jamie, his mother and Brutus the big brown and white dog went into the house and had a cup of tea. Brutus had his drink in a bowl. Then Jamie, his mother and Brutus the big brown and white dog went home. They were so glad that the little girl had got her big red ball back again.

Jamie listened carefully to this story which I have written as I told it (made up quite spontaneously the first time and then remembered). He asked for it again, twice, and when I paused at words like 'knock,' 'door,' 'Brutus,' 'ball,' 'house,' 'tea,' he made an attempt to say them. This was a simple follow-up to his mother's walk, not his, but I have included it to illustrate the simplicity of the idea using the child's name, his knowledge of a walk up a road, a ball and his own dog.

Older children on their return from visits might help their teacher to compile environment discovery charts or models. The charts could be compiled in the time when some of the children were playing and small group work was called for. The result would always mean an attractive, meaningful wall/table display to stimulate language over many days and which, when finished with in a particular classroom, could add to the display at the front of the entrance (so many schools for the mentally handicapped are still unattractive to enter) or in the corridors. If they go on buses they might have looked for one of the following:

Women with hats/women without hats/women with head scarves.
Women with baskets (various kinds), with/without bags.
Women with babies/women without/women with children other than babies.
Men with hats/caps/without either. Men with cigarettes. Men with pipes, etc.

In the streets they have looked for:
   Houses with chimneys/houses without chimneys.
   Houses with red/grey/brown/thatched roofs.
In the park they have looked for:
   Big birds/small birds and so on.
If the children are supplied with several cards each containing the one item that has to be looked for, when they see it they can give up the card to their teachers.*

When they return to school some very jolly collage work might be the outcome of this experience where particular attention was being paid to people. I remember one teacher taking the children to a café where some had tea, some had orangeade (some with straws). A simple chart was made (with cut-outs made by the teacher) showing the number of cups, glasses, glasses withstraws used.

---

* A simple method of recording without numbers. Suggested by one of my colleagues (Olwen Gregory).

8 Play understood by the adults

Many excellent books[66] and articles[67] have been written about play by enthusiasts and specialists. I am not going to spend time here therefore describing the theories of play nor pointing out the importance of play in education. To a certain extent I shall conclude that the teacher of severely subnormal children knows that play in all its forms must be a major part of the specialized approach to their education and that she must become an expert in understanding play. Appendix 3 contains a brief description of the theoretical ideas underlying the practical suggestions in this chapter. I want to stress that such an approach if carried out well is not easy. Teachers will be kept busy intellectually as well as physically if they are constantly alert to the possibilities in play for learning.

Reasons for including play in the curriculum

There are numerous reasons why opportunities for play should form an important aspect of the curriculum irrespective of the children's chronological age.* The following are perhaps the most important:

(1) Generally speaking severely subnormal children will live at too great a distance from others of the same age and stage of development to be able to have really adequate opportunities for play at home.† Normal children of the same age will be well in advance in their play activities. Even if there are brothers and sisters or friends nearby, difficulties are likely to arise because of such differences. I am not suggesting that handicapped children should never play with normal children. What I am saying in effect is that we all gain satisfaction when we are amongst our own kind. I cannot see that this might be any different on some occasions for

---

* I do not want it to be thought that I want these children to behave as children all their lives, but it seems important for the teacher to understand that *how* they develop is of equal importance to ensuring that they do develop their fullest potential.

† Play groups held in the evening for this group of children are almost unknown. Steady provision of this by voluntary workers would be enjoyable for the children and would give the parents some free time in the evenings for their own interests or for spending with the other children in the family. Parents of these children could form small play groups in each other's homes if they could arrange transport or be willing to take and collect their child.

those who are handicapped.

(2) Parents of handicapped children, unless they have a professional interest, are no more likely to understand and therefore accept and develop the play activities of their handicapped children than do some parents of normal children. They may indeed find some play activities completely unacceptable because they will be out of keeping, to their way of thinking, with what they expect from the child in terms of his physical development.

(3) Severely subnormal children need to have social experiences in play activities as all other children. They are often denied opportunities for the various levels of play, i.e. play with an adult, solitary play, spectator play, parallel play, associative play, group play, and so miss out in their social and emotional development. Particularly is this so if they have teachers and others who think that play is a waste of time and so push them prematurely into more academic forms of learning. The more opportunities the children have for play which is interpreted and developed by the teacher the more likely it is that language will be developed in both increased comprehension and expression. Jeffree found progress in a child's ability to use verbs and two-word sentences when a structured approach to doll play was carried out over a period of well-planned audio/video taped sessions.[16]

(4) Severely subnormal children, just like normal children, show us their knowledge and observation of the world around them if we take the trouble to look. The skilful teacher can use play as a vehicle for introducing relevant language at the moment when it is most needed. Then it will be understood.

(5) As the children get older, i.e. 13-15 years, they perhaps need opportunities to repeat the imitative and representational play of a younger chronological age which is usually carried out without language. If a language response from their teachers has been forthcoming over the years the majority will play at a more sophisticated level, i.e. accompanied by language.

(6) Children learn to concentrate during play activities. They become absorbed. Observations of severely subnormal children have not led me to other conclusions. As far as the evidence collected over the years as a teacher suggests, concentration on a task is something that develops over a period of time. When a child is not concentrating of his own volition we need to examine the task, the age and stage of the child and what is happening around him. We might also need to investigate undiagnosed physical defects. Clearly in the mentally handicapped population there will be some

conditions militating against our efforts. These are rare.
(7) Child psychologists, such as Piaget, see play as an important aspect of intellectual development. As far as one can see from the practical implications of these theories it would appear that the mental processes of the child will be stunted if he is not given the fullest opportunities to learn through play.

Because many teachers have been conditioned to take more account of intellectual development and achievement than of the emotional and social aspects of a child's life, these Piagetian theories seem to make a great deal of common sense, even for those working with severely subnormal children wishing to emphasize the cognitive aspects of their education in their approach. These theories are only being very slowly accepted by theorists for, as Susan Millar states, 'learning theorists have been uninterested in play in spite of the fact that play involves learning and selective response to stimulation.[68] I also need to remind teachers once more that they will largely be concerned with those stages of intellectual development, the sensori-motor and pre-operational stages, which teachers of normal children are often not considering after the child has reached seven or eight years.

In play even severely subnormal children are given the chance to reconstruct and reorganize their experiences. The implication for teachers is that they must ensure the children gain useful experiences. Particularly will this be the case when the child lives in conditions of deprivation—some homes, some hostels and still some wards of mental subnormality hospitals where the shift system of work for the nurses militates against the most important of needs, i.e. stable, meaningful consistent relationships. As Dewey[32] says, 'it is this (reconstructing and reorganizing) which adds to the meaning of experience and increases the ability to direct the course of subsequent experience!'

Insufficient attention to play as an educational approach
During the 1960s a few people only were interested in the importance of play in the education of severely subnormal children. The majority were more concerned with how to teach more academic skills and retained a formal group-teaching approach to the children throughout the day. I suspect this was mainly because:
(1) It was assumed by too many, and often too readily, that mentally handicapped children had to be taught to play or indeed that they could not play. It was not expected and was therefore not examined to any large extent by research workers or indeed by some of those training the teachers.

(2) The buildings in which the children received education were not until quite recently conducive to activities which encouraged them to become fully alive and active.

(3) Untrained staff could not be expected to understand play as an educational technique without the support and example from an ever-increasing number of professionally trained staff in their midst.

(4) The money for suitable equipment was not available in large enough amounts and teachers on low salaries could not be expected to improvise all the time to the same extent or standard that was expected during training in the past.

(5) Research workers in this field mainly concerned themselves with children in mental subnormality hospitals, and with research in rather limited settings away from the influence of other children and the response of a good teacher. Some concerned themselves with teaching the children skills which would be useful when adulthood was reached instead of examining the needs of the children in the various stages of their development and ensuring these were satisfied. Many research workers in this field of education were not always aware of the changes in the educational climates of the schools, nor of the aims of the various courses of training for teachers. I think I can safely say that, apart from the notable few, research workers in the field of mental subnormality were not well versed in the practice of how normal children function in schools where there is opportunity to develop. Some of them have even admitted to a lack of knowledge of normal child development. In the past three or four years research workers using up-to-date technological aids have been able to repeat the innovated observational techniques of the early 'sixties and, using the work of skilled observers among the teachers, are being able to begin to compile more scientific observation systems. Perhaps these recent methods will give us the descriptive accounts of the process of change from more authoritarian-structured classrooms to those where cooperative work and the development of children is a vital criterion, for, as Leonard Marsh writes[31] in *Alongside the Child in the Primary School*, 'such accounts would do much to share on a wider scale the professional expertise that is already available. Such studies depend on a firm acceptance of observational techniques as the fundamental tool of educational research rather than experimental methods.'

If the spate of research in the past twenty-five years using experimental design has, as is suggested, succeeded in bringing about a measure of change in 'probably rather less than two-thirds of our primary schools,' I would like to suggest that we need to pay immediate need to the lesson illustrated and bring about radical changes in research methods in the field of the mentally handicapped. The full-time research worker in this field is presently in a splendid position to share the teachers' expertise with other teachers. He is perhaps also in an excellent position to see how teachers learn, and to measure how their attitudes to changes come/do not come about.

(6) Play and intellectual development have not been closely linked in the eyes of the teacher or the research worker.

(7) It was assumed that the children were wasting time if they were playing. Some workers perhaps wanted a similar approach to that which was being made to socially deprived children both in this country and in America (following the research of Bereiter and Engelmann.[69] The provision for play in such an approach, even from a very early age, is minimal. It is assumed that the children play enough out of school and need a more structured intellectual approach in school in order to 'catch up' with children not socially deprived. What workers might tend to forget is that some socially deprived children are potentially normal or above normal in intelligence and so therefore there is value indeed in helping them to catch up. Severely subnormal children will never catch up. We need to accept too that social education is the most vital part of our work with this group of children and that this can probably best be fostered in play activities developed by teachers understanding the importance of play. It must also be pointed out that the premise about socially deprived children having enough play out of school certainly does not apply, as I have already stated (page 117) in the case of severely subnormal children. We need also to imagine (or better still go and see) the lives some of these children lead at home in homes where adults and siblings are coming to terms with a fundamental major life disappointment. Then we shall be more likely to give the children a wonderful life in school.

Research and play. The 'sixties.
Tizard and 'Brooklands'
In the late 'fifties Professor Jack Tizard, with the help of a research grant and a teacher of young children, Pat Daley, demonstrated the positive responses of severely subnormal children from an institutionalized hospital setting to a play-oriented situation. A clear description of the work is given in *Community Services for the*

Mentally Handicapped.⁶ There is no doubt at all that the approach influenced the practice of teachers working with the severely subnormal in the 'sixties and even some of the teachers in the hospital schools. Teachers who are seriously concerned with the emotional and social development of children will certainly benefit from reading the account of this work in full. Two comments in particular merit attention: 'They were eager (after two years of work), active, purposeful, and in this way presented a striking contrast to their behaviour on arrival at Brooklands.* This was aggressive, apathetic and disturbed. They were affectionate and happy children (remember they had been in a large mental subnormality hospital for varying periods of time and were deprived emotionally and seriously disturbed children), usually busy and interested in what they were doing, confident and full of fun.'

To those teachers who do not yet know the severely subnormal child what better encouragement could they receive to work with them; what better values against which to measure the results of the work which they might wish to achieve?

Woodward, Piaget and the severely subnormal

Dr. Mary Woodward in a paper, *The Behaviour of Idiots Interpreted by Piaget's Theory of Sensori-motor Development*⁷⁰ shows teachers in a very positive way that all behaviour is meaningful. Her results show how even what had been considered aimless behaviour on the part of idiot children and adults has a meaning if it is understood in the context of Piaget's theories of intellectual development in the first eighteen months of life. One of the implications of these findings for teachers of severely subnormal children is that they must be sure to examine the spontaneous activity of the children and see where it fits into a general pattern of development. Thinking of the majority of the children in this group, when activity is not forthcoming, the teacher needs to look at what she has provided to stimulate it.

If teachers watch behaviour conscientiously they are more likely to provide sufficient time at each level to enrich the quality of the play displayed. If teachers refer to the many developmental scales that are available their imagination will be stimulated and from time to time they will be able to measure progress more objectively. Another source of ideas which will undoubtedly enable teachers to see what kind of behaviour to expect (if they provide) in the first

---

* A large mansion, housing 16 children and the helpers in the experiment.

important stages of intellectual development, irrespective of chronological age, are the recorded observations of Piaget himself as he played with his own children. Whilst the expositions of his theories are perhaps too difficult for many of us to understand the records are easy to read and are interesting. The records provide us with sufficient concrete examples to trigger off our own thinking about play.

Queen Mary's Hospital, Carshalton
In the mid-sixties research workers at this hospital, undoubtedly prompted by Tizard's work at Brooklands, experimented once more with specially devized play programmes in family group arrangements with children of 4-12 years and having mental ages between one year and four years. The work is interestingly described in the journal *Special Education* by Elspeth Stephens and Jean Robertson.[71] The results generally speaking were educationally positive, for we read that after two years the children: 'can handle sand, can choose their own activities, can pursue them with little direct help from an adult, can be relied upon to find their own apron and wash hands after play.'

It was also found that:
(a) more equipment could be introduced into the environment;
(b) the children became distressed if classroom pictures were found torn;
(c) dolls thrown by one child would be rescued and 'tucked' into bed by another;
(d) the children's attention span lengthened;
(e) frustration was more easily tolerated;
(f) there was an increase in social interactions;
(g) the ability to use language developed alongside the beginnings of imaginative play.

Those of us who know well the hospital population of children fully understand the importance of the findings of this research, particularly in view of the emotional and material deprivations of these children, and the very wide variety of clinical conditions that exist. Teachers of normal young children and teachers who have developed an informal approach to children will appreciate the results. They might not so easily understand why the recording of such findings have been so epoch-making, particularly when to them a seemingly obvious approach to the education of all children is initially through play. I must remind them that until quite recently such teachers have not known a great deal about these children or their whereabouts.

Research such as this however should encourage future teachers in special education. It will act as a constant reminder that positive results can be gained even by those children with the most severe handicaps if optimum conditions for learning are provided over a long period of time and on condition that the results worked towards are within the children's capacity to achieve. Clearly the kind of results we are working towards with these profoundly handicapped children will very much depend upon our own value system in terms of what we consider positive (cf. page 141).

Play and the training of teachers

One of the advantages I appreciated whilst training teachers was the opportunity of seeing the development of educational ideas in a large number of schools and subnormality hospitals. I could also spend a good proportion of time observing the work of my students and recording some of the interesting play activities of the children.

The findings of these research workers though based on rather limited populations of children will almost certainly apply to most severely subnormal children having maximum opportunities to learn through play. The difference might possibly lie in the shorter time it will take children living at home to achieve some of the goals listed and to adapt to the educational approach suggested throughout this book.

I can recall the difficulties my students experienced when in 1962 they first introduced a play approach in classes where the children had been encouraged to sit at table occupations. The relative speed with which most of the children adapted to change in terms of the personnel and equipment (according to the skill and provision of the student concerned) never ceases to amaze me. Their response to change certainly seemed similar to that of normal children given opportunities for choosing their own activities after becoming accustomed to class teaching methods, i.e. they are not sure what to do at the beginning and have to be encouraged; they sometimes ask if they can do a particular thing, they rush around touching, feeling and exploring everything that is available; they try out the response of a new teacher.

We still come across classes where children sit with table activities for too long, even when teachers have plenty of help and could provide for the children to become active immediately they come into school. However, within a week or so of a different approach, and according to their particular level of achievement in self activity, they will pursue their own activities in an independent fashion provided the provision of materials is sufficient and appropriate.

I feel it is important to draw teachers' attention to this fact for often they do not rearrange their classrooms and introduce new, exciting equipment into it because they fear the children's response. We need teachers who can meet the challenge such changes present and so initiate the topics of research in the interests of the children they serve. Particularly will this be so if they see research workers complementing their work.

These pieces of research were conducted on children from subnormality hospitals. An important piece of work not so well known by teachers is that of Hulme and Lunzer. Its implications as I see them have been important for teachers. Their paper, *Play, Language and Reasoning in the Severely Subnormal Child* describes the methods and the design of the research carried out in schools in 1964.[43]

Its main purpose was to compare the play, language and reasoning of a group of severely subnormal children with those of a group of normal children of similar mental age. The management of the children in both groups took place in an environment which approximates to the pattern of general nursery education. The findings relating to play were as follows:

'(1) Almost from the outset it was found that the severely subnormal children were able to accommodate to their increased freedom so that the general impression they produced was one of activity and enjoyment.
(2) The organization of their play was not easily distinguishable from that of normal children of comparable mental ages.
(3) There were considerable differences in the levels of language responses between the groups of children and in the amount they used.'

This research is useful, for its main findings reinforce in a more objective way the impressions gained by those seeing hundreds of mentally handicapped children playing in well-planned environments during our students' teaching practices.*

---

* Although we must remember that, at the time that this research was carried out, training centres were only just beginning to hear that a different approach was possible. Opportunities for play were almost unknown except for the Play Hour in between the morning and afternoon sessions. The children played with whatever was available but this was in no way structured or developed by the teachers. Many of the children studied in this research were known to me and for the most part were used to 'sitting-down' activities with their own class teacher. One of my students was in fact responsible for setting up the active environment in which Mrs. Hulme did her observations.

Its future value lies in the implications suggested by the authors for future investigations, viz.:

'(1) That comparable observations should now be made over a longer period of time than was the case in this research.
(2) The possibility that subnormal children are more content to repeat familiar routines with the different materials available than are normal children of similar mental age should be examined.
(3) To investigate the use of spontaneous language in severely subnormal children.
(4) To investigate the hypothesis that language is not used by severely subnormal children in the regulation of their behaviour.'

This traditional style research was the first piece of published work designed to examine the spontaneous reactions of non-institutionalized severely subnormal children and their ability to initiate fruitful interactions with their environment in a non-directive setting.

In those schools for the severely subnormal where play as an educational medium was used over a period of years in conjunction with a wide variety of other educational activities:

(1) The quality of the children's play generally increased in terms of the amount of imaginative and representational play.*
(2) More children seemed to be using spontaneous language in their play activities.
(3) More children seemed to be using intelligible language and asking questions.

I must be cautious in such claims for observations in the main were spasmodic rather than continuous and the following considerations must be taken into account:

(a) The observers might have been biased because of the personal involvements regarding the particular educational approach they tried to encourage and develop because of its relevance.
(b) The observations always took place in conditions usually providing the children with more varied stimulation and equipment than was the case when the class teacher was in charge, for students were working with the children.†

---

* On reflection I might question the statement that severely subnormal children do not use language in the regulation of their behaviour. My ears must have deceived me on many occasions. Perhaps future research will clarify this point. I would also suggest that wherever imagination in the use of materials by these children is lacking, or not developing, the teacher's response and her imagination in providing materials and arranging these should be carefully assessed.

† In order to bring about change in attitudes Headteachers were asked[23] to

(c) As informal methods became more accepted by the teachers, students were able to continue the work provided by the class teacher and were therefore able to develop the play rather than introduce a play environment.
(d) More teachers were qualified and were therefore giving the children more appropriate educational experiences.
(e) The importance of the teacher's language contribution[23] in the play situation was constantly emphasized during training.
(f) Teachers were using much more imagination in the provision of new and interesting equipment.
(g) The parents, seeing the teachers taking their children out into the community, were probably doing so too and thus giving them extra out-of-school experiences.

An experimental approach to direct observation of the play of severely subnormal children by student teachers (1963-4)*

No literature existed at the beginning of the 'sixties regarding methods designed to train teachers to become interested in developing systematic habits of observation of individual children in order to arrange their education. An exploratory experimental approach was therefore introduced to 29 students training to become teachers of the mentally handicapped on a one-year course of initial training in order that they might acquire this interest. Ten severely subnormal children aged 11-16 visited the course centre on one afternoon weekly over a period of 16 weeks. On each occasion their stay lasted for an hour and a half. There were four boys and six girls in the group. This particular age group was chosen because there was little recorded information about the spontaneous behaviour of such a group in a non-directive but enriched setting. It was hoped that students might begin to see individual differences in this situation and begin to think about teaching methods where they could consider the needs of the children more diagnostically and see the possibilities in one-to-one situations. It was also surmised that the students would see the growth of social relationships in a free situation and therefore accept more easily their role in providing possibilities for this in their own classes.

give students the opportunity of having the class and the classroom to themselves during teaching practice. In this way new approaches, new ideas were presented as the years went on with minimum interference from the class teacher (so many of whom of course were untrained). These expectations for students were high but few failed to respond to them.

* Précis of paper presented by the author and published in the Conference Proceedings of the International Association for the Scientific Study of Mental Deficiency, Copenhagen, 1964 [14].

Students were encouraged to plan a lively and developing indoor environment.* Discussions of their own records enabled them to decide when new equipment was to be added to that available. Diagrams were made weekly of the placing of equipment and the new pieces added. Equipment for woodwork, sewing, real baking, pasting, painting, cutting out, modelling in a variety of media and printing patterns was available. Equipment for imaginative play included that needed for house play (at a size appropriate to the physical size of the children), collections of small toys, large boxes, dressing-up materials, a case, an assortment of hats, cardboard and paper, a tent, a bus made with chairs and a conductor's hat and collecting bag, a long wooden boat shape. Other experimental materials consisted of water-play equipment, wet and dry sand, weighing possibilities, improvised musical instruments, blowing games, inch and two-inch cubes, a mirror, a small wheelbarrow, a selection of puppets and a book corner.

It was envisaged that the children would need some help in this environment so three students were also among them though they were asked not to teach. Different students were initially put amongst the children but then it was decided in this experimental year that the same three students should remain with them and that these students should always get out the materials and set out the room.† The rest of the student group sat at the end of the room separated from the children by long benches stretched across the room. They were instructed not to talk to the children. Each child was observed by at least two students who were instructed to write all they could about what they saw/heard. Their records were checked in the first few weeks in order to see that they did not draw conclusions about a piece of behaviour and that they did not draw inferences. This habit was soon established by the majority in this supervised situation.

Some students were anxious lest the children would be disturbed by their presence. During the first few weeks their presence was completely ignored by the children. Over five thousand observations (each one written separately on a small slip of paper) were examined.

Impressions gained from these observations indicated:
(a) the children's need to move, to explore, to experiment with and manipulate all the materials and the equipment;
(b) curiosity about other children's behaviour and activities;

---

* The course only had £150 per annum for all stock so this was developed by communal effort.
† They were invited to comment on their observations (recalled) in the seminars immediately following the session.

(c) imaginative and creative play arose in many instances as a direct consequence of the equipment, e.g. a torch stimulated one girl to arrange the chairs in rows and then 'show people to their seats in the cinema;'
(d) sand and water was a favourite with all the children;
(e) the musical instruments were used by all the children;
(f) the books were never taken from the shelves;
(g) the children experimented in social relationships;
(h) the children were nearly always friendly towards the adults and some children demanded constant attention from them;
(i) some aggressive behaviour towards each other was observed amongst the children, sometimes happening as a result of teasing, sometimes through irritation;
(j) they liked the adults to join in their creative play—on the bus, in their parties, and at their weddings;
(k) frustration with materials when help was not immediately forthcoming was shown by a rapid change of activity;
(l) more concentration on one activity and some were able to complete a task started;
(m) some play in twos and threes and more communciation through language in the last two or three sessions.

Value to students. They saw the ability of the children to be active with self-chosen tasks. They also saw the way in which the children used the variety of first hand experiences with materials. In some ways their appreciation of the importance of recording precise details was increased.

Evaluation of the experience by students. Difficult but useful. They emphasized that they had begun to understand individual needs perhaps for the first time and they saw the children's need to be talked to about their activities (cf. with Dutch research). They considered that the practice they had had during the sessions had facilitated their powers of observation during their final teaching practice and had made them more aware of the kind of equipment the children needed to stimulate curiosity, imagination and social relationships.

This experiment was the first of its kind in the education of severely subnormal children. Whilst I imposed a hard discipline on the students in this experience, we all learnt so much not only about the children but about the importance of observation and recording as a starting point for our work.

Suggestions for further research on play

(1) Comparing the play of children in the same school:
   (a) those with language; those without language (at all ages);

(b) boys; girls;
(c) those who are expected to achieve reading skills; those who are not;
(d) those with brothers; those without;
(e) those with young parents; those with older parents.
(2) Comparing the play of children in schools where the equipment is always the same/is developed as the children's needs are observed.
(3) Comparing the play of children coming from schools where much experience is gained from outings into the community/is not gained thus.
(4) A longitudinal study of the play (free choice of activities) of ten children throughout their teens.
(5) Comparing the play of severely subnormal children and normal children under five in the same conditions.
(6) The play of severely subnormal children in their own homes.
(7) The play of severely subnormal children from formal/informal schools.
(8) The spontaneous activities of those attending Gateway Clubs (clubs for those attending Adult Training Centres).
(9) Comparing the play of babies with severely subnormal children under two given the same optimum conditions.
(10) Representation in the play of the severely subnormal.
(11) The design and use of table games for the severely subnormal adolescent.
(12) The function of looking behaviour in the play situation (records of the play activities of ten severely subnormal children over a period of three years suggest that looking behaviour forms an important part of the play experience).

It is suggested that whenever research on play is carried out the following must be attended to:
(a) the details of the equipment provided in the first session must be described fully (and then checked each time);
(b) the reactions of the children and the development of their play when new equipment is added to the play materials already available;
(c) the teacher's response and involvement (language, provision);
(d) the outstanding events surrounding the child, e.g. special outings, family difficulties/experiences;
(e) social class and condition of child.

Equipment stimulating exploratory, imaginative, dramatic, representative play

There is little doubt in my mind that the play I have seen amongst groups of severely subnormal children over twelve years has resulted in many instances because of the equipment which hardworking students and teachers have provided and because of their ingenuity in arranging and placing this in the environment.* Whilst imaginative teachers will have thought out most of the following for themselves, lists of items are always useful to the busy teacher. They also trigger off one's own thoughts.

Dressing-up materials with wardrobe to contain them
A beret with two thick plaits (black, brown) of wool attached. Wigs. Sun hat. Spanish hat. Soldiers' helmets. Policeman, postman, etc., hats. Party hats. Children can make hats themselves with the help of the teacher.
Shoes. Arrange in sizes. Flat heels, high heels. Boots.
Long stockings. Short socks. Tights.
Glasses you can see through. Glasses you cannot see through. Sunglasses. Glasses with various colours of cellophane as lenses.
Gloves. Varying sizes and textures. A long fur. Veiling.
Long and short dresses. Ties. Ribbons. Indian costume and headdresses.
Clown's suit. Other circus and pantomime characters. Masks of people and animals. Batman outfit.
Boxing gloves.
Clothes hangers for all dressing-up clothes with something suitable for hanging them on.
Postman's leather bag. Umbrella. Sunshade.
Cloaks. Aprons. Nurse outfits.
A large cardboard dalek (made by child with teacher).
Large suitcase for packing and unpacking activities. Small case (cf. Chapter on Adolescence).
Hair rollers. Hairdresser's cape. Plastic scissors.
Ballet shoes. Ballet dress.
Necklaces,. Bracelets. Manicure sets. Perfume bottles, etc.
Pipes.
Pretend shaving equipment.

Dolls
A collection of dolls of all shapes and sizes with the appropriate clothes for

---

* Cardboard cones placed in a shop by one student encouraged a child to pretend they were ice-cream cornets and to make them for her friends and the teacher. The same apparatus put in the home corner along with a tea towel stimulated a group of children to play at hairdressers and to use the cones as hairdryers. Placed in the hospital corner a cone became a stethoscope and an instrument which examined ears! Increased attention is placed upon giving children colour concepts in normal infant schools by having the 'red' table. Teachers need to expand this concept formation idea by providing red cups, knives, forks, cushion covers, etc. in the home corner. Displays tell the adult something. Nothing however can be done with them by the children unless the teacher is constantly referring to them. One wonders sometimes what the children are gaining in measurable terms.

occasions and seasons. Beds to fit the dolls, to stimulate thinking of all kinds, as well as role play. Doll's combs.
Life-size prams and trolleys (think of the physical size of the child here).
Dolls' wardrobes in cardboard or wood complete with hangers.
Inflatable toys. Diddy man, Yogi Bear.
Hairbrushes near dolls with hair will stimulate reality play—brushing the hair and styling it. One teacher of Home Economics (Denise Farr, Macclesfield) has a very large doll and hairdressing/hair-washing equipment. This links up with her group work in this self-help area and enables the children to later reconstruct dramatically.

Experimental toys

Opera glasses. Old box camera. Kaleidoscope. Telescope. Magnifying glasses. Boats to sail on large expanses of water. Humming tops (varying sizes). Football rattle.
Mechanical toys. Bicycle bell fixed to piece of wood, inclined plastic channels/tubes to run marbles/balls down (plumber's guttering useful).
Plant pots (plastic) used as nesting cups. Typewriter. Telephones (real if possible). Camp bed. Wigwam. A table with shelf underneath could contain pulley/lift to draw up cars 'on to the road from the underground car park.'
A sheet with roads, fields, rivers and railway lines painted on for arrangement play with small cars, people, trains, etc. Locks. Keys. Puppets.
Papier mâché and wooden 'hills to roll cars and small tyres down, to run after. Windmills in the sand. Tip-up lorries and vans for the sand play.
Yo-Yo. Ball attached by elastic to a bat. Walking spring.
Punch bags (children can help to sew and stuff these).
Torches. Pinging clock. Giant egg-timer. A tricycle/bicycle fixed to wooden batten cemented into floor. India-rubbers and pencils.
Guitar, violin, banjo, zither, calypso blowers.
Cardboard and plastic cones (obtainable from hosiery mills).
Mechanical toys giving quick/slow, loud/soft experiences.

Shops

Real money. Cash box.
Different kinds of shops provided, e.g. grocers, cake shop, chemists, ice-cream booth, florists, greengrocers, chip shop, lemonade bar, Post Office, supermarket.
Clothes shop (Norfolk teachers, 1974).
Shoe shop (hygiene noted here).
Variety of shopping bags most useful: paper/string/'trendy'/cane baskets in a variety of sizes and shapes/supermarket basket.
Paper bags.
Flour and salt items—meat pies, sausage rolls, bread shapes, pies and tarts.
Papier mâché fruit and vegetables. Real fruit and vegetables.
Cash registers, toy and real ones.
Cardboard cones (obtainable from mills).
Plastic flowers. Strawberry baskets containing lots of paper flowers (made by children with teacher).
'Lollipops' (circles of thick card glued on to lolly sticks).
Wafers (blocks of wood covered on either side with cream-coloured card).

Ice lollies (plaster-shaped and moulded round lolly sticks).
Parcels of all weights and sizes in a variety of coloured wrappings.
Scales of various kinds. Objects to balance, e.g. stones, buttons, peas, beans, beads, corks, macaroni, dog biscuits, bottle tops, fir cones, flour and salt sweets (wrapped/unwrapped), empty cotton reels, empty sellotape reels.
Shoe boxes glued together in rows of four or five make excellent containers.
Plastic fruit obtainable from markets or chain stores.
Shelves improvised from cardboard boxes fixed together by sellotape or glue.
Shelves containing just so many tins, e.g. four, of which three are the same, one is different.
Thick Smartie tubes. Thin Smartie tubes.
Arrangement of shop items important for learning, e.g. cigarettes and matches to go together. Salt, pepper, mustard, vinegar. Coffee, tea, Ovaltine, etc.
Egg boxes containing 'eggs' made of clay/pot eggs (available in pet shops).

Home corner play
'Trendy' wallpaper/paper to attract attention.
Cuckoo clock. 'Play' sausages and chips and chops.
Carpet on floor. Brush. Vacuum cleaner. Bucket and sponge.
Full-size iron. Disused stove. Round mirror on square background.
Blanket. Cardboard boxes fitted to wall to simulate kitchen cupboards.
Old TV cabinet. An armchair.
Shaving items, e.g. razor (minus blades), shaving brush, shell of electric razor.
Bowl for washing dolls' clothes. Overalls. Tea towels and towels.
Cushions in a variety of shapes and colours. Pouffes. Tin plates and spoons.
Curtains. Pictures (children's framed) on the wall. Plastic flowers and plastic vases.

Throwing, rolling, wheeling, pulling, building
A very large cardboard face with eyes, nose and mouth attached to springs—aiming game—movement of face parts stimulates laughter.
Clothes basket on wheels or castors/without wheels or castors with rope attached to stimulate pulling about.
Cable drums for rolling (covered with tinfoil to make attractive).
Cardboard boxes of all sizes, filled with foam rubber or paper and sealed, make excellent bricks for building. Skittles, quoits, soft balls.

Miscellaneous
An 8 to 10-foot (240–300 cm.) space ship made by teacher in thick card with the help of the children. Door in side encourages much imaginative play (Crosland Ward, 1969).
Paper bags for blowing up and popping.
Bubbles.
Large-size pulley cable with crane attachment for 'hooking' up objects from ground (Crosland Ward).
A length of rope. Stilts. Soft toys of all kinds. Watering cans. Small fork and trowel. A see-through string bag for water and sand play equipment.
Balloons. Boxes of small toys—cars, animals, people.* Boxes of cardboard

---

* An idea given to us by a physiotherapist might be implemented wherever

people dressed in familiar outfits. Telephone booth large enough for older child. Toy dogs with leads round necks, blow football. Car made from wooden packing case with steering wheel, car seat, number plates and two large tin lids to act as headlights. Wooden floor mazes. Playground maze.

Equipment stimulating group cooperation

Table games

During the course 1967-9 I played a simple table game with Susan, a mongol child of 11 years, who visited college one morning a week as part of the 'observation/getting to know a child' exercise we all so much enjoyed (including the child). I had devised a game based on the left to right, then down and left to right again of the snakes and ladders type, but my colleague, Mr. Narey, suggested that perhaps a circular type of movement round a board/card might be more appropriate for Susan. This encouraged my thinking about how we would end the game. The following game emerged and also the request to students to make games on their final teaching practice which used a dice, which had an end to motivate the child to continue.

Equipment:
 a path of squares placed in a circle;
 a dice with dots up to three only (could be two) on all sides except one;
 container to throw the dice;
 a small replica of a boy and girl doll (cut out in card);
 a toy swing placed on one of the squares (the end).
 Aim of the game—to see which doll arrives to have a swing first.

The circle can be of any number of squares according to the children's ability to stay at the game long enough to finish it (with an adult/with another child).

A small model letter box could be the end of the game with the dolls holding letters to post.

As developmentally a child copies a straight horizontal line before a vertical one and before a circle, the game might be played on a straight path before a circle.

Although many of the students compiled very simple, interesting games we looked at them all but did not make a record for each other. However, two teachers with whom I have recently been in personal contact have reminded me of their games. A description of them will give teachers and others ideas to develop their own better versions.

Elaine Osborne (neeTeale) now of Ivy House School, Derby, has compiled the following games:

---

there is a child who has difficulty in picking up toys from a hard surface. A piece of foam rubber attached to the table or tray at which the child is playing will facilitate his manipulation of the toys before him.

Traffic lights game. Each child has a card showing two sets of traffic lights (a vertical line game) and also six discs two of each colour—red, amber, green. A wooden cube acts as the dice. Each side is coloured except one. As a child throws an appropriate colour he places his disc on the traffic light colour. The game continues until the traffic lights are both filled.

Such a game enables the teacher to talk about the traffic light colours and enables the children to take turns, to match and to wait for a result.

Football Game. Big card painted green represents a football pitch. Centre line and goals indicated. The pitch is divided into squares all over. Each player has four balls. The dice (specially made) contains spots up to three. (This could vary according to the child. The dice might contain the symbols up to 2/3/4, etc.)

The players sit at each goal. As the dice is thrown and the numbers shown, the ball is moved up towards the opposite goal. This game gives the child the opportunity of playing one or more balls at a time.

Fishing game. Adapted from number/spelling fish game.

Equipment:

large cut-outs of fish contain a paper clip;
the line has a magnet on the end of it;
each fish contains a picture of a fruit, a piece of clothing, a feature of a face, furniture pictures.

Four children play. Each child has a card containing the same group of pictures as are on the fish. As he fishes in turn he places the caught fish containing a picture from his group on the card. If he catches a fish containing a picture on someone else's card he throws it back.

This game can be used for simple matching and classifying of objects. There is no limit to the kind of pictures the teacher introduces.

Shopping game. Two possibilities. Large colourful picture of items that can be bought for a few pence. Price at the side. Each child has 6-8 cards of items (similar to those on the large card). Dice has the money value on each side. Leave one side free (makes it more exciting when a child cannot go). As the child throws the dice he looks at the money value on it, compares it with the large picture of items, and if he has a card of an item the same price he places the card in a pile. First to lose all cards wins.

Real money in a bowl. As above but when the price of the item is matched the child takes out the money from the bowl and places the amount on the appropriate card. The first one to fill up his cards with the correct money wins.

Shape game. Compare the qualitative difference in playing this as a matching exercise only and playing with the shapes as part of a game in a group. Each child has a picture made up of shapes. Each child has a box of the shapes used to compose the pictures. Shapes are on the sides of the dice. As dice is thrown the child makes up the pictures from his own store.

Mr. Fruit Game. Each child has a picture of a man (it could be a woman) made up of apple for his head, orange for his body, bananas for his legs, strawberries for his feet, etc. Large card contains pictures of the fruit used with a number at the side. The dice contains the numbers. The game is to make up the man.

Mrs. Osborne has an adolescent group and says that they enjoy playing all of these games; the language that is elicited as a result of playing them is 'fabulous' she says.

Miss Louise Knight, now teaching at a school for the mentally handicapped in Devon, has compiled the following games:

Each child has a stand-up figure of a man/woman with pieces of Velcro attached to it. Each child has a pile of body parts in front of him—the parts also have a piece of Velcro on the underside. A pile of cards in the middle contains pictures of the body parts, although some are blank cards. The children take a card each in turn. If they have the body part indicated on the picture they fix it on their stand-up.

Model of road going through a model village. On the road there is a bridge for going *under*, a hill for going *over*, a telephone kiosk for going *past*, etc. The road winds through the village and is divided into squares. The children (two) or child and adult have a car each. The dice has spots on it. The car moves along the squares according to the number of spots turned up. The game is over when the cars go *into* a garage.

Making a bed game (Joan Fenwick/adapted Stevens)
Equipment for four players:
    a model bed each,
    replicas of a pair of sheets, a mattress, two pillows,
    2 blankets, an eider-down, a bedspread.

Cards depicting these items (several cards of each item) should be arranged in a circle. Each player spins a pointer and as the appropriate item sequence-wise is gained by a player the bed 'is made.' The picture cards could be piled in the middle with some blank ones amongst them. As the player turned up an appropriate card the bed could be made up.

The children would 'see sequence' in a real life activity, i.e. the correct order of the bed-clothes being placed on the bed.

Spin the pointer games can be applied to a wide variety of matching, classifying and sequencing games—according to the needs of either an individual child or a group.

Research on play published in the 'seventies

Since the late 'sixties and early 'seventies much more has been written about play and the mentally handicapped. Some of the work has caught my attention and I want to share it with you. My comments on some of the work will be brief but I know that a deeper acquaintance with the original work will further stimulate the reader's thought about the meaning of play.

The characteristics of 120 children attending Day Centres in Glasgow[19]
(cf. Footnote, page 46).

In addition to the study that was made during assessments using the Uzgiriz and Hunt scale, very detailed observations and records of the children's play behaviour were made.

Improving the children's play[72]

Sample: Six children (9-13 years with mental ages 15-24 months) 4/6 behaviour disturbances; 2 of these children had no speech. 4/6 no speech. 2/6 C.P. with left hemiplegia; 1/6 epileptic. 4/6 had attended school but had been excluded—no progress.

Personnel: (a) a psychology graduate; (b) an assistant to him for 20 weeks (13 weeks alone).

Methods:
(1) Time out room alongside play room.
(2) Time out for undesirable behaviour.
(3) Smallest sign of desirable behaviour rewarded initially.
(4) Morgenstern/Beer/Morgenstern toys used.
(5) Personnel taught and supervized initially to apply behaviour modification techniques.
(6) Sweets, crisps, (a car for one child), plus verbal praise/pat/stroke (cf. Stevens page 26 and page 78).
(7) Use of verbal cue 'NO' with time out.
(8) Same toys five days weekly presented to child in the order in which the child initially showed interest.

Results:
(a) Verbal praise sufficient after limited (no quantifying of time stated) period of intensive behaviour modification.
(b) Children soon learnt that 'NO' meant behaviour was unacceptable to the adult.
(c) 1st week, toys not used successfully; 2nd week, 14 per cent used successfully; 13th week, 89 per cent used successfully.
(d) Total time spent in playing increased for all children from five minutes to 30 minutes (cf. Adrian, page 90).
(e) By 6th week, time out progressively declined, by 10th week used only sporadically.
(f) Throwing of toys diminished to extinction by eight weeks (cf. page 54).
(g) Chewing rapidly increased after first week until by the third week it was so bad that 'time out' was used continuously. By week eleven no child was chewing toys.

Follow-up at the end of the study: Two children maintained their improved behaviour in those wards where behaviour modification techniques were being encouraged. Four children returned to former undesirable behaviour patterns.

As a teacher I found this description of how a group of profoundly handicapped children gained some intensive individual attention most interesting. It would have been of even more interest if the same group of children had had similar parallel attention over the same period of time with an experienced teacher of young normal children who introduced them to a wider variety of toys (pages 85-97) and used her own teaching skills. Unfortunately we are not told about the amount of time the children had had with an adult in any meaningful continuous play experience six months prior to the work being done.

The children seemed to adapt to what was wanted of them in a relatively short time. The pity is that, in view of my suggestions (page 146) that these severely subnormal children need the same adult over a long period of time before we can see progress that takes them on to the next stage as it were, 20 weeks was considered long enough to begin such an exciting piece of work.

The value of the research is that it reinforces my own belief in the positivity of these children. The method must always depend upon the personality and skill of the adult concerned, but the hopefulness engendered by more precise results being presented by research workers such as these gives the support needed:
(a) sometimes to begin with such children;
(b) to continue working with them;
(c) to be positive with them.

I was interested in the chewing behaviour of the children and linked this in my thinking with the development of mouthing in Piaget's Development of Schemas (page 49). Particularly was this so in view of the fact that it is highly probable that these children had not previously had the opportunity of handling play equipment such as was provided for them.

It is also not surprising that chewing vanished before throwing. If we examine again Piaget's Development of Schemas* in relation to objects and take the mental ages of these educationally deprived children into account, we shall note that throwing is indeed part of this normal development and occurs later than mouthing (page 49). As it is part of this development it cannot therefore be considered undesirable. What the possession of this feature in a child's repertoire of behaviour suggests is that the materials provided for throwing should be non-hurtful to persons or property (remember pillow fights); they should give the child a wide variety of interesting experiences and enjoyment. Future research might be interested in the trajectory paths made by one child throwing objects over a period of time, i.e. until the child because of his own development turns his attention to another characteristic of the object.

Play and non-verbal learning in the profoundly handicapped.[33] (Refer back to page 77/78).
Mental levels 15–24 months as above (Polish Research).
Growing up in hospital[71, 74] Robertson and Stephens.
This report, written in a simple, uncomplicated style, gives us a clear description of all that a child living in hospital should have to afford maximum opportunities for development (that is to say with the

---

* Sequence of motor/mental actions.

exception of real parent figures in constant attention as parents in a home). Twenty out of 116 children took part in the research.

The work and findings now published were carried out over a three-year period (1964-7). Changing the wards and attitudes included:

parents and aunties visiting on a more regular basis;
involvement of others in the lives of the children;
family group care;
wall charts as an aid to junior staff—the vocabulary to be used for the school children, the play programme and self-help programme;*
rooms made more homelike—armchairs, settee, carpet, and three-tiered bunk beds used as room dividers;
weekly meetings;
a structured play programme;
men and women involved with a mixed group of children;†
treating the children as individuals in terms of their clothing and appearance;
an interesting educational programme;
cooperation between the school and the ward;
devising an observation scale based on the Lunzer Scale for measuring 'adaptiveness in the use of play materials.'[75]

Detailed descriptions then follow of the toys that were used on the wards, the way they were reinforced for rough handling and some very useful recommendations, (two of which are worth citing here):

(1) A high standard of care for play material should be maintained.
(2) There should be someone whose special responsibility is to repair and reinforce toys and other equipment, and it is suggested that as much of this as is possible should be done on the spot. I would like to extend this idea and say that all schools need someone to make up, in card or wood, teaching aids to teachers' design and specification. Few commercial firms are going to be bothered making up material to a teacher's design unless they know there is a good market, and also most of the materials that are needed by teachers anyway need to be made to satisfy a particular child's need. Few teachers will have the skill or perhaps even the energy to make materials themselves but most of them wanting to work with

---

* I am reminded here of the wall chart put up by one of my former students, Judy Coupe, in her classroom for the classroom assistants 'Words to use in the water play.'

† It is very odd to see male nurses completely in charge of little boys, even those of one and two years old.

the handicapped should be encouraged to have ideas regarding relevant teaching equipment. The present use of infant table material is not always valid for the older mentally handicapped child.

An adventure playground is carefully described, as is a parents' involvement scheme. Critical evaluations are made on all aspects of the work throughout.

Perhaps the most important aspect of this work is the reporting of the attainments of these children and the measures used to assess both the control and experimental group.

I shall not describe the results for those children within the moderately retarded range of ability, for in the main they were what one would expect—except to say that some results were obtained that were different from those found in the Tizard Brooklands experiment, with regard to progress in non-verbal areas, although significant changes were noted in verbal areas of language and socialization. The results were not so encouraging in non-verbal aspects of learning.

These differences were accounted for by the fact that (a) the initial means for the verbal and non-verbal mental ages were much closer together than the children in Brooklands; (b) the children had been given a wider variety of experiences in using their hands; and (c) school activities were continued in the wards. I should also like to suggest that, by this time too, more teachers had a better idea of what to do with these children because of educationally oriented courses of training and annual refresher courses run by the N.A.M.H.*

However, the amount of well-documented knowledge of use to those planning the care and education of the profoundly handicapped is so sparse that I will spend some time on this aspect. Professor Tizard sums the results up in the Foreword of the book in which a description of this work appears. He writes, quoting the researchers, 'but the most striking feature was the limited amount of change which took place . . . this experimental group was of such low ability that marked changes could not reasonably be expected . . . there was some evidence that the experimental group achieved a better emotional adjustment than their controls.'

Perhaps this research is the most informative work that has been carried out with the profoundly handicapped in Britain over a period of time. We are certainly made aware of the kind of results we are likely to achieve in an institutional setting.

---

* National Association for Mental Health, now MIND.

	1964 Active Positive Ignoring	1966 Active Positive Ignoring
Response to adults	1 4 3	4 2 2
Response to children	0 5 3	2 2 4

	1964	1967
Response to play material	5/8 repetitive banging/shaking 2/8 sucked toys together 1/8 used 2 things together 1/8 building bricks	6/8 banging/shaking 1/8 used 2 things together 1/8 used several

	1964	1967
Vocalizations	6/8 made no attempt 1/8 used sounds to register protest 1/8 used sounds to attract attention	3/8 used sounds to communicate to attract attention

Direct observation of eight children was used to assess their progress. This was carried out by nurses and others involved with the children. The children's ages ranged from 4 years to 8 years 2 months

These two well-known psychologists have given us an extremely useful picture of the minimal progress made in three years by these profoundly handicapped institutionalized children (of course it was an extremely small sample). Whilst they initially pose the question (Reference 74 page 158) about the usefulness of giving them toys, they immediately say 'that most of them were capable of responding at a simple level and the human approach would be to provide them with such stimulation as they can use.'

They discuss staffing problems in terms of training and recruitment in their paper, and bring up the question of whether these children should not rather be in smaller units.[76, 77]

In view of the significant differences in emotional tone of the experimental group compared to the control group (cf. page 158), I should consider the approach with play and toys as not only successful but highly desirable. The children for the most part cannot be left to themselves (this has been so for too long already) and the adults concerned with them cannot remain passive and satisfied jobwise, so it seems that we must make quite sure of the following:

(1) All the adults working with these children should be well versed in how to play with children and in the structure of simple play levels. They need practical workshop courses on play to stimulate their imagination. They need to see themselves as 'big toys'.

(2) They should be helped to understand the rate of development in these children. Thus Robinson and Robinson[78] in describing profoundly handicapped children as adults say that their mental levels will be round about three years. If we turn this into months we shall see that, even if there was even development every year, each year would only mean two months of development. Without a longitudinal study of a group of profoundly handicapped children being carried out (where precise annual measurements of their intellectual development are made) we shall never know whether there are years when they do not develop at all and years when they develop more than the possible 2 months. A highly theoretical problem, but equally as important it seems to me, if a child is alive, as the medical decision to preserve life in order sometimes to discover the causes and thus prevent further cases with the same condition in the future. By six years of age they might be at a one-year level, twelve years a two-year level and by eighteen years at a three-year level.*

(3) That the adults concerned should be aware of the slight qualitative differences found by Gregory[19] that might be observed if they become skilled observers—this needs practice as I have been saying for a long time.

(4) That those working with these children should always be in full receipt of the implications of their special medical conditions—i.e. some children will deteriorate.

Perhaps one of the important omissions in this survey for me at least was a really detailed report on what the adults did with the children, session by session, and the amount of time each child received in any one block of intensive handling playwise. Perhaps the

---

* This research made me rethink the practicalities of considering the concept of rate of development and try to work it out in such terms, however crudely.

results would have been the same, for indeed the children studied were *the* most handicapped children, but if we are going to make recommendations about staff then we do need perhaps to follow the example of Gardener and Cass in the field of normal infant school education and observe personnel at work in some detail.*

Symbolic play and language development.[62]
(1) Two classes of 7-8 children ($2\frac{1}{2}$–$4\frac{1}{2}$ years), (whose language handicap is severe and specific compared with performance), have $4\frac{1}{2}$ days weekly with a teacher assisted by an assistant.
(2) Symbolic play material (large dolls, tea-sets, model village, etc.) easily available and affording flexibility for the adults/children.
(3) Specific instructions to the adults regarding the use of their own language (cf. pp. 150/151), the use of gesture and the importance of concentrating more on building up a 'sound basis of symbolic understanding than on eliciting expressive language.'
(4) Weekly conference with speech therapist and psychologist for consultation.
Design of Experiment: Comparison of results on a wide variety of tests with two other groups:
(a) having individual speech therapy locally;
(b) having no special help with language.
Results after a year (tentative): The language class children did as well in verbal comprehension and expressive language as those in (a) and considerably better than those in (b).

Dr. Reynell points out the difficulties in planning such remedial work, but the description she gives of underlying principles of helping these children language-wise, of a specific method and of her results should influence those training teachers of the handicapped to devise ways and means of giving students opportunities under supervision to practise, using symbolic play material with individual children and small groups.

If my own experience with Adrian in particular (2 years) is meaningful in this context, it would appear that when one has observed most of the development posed by the Uzgiriz and Hunt Assessment Scale and the child can remain alongside the adult *of his own volition* for increasing lengths of time, the time is ripe for the kind of symbolic play suggested in this research. The reader will see how my own play materials (page 89) have in fact allowed this kind of play and adult response to take place.

---

* Mein at Harperbury Subnormality Hospital used a 16-year-old volunteer to observe each child for ten minutes in a play situation. On the basis of the observational records made by this young man, a play group was set up in this hospital. Is there a lesson for us here with regard to collecting information about personnel, with their knowledge and sanction of course?

Indeed it seems a logical development in the curriculum for teaching the young mentally handicapped child—the next step forward as it were from the kind of play between a child and an adult that has taken into account gross motor activity, exploration of objects, sensation of the body in space, the conservation of the body parts (page 56) and activities designed to arouse and keep the child's spontaneous attention over longer and longer periods of time. Dorothy Jeffree discussing this paper[62] after its presentation expressed this more precisely, viz 'It would seem that some awareness of the relationships of objects and permanence of objects was a prerequisite to such a programme.'

Improving language by doll play.[16] Dorothy Jeffree (cf. pp. 118)

Development, play and handicap[79] *and The communication of young severely handicapped children*[60]
Two useful papers outlining the theoretical constructs underlining the value of play in helping handicapped children, and the work presently being carried out using audio/video techniques on mother/child reaction in play situations. The second paper mentioned is important for me as a teacher for:
(a) it describes some of the developmental origins of communication;
(b) it extended my thinking about sequence in development, particularly in connection with different types of attention:
   (i) to mother's face
   (ii) to rattle
   (iii) to rattle, then to mother's face, then back to rattle (cf. page 54);
(c) it reinforced my own experience regarding the importance of looking behaviour in the development of social response for Mogford writes: 'many handicapped children may have failed to develop the most basic responses of looking at and responding to other human beings' (cf. page 54);
(d) it emphasized the importance of the significance of an event to the *two* people playing, if social relationships are going to be formed and made use of in the learning situation;
(e) it emphasized understanding the 'wealth of pre-verbal and pre-linguistic concepts that normal infants acquire and the features of interaction that makes this acquisition possible;'
(f) it points out the dangers of behaviour modification techniques unless the social aspects of communication are taken into consideration too. 'Such techniques cannot help but provide an artificial context for the use of speech or, applying over-simplified criteria

for its appropriate use, they may only provide the child with behaviour that fits a superficial criterion of speech.'

Play alone is not sufficient
Teachers who show they understand play by:
(a) continuous provision of stimulating materials based upon the observed needs of the children;
(b) relevant and well chosen language;
(c) continuous intervention to extend the children's play;
will have their critics. If the programme only contained opportunities for play I would say that such criticism would be entirely justified. Alongside such an approach there must be, as I have already said, a systematic approach to the individual child; the teacher spending a proportion of her time each day teaching in a one-to-one situation. As I see it these two approaches must go hand in hand and a balance between the two achieved with teachers always being responsible for the organization and the evaluation of objectives. In working towards the ideal of some one-to-one teaching in Special Education, the teacher must never lose sight of her major responsibility for the group and its work. Classroom assistants must never become second-class teachers and 'mind' the children even in a rich stimulating environment whilst the teacher is teaching one child.

Perhaps the success of one is dependent upon the other. There must be time for *both* in the school life of the severely subnormal child. The teacher will be sorely at a disadvantage if she does not see and understand the play of the children. It will tell her much about their levels of development if she constantly takes the trouble to refer to the developmental scales available. It will provide her with some of the starting points for each individual child's work with her.

9 A special kind of teacher

Severely subnormal children, like normal children, must get to know their teachers. Of even greater importance is the fact that the teacher must have time not only to discover the individual needs of the children and diagnose difficulties but also to see that some of these needs are met. Time is needed by the child and the teacher if any measure of continuity of approach and teaching method is to exist.

It has not been unusual in the past for teachers in some schools to be transferred almost without warning to other schools in the area. Some heads adopt the practice of constantly moving their teachers around the classes each term. Such actions have certainly not taken into account the security of the children or the pride of the teacher in her work as she helps the children to learn.

In some schools there is a 'specialist' programme, teachers being responsible for 'subjects' on the curriculum. In such cases the Heads are usually unaware of the value of these children having the same teacher over a long period of time. I have seen some of the benefits however, when this idea has been adopted, particularly when the subject has been language. One school* in Derbyshire has appointed a teacher† to carry out individual language programmes with all the children in the first years of school. This is only one of many new interesting experiments in the education of severely subnormal children. It does not mean that a teacher's special gifts should not be used. What it might suggest is that teachers of these children should have a good measure of personal skill and achievement in all aspects of creative and prescriptive education and be able to use this.

By suggesting that the teacher should stay with her group for a long time I am not saying that this policy should be a rigid one; I am not saying that the children should not have contact with teachers having special gifts—in fact when more schools work on an open-plan system the children will spontaneously move amongst all the adults available—what I am suggesting is that one teacher will be responsible for the intensive individual diagnosis and teaching that will be done with the members of a particular group as well as for some of the group activities.

---

* Parkwood, Alfreton.
† Under the guidance of a psychologist research worker employed by the L.E.A. as an educational psychologist.

The opportunities the children will have of meeting a wide variety of people, both inside school and out of it, will depend to a large extent upon the teacher's resourcefulness. The children will meet people when they go shopping, go for a walk, go on a bus, or into a café. Their teachers will be inviting a policeman, a fireman, a musician, a postman, into the school. They might be inviting the children from another school to a puppet show, a concert or, as arranged by one head,* to a lunch which the children had prepared themselves for their visitors. In another school some of the children have creative dance with a group of Primary School children visiting their school once a week. In practical ways like this the children's needs to have contact with other human beings will be satisfied.

A SPECIAL KIND OF TEACHER

Few teachers take the opportunities of teaching all ability levels or all age levels even if this might be considered a useful professional experience. Few want to teach a wide range of pupils, for most realize their success in a particular field and remain within it, preferring to savour the depths rather than the breadths of teaching experience. Attempts have been made, mainly in American literature, to describe the qualities of the successful teacher of retarded children. In Miss Neale's book too[80] we can gain some useful insights. Nothing that I know in English literature on the teaching of the mentally handicapped has attempted a similar qualitative assessment. Traditionalists with only their own experience to draw upon claim that these children should have teachers initially very experienced in teaching normal children and who later take extra advanced courses in education.

Some of us had the opportunity of discovering that young teachers with a particular feeling of commitment and involvement, flair and need for working with such children can be successful, if not better, after special training, than more experienced, qualified teachers without the inherent qualities or training. Of course these young people generally needed the support of mature, experienced Heads. The severely subnormal need energetic, lively, adventurous, hard-working and imaginative teachers of both sexes. They have been deprived of men teachers in the 'sixties for schools in the main have been staffed by women willing to receive the poor salaries paid.

If we cling to the idea that only experienced teachers with advanced educational qualifications should teach the severely subnormal (and I am anxious lest this idea take too strong a hold, for most of the

---

* Mrs. Penny, Piper Hill School, Manchester.

advanced courses do not prepare teachers to work with these children) a potential source of very suitable, flexible, adaptable young people will be lost. The children will also be deprived. No one is suggesting that young teachers should remain with the severely subnormal all their teaching lives but at a time in history when young people seem to need 'causes' to combat the terrifying growth of a materialistic society their enthusiasms and vigour might be successfully channelled to benefit a group of children denied their rights for so long.

It seems a matter of aptitude for the job and special training (as with infant teachers or those in comprehensive schools with special subjects) rather than of age and of a fixed amount of teaching experience—experience which might in fact establish habits and skills needing to be unlearned if one is to work successfully with this group of children.

Personal qualities needed
(1)   Intellectual curiosity
By this I mean the kind of curiosity which wants to know how these children learn, which is fascinated by the many things which the handicapped can achieve in some activities (e.g. physical skills, some features of observation, social adaptation) alongside their obvious difficulties in others (e.g. academic learning). Linked to this intellectual curiosity the teacher must be a 'book dipper' for she will constantly want to know how to deal with a child with this or that particular handicap and difficulty at this or that particular stage of learning. She will not become a really successful teacher unless she puts time aside for referring to books. Her curiosity should stimulate the habit.

(2)   Pleasure in simple experiences
She needs to be a person who gains deep pleasure herself in simple life experiences. She will then be more likely to see what the children need as part of their experience and enjoy providing it for them. In other words she must like what these children like doing and be interested in their pursuits at whatever level these present themselves.

(3)   Personal appearance and private life
She should try to look as attractive as possible in appearance and dress.

She needs to be a developing person herself with an interesting private life.

(4) Imagination

Not only does the teacher of this group need to be a skilled observer of the children's behaviour; she must know *what to do* when she has observed. For this she has to develop her own imagination as well as her knowledge of child development. Sustained reading habits and continued attendance at lectures and specially designed In-Service workshops will enable these qualities to be fully stimulated, though we must not forget how the children can also stimulate us if we watch them closely as we work with them.

(5) *Skilled in keeping records*

She must also know how to keep detailed records of her observations of the children and the work she does with each one. She must know about the kind of records to keep. The following sources could be useful in assessing achievement and diagnosing difficulties:

(a) her own testing programme (Chapter 11);
(b) standardized tests given by herself or other specialists;
(c) developmental scales and assessment charts;
(d) observing in free and structured situations;
(e) taped interviews with parents in the home;
(f) records of other teachers;
(g) the social workers (teachers might usefully ascertain whether other visitors are seeing the home situation and are willing to share impressions, e.g. a psychiatric worker if there is mental illness in the home, the health visitor.

Descriptive records are often tedious to keep but some form of brief notes seems a necessity. Sessions with very young children perhaps need tape-recording, for, however skilled an observer the teacher is, the recall of her activities and the response of the child will be difficult.

(6) *Ability for constructive discussion with specialists* (including own colleagues)

Regular discussions amongst the teachers about each child and his educational needs should be held at intervals, however time-consuming. Sometimes these should include other experts. In a variety of ways we trained students to discuss individual children throughout their course of training.

(7) *Ability to have constructive discussions with parents*

During such discussions she will have to judge when she can legitimately 'offend' the parent in order to bring about any necessary changes in attitudes they might have towards their offspring. I think that what the teacher has to do here is to help the parents to trust her and this can only be done over a period of time. When they feel that she is genuinely interested in their particular problem they will be more likely to listen to her and perhaps act upon her suggestions.

(8) Ability to dare to play a positive part with those in loco parentis *in hostels and hospitals*
Those in the hostels and hospitals responsible for the children's home welfare should invite the teachers to have tea with the children from time to time. Nurse/teacher workshops might copy the Parent Workshops initiated in the North West by Jeffree and Cunningham, supported by a grant from the National Society for Mentally Handicapped Children (Manchester).

Further qualities required in the teaching situation
(1) The teacher must be able to build up confidence in each child and thus help him to become independent of her rather than dependent on her. To do this she must work fully convinced of her own ability to bring about learning in such children however handicapped they are (cf. page 44). She must also consider how confidence is built up through appropriate experiences bringing about feelings of success and happiness, through encouragement and praise and through her own caring.
(2) She must have a gift for seeing what she can make of the child's behaviour in terms of a positive response; for seeing when she has to go back to the simplest beginnings in experience in learning with individual children and whatever their chronological age without heeding the pressures from: (a) colleagues, (b) parents, (c) other specialists.
(3) She must be able to break down experiences and teaching materials into small graded steps.
(4) She must have the capacity for ignoring negative behaviour (or what seems to be so at the time) and knowing how to exploit it positively; how to interpret so called 'negative' behaviour in terms of its communication aspects.
(5) She must be able to choose as well as design and sometimes make relevant equipment.
(6) She must be a listening teacher in order to assess a child's language level. She must also cultivate the habit of listening to her own language structure and noting each child's response to it. She needs to be constantly aware of what the child is hearing of her language and what he is imitating, missing.

(7) She must be a 'talking' teacher who:
   (a) can use her voice continually without straining it;
   (b) can structure the grammar of her own spoken language and adapt it to the needs and level of each child;*
   (c) knows how long to make her sentences;
   (d) knows how much repetition of language to give in order to gain a response, i.e. how many times to repeat an instruction, command or comment, and whether to accompany this with gesture or not (cf. Dutch research page 59);
   (e) can hazard a guess at the length of time she sometimes needs to pause for a child to make a reply or follow out an 'instruction' before repeating what she has said;
   (f) can understand the need children apparently have for their actual words (sounds) to be imitated by the teacher in order that they may be motivated to use more words and to extend their thinking, e.g. if the teacher asks a question about an object, a picture or an activity and fails to elicit the 'correct' answer she should not become impatient or continue to try to get the correct answer. She should be more interested in the 'error'.[65] She should follow the lead suggested by the child. In this way the child's passive language will be elicited, surely, as I have said before, one of the main aims of the teacher of these children. She must be a teacher, genuinely wanting to interpret the CHILD'S meaning and to help him to comprehend.
(8) She has to present tasks in such a way that the child understands what is expected of him and so that he can learn what is necessary.
(9) She must be able to recognize the 'readiness' signals for the next stage of learning. She should be encouraging any signs of independence which indicate growing feelings of maturity.
(10) She must be able to help the child to learn what it is she wants him to learn. She must give him opportunities to learn before assessing what he is capable of (cf. ref. 35, page 36).
(11) She must ensure that no child is allowed to fall into or remain in a 'cabbage'-like existence because of inadequate assessment of his present attainments and future needs because there is an expressed

---

* I think that this constitutes one of the major differences in teaching young children who are 'normal' (and not deprived) and this group. It constitutes one of the main difficulties too, for it is an exacting technique for her mental and physical energies. It also plays havoc over a period of time with her own vocabulary and structure of language. Because of this the teacher must give herself plenty of opportunities in other social situations to discuss at adult levels and to use her own spread of vocabulary.

feeling of 'it's a waste of our time.'
(12) She must keep an eye over the general health of each child and be quick to refer a child for treatment. It is better to be too enthusiastic here than not to bother 'because the child is mentally handicapped.'
(13) She must have the ability to integrate auxiliary staff into her programme and plan their work each day as well as her own.

Emotional qualities

Involvement is essential as are certain emotional attitudes.
(1) Affection—this must be shown overtly (p. 81).
(2) Acceptance of the child in order to help him feel he belongs to a group.
(3) Interest in him and his activities in order to give him feelings of importance.
(4) Balanced approach between permissive attitudes which enable her to see what he is able to do and those which enforce reasonable limits on his behaviour (and the ones she imposes will depend on her ever-increasing knowledge of children's development, her own expectations and her ability to tolerate without strain different aspects of a child's behaviour).
(5) Lack of rigidity and demand for exact ritual

Emotional involvement

The teacher must become involved and have attitudes which can only be described as springing from the emotions. I would point out by this that I do not mean that she should become emotionally entangled. The phrase 'emotionally involved'—an expression used by a social worker (BBC, 1974)—needs explanation because teachers are often told not to be, but are not always sure what it means in the practical day-to-day handling of handicapped children.

Since nearly all of these children are loved by parents we must never think of them as our own nor seek ways in which to make them emotionally dependent upon us. We should know the part we have played in their total development but be pleased to send them on to someone else who can take them on just that little 'bit further' in their learning because of their personal skills and attitudes. If we become emotionally involved with a handicapped child and his family it can be most difficult to stand aside and look objectively at his measured progress. We can assume all too readily that because we have taught him then he must have progressed. If we achieve any skill in giving standardized tests we shall find it difficult not to help him in the items he finds difficulty in doing if we are emotionally involved. We might find it difficult to suppress any desire to say to ourselves, or aloud if there is someone else present, 'Well, I know he can do it. He's done it before for me.' One expects this of parents for they are naturally emotionally involved, but one has to resist it as a teacher unless one has recorded evidence to the contrary and this is quite feasible. If one remains emotionally uninvolved it is more likely that all the children in a group will have their fair share of attention. Otherwise a teacher might find some children much more appealing to her feelings of protectiveness, of pity, love, or even pride in her own ability to teach, and so neglect the others.

Another pointer to testing our own emotional involvement (and insight might help to curb it) is to become aware of our feelings when another member of staff concerns herself spontaneously with a child who is in our particular group. Ideally speaking, although the mentally handicapped child needs his teacher for a long period of time he should nevertheless be the immediate concern of all the teachers in the school whenever he happens to be in their presence.

Perhaps a certain amount of observed possessiveness is one of the reasons why the children in most schools were not encouraged to wander from classroom to classroom and in and out of the Head's room. No teacher of insight and experience will deny that as a young teacher she had all or most of the feelings I have described in relationship to the children she has taught. She will agree that as she has matured her feelings have become modified.

I think the important point we must bear in mind is that it is time to let the children go when *they* no longer need us. Teachers who become emotionally involved with severely subnormal children find difficulty in accepting that the overt friendliness which is so apparent to the visiting stranger (sometimes welcomed as a 'long lost friend') is so often a feature of their handicap. If they can accept this with some measure of understanding they will be just that little bit nearer to understanding the role of the teacher in coming to terms with the problem of mental handicap.

10 *An interesting dynamic programme and curriculum*

I should like to begin this chapter by describing the way in which one school for the severely subnormal began the day for, although no schools for the mentally handicapped exist in old church halls any longer, there are many still existing not satisfying the needs of children when they come to school in the morning; still imposing formal methods on the children even at the beginning of the day. As the activities of the children were carried out before my eyes I felt the life, the purpose, the dynamism.

It was half-past nine in the morning. I had just entered the door of an old church building. A number of adults each accompanied by a severely subnormal child had just alighted at nearby bus stops. We had arrived at the same time. Inside, it was a hive of activity. Peeping into a small room I saw two girls aged 13 and 15 years spreading slices of bread with butter, cutting them into two and placing them attractively on several large plates. Two boys were keen to arrange the tables with beakers and a serviette in the 'milk bar' space set aside in a corner of the only large room of this school. Yet another boy was setting out the bottles of milk on a table nearby ready for the children to 'buy.' After changing into plimsoles, other children were helping their teacher to bring out all the equipment for the day's activities from the storeroom at the end of the large room. There was an atmosphere of friendliness, liveliness and serious purpose behind all the activities I saw. The children were learning to do things for themselves and to concentrate. They had to help each other to carry the large boxes. They listened to instructions which were repeated and spoken clearly in words consciously chosen by the teacher. Sometimes they had to communicate with each other.

One of the teachers helped the children choose a real coin (1p, 2p, 5p) from a special box to spend at the 'milk bar.' They could 'buy' a slice of bread or a biscuit and a bottle of milk and sit at a table of their own choosing. Taking it in turns, the children chose their coin, were talked to by the teacher and walked over to the 'milk bar' for their purchases.

The other teacher was supervising the changing of shoes and encouraging the children to go and choose from the activities and equipment brought out by the early arrivers. The children's immediate return to activities either in their own classroom or in the hall after a short stay in their 'milk bar' meant that *no time was wasted*. All the time was purposefully spent. The children did not have to wait for their teacher to help them become busy. They moved quite naturally to the activity in which they were most interested.

What a lovely way to begin the day; with a well-thought-out programme to absorb the children's attention and activity straightaway on their arrival.

PLANNING A SUITABLE PROGRAMME

Many factors must be taken into account in thinking about a suitable programme to afford the teacher time for all the activities she needs to introduce to the children and for them to gain the maximum benefit from these. Long periods of time should be available during the day for the children to choose their own activities and for the teacher to organize her individual teaching sessions. There should be complete flexibility in the teacher's own classroom and in the school generally (so that she might arrange activities according to the children's needs, except where another teacher and group is concerned), e.g. in using the hall, the kitchen, etc., at specific times. A balance needs to be kept between the indoor and outdoor activities undertaken daily by the various age groups, and there should be ample opportunity for both boisterous and quieter activities. These should exist alongside each other on some occasions. There should be a balance in the teacher's plans between the group's activities and the individual work that is done with each child. The increase in classroom assistants should make the teacher's task easier here.

Practical considerations

A successful programme depends for its success on detailed preparation beforehand. The following factors also need consideration:
(a) Thought about the children as individuals and as a group.
(b) Thought about the classroom environment in terms of the teacher's attitudes, provision of materials and suitable activities, the requisitioning of materials and apparatus, the attractiveness of the classroom, the interest of the children in the teacher and in the classroom.
(c) Thought about the suitability of the materials as well as the care, cleanliness, renewal, making and mending of these (cf. reference 71, page 139).
(d) The amount of time spent at the beginning or end of each day jotting down ideas about the children, what should be taught; in

arranging the classroom so that all the materials are accessible to the children.* I would like to suggest that no adequate teaching can be carried out unless at least an hour a day and some time at weekend is spent in preparing; and this is an absolute minimum.

EXAMPLES OF DAILY PROGRAMMES

These should never be thought of in terms of subjects or short fixed periods of time. They should be considered in terms of children's needs and the best use of time and opportunities. The greater the problems of individual differences there are within any one group the more the teacher has to rely upon her own skill and judgement and upon her own professional integrity in planning the programme and carrying it out. Perhaps a glance at three suggested programmes for children of different ability levels will explain more clearly and enable the teacher to devize her own schemes.

Youngest children and those of lowest ability
A glance at the programme (page 157) might produce the comment 'What an easy day!' The chapter on understood play and on planning for the individual child will explain why the day is fairly unstructured and where the beginning and ending of session only really depends upon the arrival and departure of the children and their lunch time. Generally speaking the day should be organized to meet their individual needs. The thoughts of Professor Tizard concerning that now classic educational experiment at Brooklands[6] might sum up the suggestions I am putting forward. Young children 'will be found to be the best judges of what is good for them. It is diversity of experience rather than mere repetition that makes for useful learning.' When one is considering the young handicapped child in school he needs time, before our eyes as it were, to have the opportunity of showing what he has assimilated of his experience at home and in the individual learning he does in school.

---

* Gardener and Cass, when questioning sixteen teachers (using an active approach) about the amount of time they spent *out of school hours* in preparation for their work (and remember most classes would contain more than 30 children), discovered the following:

Number of hours per week	2	3	5	6	7	10
Teachers	2	2	1	2	1	1

The rest said it varied according to the needs of the children.

SAMPLE PROGRAMME FOR YOUNG OR LOW-ABILITY CHILDREN

Day	Early activities	Mid-morning	Transition	Late morning	Closing
Monday	Jobs in the classroom. Getting out the toys and equipment. Helping the teacher to mix the paints, to set the table for milk. Fetching and carrying small equipment	Free play inside/outside Individual work Mother's work	Clearing away together Movement Story-telling Music	Free play Individual work	Clearing away together Music Storytelling
Tuesday		Free play inside/outside Individual work Walk		Free play Simple creative work*	
Wednesday		Free play inside/outside Individual work Mother's work		Free play Individual work	
Thursday		Free play inside/outside Walk/swimming		Free play Simple creative work	
Friday		Free play inside/outside Individual work Mother's work		Free play Walk	

If we look at the programme as it is written I should say that, in any free-play session of an hour and a half or more even, the teacher should have been able to work with two or three children individually (cf. Chapters 4 and 11) (and these will be different each day so that they all have a turn according to a plan), to mingle, chat and play with the rest of the children and to carry out a mother's work task.† If she achieves this each day she will truly have participated in the learning situation. She should also try to fit in a 'sit down and do' session. By this I mean that *she* should paint, do a puzzle, build up nesting blocks or bricks, etc., in front of the children. This needs to take up only five to ten minutes a day. She will find it valuable in stimulating the children's curiosity and she will also be taking into account assimilation and imitation in the learning process.

---

* I have used the term 'simple creative work' to suggest to the teacher that whilst the children are playing she can work with small groups of willing children on collage with exciting materials, painting, etc. I have called it work to suggest to the teacher that it is something she prepares for the children and which she guides.

† I have explained this more fully elsewhere but it might be useful to describe this technique in the present volume. Briefly, it entails the teacher doing an activity (usually carried out at home by the mother) amongst the

A further look at the programme will suggest that some part of every day should be spent in creative movement, music, storytelling, even if only a few children in the group are ready to join in. Children who are not ready should be free to find and continue with their own activity. This might mean watching the group activity from a distance. Storytelling will be at the simplest level, looking at objects, looking at pictures and talking about them, saying rhymes. I think that it is important here to mention that the storytelling, music and movement sessions or just talking to the children in a comfortable 'family group' should be given adequate time according to the levels of development of the children. They should never be 'filling in' or 'waiting for lunch or home time to come round' sessions. Preparation and thought for them is as necessary as for all other parts of the programme.

During the day there should be *natural* opportunities to help the children with toileting, washing, cleaning teeth and combing hair skills. Outings and changing for movement will motivate dressing skills and afford much-needed practice. The children's individual needs and rhythms should be regarded. They need to be given plenty of opportunities to become self-regulated. The teacher should constantly remind herself that the 'acquisition of various skills is dependent on maturation of the nervous system. No amount of practice can make a child acquire skills until his nervous system is ready for it. Not giving children opportunities to practise their skills on the other hand when they are ready might cause delay and more retardation in the skill than is necessary.' Here is yet another reason why the teacher must increase her skill in observation so that she is ready to use the child's readiness and his particular form of communication.

Outdoor activities
One of the most needed changes in the schools prior to 1st April, 1971 was in the amount of time which is spent by the children out of doors. So long as the weather is fine, even if it is cold, and provided there is plenty of equipment, the children should be out in the open air climbing, sliding, playing with pushing and pulling toys, balls, tyres, hoops, tricycles. Since reorganization with the L.E.A.'s, many more

---

children at play. If she spends about twenty minutes daily on such activities she will find that they stimulate curiosity, enable her to give the words of the activity in an ordered, systematic fashion, command the children's attention and encourage communication both through gesture and through words. Now the teachers have classroom assistants this can be effective if they too are invited to think about the words they use when doing jobs.

AN INTERESTING DYNAMIC PROGRAMME AND CURRICULUM

schools have introduced and developed weekly pony riding classes. Warwickshire has enabled all its schools for the mentally handicapped to have exciting Adventure Playgrounds. They are well worth a visit. Maybe future architects will ensure that each classroom opens on to a safe play space (perhaps roofed over). In this way the children can change at will from indoor to outdoor play. Whenever there is enough help, and this can be reinforced by kindly ladies from the district, by young people desirous of gaining experience with the handicapped before entering a College to do a course in Mental Handicap, or by young people in their last year at school, the children should be taken out for a short walk, those who cannot walk and those who tire easily in a pram. Determined students took out a group of tiny children in a wheelbarrow—more prams and trolleys please and more help! Such a walk will give the teacher plenty of opportunity for talking to the children.

Middle years, i.e. 10-13+ years

SAMPLE PROGRAMME FOR MIDDLE YEARS

Day	Preparation (vertical)	Morning activity	Middle (vertical)	Lunch	Afternoon activity	Clearing (vertical)
Monday	Getting equipment and materials ready with the teacher's help. Nature table arrangements and care. Mixing paint. Sorting out 'bit boxes'. Arranging interest tables and home corners.	P.E. / Free choice / Individual work	Clearing away together / Drama / Music / Storytelling	L U N C H	Music/Storytelling / Free choice	Clearing away together.
Tuesday		Free choice / Individual work			P.E. / Free choice	
Wednesday		Walk/visits / Swimming			Guided creative work	
Thursday		P.E. / Free choice / Individual work			Free choice / Cookery with/for children / Music/Story	
Friday		Free choice / Individual work		P.E.	Music/Story / Drama	

The children still need plenty of opportunities for choosing their own activities. The teacher needs time in which to work with individual children. Group work with three or four children at a time will become possible and natural.

There will still be children within this age range however who are not ready to join in with a group. Their behaviour should not be considered negative. Rather should it be seen as part of their natural development. Playing amd working alonside of, but not with, other children will continue for a very much longer time with severely subnormal children, until ten, eleven or even twelve with the most handicapped. The positive teacher will encourage but not force the pace. I might add here that I do not think that one child should be allowed to spoil the activity of the others by behaviour which is preventing a group activity. There should be a place where his momentary needs can be met; for short spells of time this might be in another group in the school or doing something with the Headteacher. There must be freedom within the school for flexible human relationships so that no teacher feels left to cope alone, sometimes with insuperable problems. In this way the best can be made of whatever stage of behaviour is presented and a positive approach adopted.

Associative play
A great deal of the observed play of this group is that which is called associative play. By this is meant that the child plays along with other children but not in any way which suggests that there is a common group aim in the play. This comes at a later stage in the children's development. In observing associative play happening spontaneously teachers can expect the children to be more ready to join in group activities of a more structured kind. In other words such behaviour is a readiness pointer.

Working with individuals
During one of the long free choice sessions the teacher should concern herself initially with testing the children and, on the basis of the results of her testing programme (pp. 175-182) and her records of interests, she can work individually with each member of the group. If she has provided well the rest of the group will be able to work and play fairly independently. She will need varying amounts of determination to continue working with an individual child without being deflected from her purpose. However, the children have to learn (and they can learn) to accept that the teacher will take them when it is their turn.

She should not become over-anxious if other children gather to watch her whilst she is working with one child, for watching as an activity is part of learning. They will gradually learn how to 'get on' with their own work. As I see it (and have carried it out myself as a teacher when I worked educationally with a group of very low-grade institutionalized men one evening a week over a period of two years) 10 minutes* might be spent with one child from the hour and a half, 20 minutes could be spent mingling amongst and working with the groups needing help and then a return to working individually with a second child and so on. This could form a useful working plan for an approach where the individual matters—to the extent that he has work specially prepared for him. Each teacher, each special school, has to work this out independently. If one of the aims of the teacher is to attend to the needs of individual children a way will be discovered.

'Useful' work
During these years the number of 'jobs' the children can carry out with their teacher will not only increase in complexity but also in number. Too often do we still see the children having too much done for them by their teachers. In an active atmosphere a great deal more responsibility can be given to the children for getting the room ready for all kinds of activities; for fetching and carrying equipment from the storerooms, cupboards and boxes; for preparing the tables for dinner; for arranging the interest corners, the milk bar, the tables for the mid-morning drink. Whilst on this subject I should like to refer to the habit which some children are encouraged to continue both by their parents and teachers, i.e. the one of letting them have a 'lunch' midway between arriving and lunch. In view of the very short morning it means that the child probably only has a complete hour in which to 'get going' with his work. It is also surely bad dietetically. I should like to see many more teachers introducing the children to a carrot or a piece of fruit (if they must eat in between meals) and discouraging packets of sandwiches and biscuits. A school shop selling such 'wholesome' fare might become a healthy useful feature of the school.

Free choice sessions
You will see that I have changed the term 'free play' in this second programme to the words 'free choice.' This is not because I am considering that play as such will stop at this stage. Indeed if it is

---

* Ten minutes is indeed a very short time to spend with a handicapped child—it will certainly mean that the teacher will have to have selected something very specific that she wishes to do with the child and have her materials ready. As far as my experience with very young handicapped children is concerned, one hour of structured play with an adult is both relevant and possible. Unless one has a large number of adults to help, the school situation might not afford teachers to work so concentratedly.

allowed and understood properly by the teacher as an integral part of the child's development there will be opportunities for the children to have some means for play during their school life. The observant and knowledgeable teacher will see how the quality of their play develops as the child matures and will know its value to the child. My reason for using the term 'free choice' is to suggest to the teacher that her role is different now in that she has additional responsibilities. The successful teacher will encourage the children to develop their interests and to sustain them. She will make sure that the activities are purposeful and 'lead somewhere.' A useful maxim to keep in mind seems to be that each free choice session should have *something achieved* at the end, perhaps something achieved that can be seen. This will only happen if the teacher has a goal in mind and if the children are in an environment where something new is always happening. The classroom displays will indicate the way in which the teacher develops purposeful activities.

Some purposeful activities
(1) Cover storage boxes with their own painting, shape printing, wallpaper.
(2) Wallpaper the walls of the home corner, paint the 'walls' of the house, make the 'roof' for the house.
(3) Paint boxes to make extra storage shelves in the classroom.
(4) Start a frieze or a simple model to follow up a visit or a story or a special experience. For example:
  (i) Some children had been to a cafe the day before. Some had had orange juice, some had had tea. The teacher had prepared templates of glasses, cups and saucers for the children to cut out and colour and paste on to a chart. It showed the children in a pictorial form how many had juice, how many tea, etc. It provided a lot to talk about.
  (ii) A policeman had visited the classroom. He wore a flat peaked cap and long black boots. What fun the children had the following day colouring-in the teacher's drawings of the caps and the boots. What fun they had another day painting the giant-sized cardboard boot which reached almost to the top of the ceiling!
(5) Sort out the 'bit box'/the shop. Rearrange the items in the cupboard.
(6) Make the 'fruit', 'cakes', 'bread', for the shop.
(7) Make the 'stove' for the home corner and any other unit that is needed.

(8) Rearrange the nature table, the interest corner, the music table, the dressing-up clothes.
(9) Make own instrument for the music table or to take home.
(10) Plant bulbs, seeds, etc., for the indoor garden.
(11) Start to make simple puppets.
(12) Arrange an exhibition of the other children's paintings with the teacher.
(13) Make a puppet box for the classroom.
(14) Wash the dolls' clothes, the dressing-up clothes.
(15) Help teacher to stuff a pillow/mattress for the dolls' bed.
(16) Paint the bricks on the wall of the house.
(17) Make mats from foam rubber/cardboard/other material for the table at lunch time.
(18) Fill vases with flowers or with leaves.
(19) Start to make the milk bar with the teacher.
(20) Paint the shoe cut-outs which will decorate the box housing the shoes in the dressing-up corner.
(21) Clean out the pet cage.
(22) Water the plants.

The number of purposeful activities which can be carried out with the children are numerous; the observant teacher will be guided by the children and see which are likely to be meaningful to them.

In making these suggestions I am not intending that the children carry out all the particular activities listed. They are included in order to indicate the kind of activity I am referring to and to trigger off the teacher's imagination in the situation in which she finds herself. They are mentioned to reinforce the point I am trying to make about the children being free to choose their own activities; for some children these will be the ones the teacher is organizing. The teacher is *not free*. The whole success of such an approach depends upon the teacher identifying with this concept.

Outings

As the children develop physically and become more group oriented they will gain much from more visits to places of interest. These are now a regular and recognized feature of the programme. The many gifts of mini-coaches to the schools mean that the children can go further afield. This should not mean that the teacher underestimates the value of visits immediately outside the school building. It would appear that the impressions gained by the children whilst they are on these outings will stimulate their use of language and widen their vocabulary. All visits should be carefully discussed with the children on their return to school either individually or in small groups when the real experience is over. Using a tape recording will make it even more interesting, for the children like to hear themselves. Perhaps it is difficult for some of the children to take in impressions from the stimuli around them and talk about them at the same time. This might be one of the valid reasons for casual observers to say 'how well behaved' they are; the main reason for describing the behaviour of normal children on the same kind of outing as not so perfect is because usually they make a 'noise' on account of their spontaneous chatter. The teacher therefore must see this 'good' behaviour generally speaking as a characteristic of the mentally handicapped child and because of it provide well for the verbalized expression of the experience when the stimulus is no longer visually present. Recalling the sequence of the events during the outing through drama, story-telling and movement, is yet another method of ensuring that the children record, represent and relive their experiences. If there are specialist drama or movement teachers they should be informed of these sequences in order to make use of them in their sessions.

Group activities
As normal children mature intellectually they are usually capable of taking more guidance in some of their pursuits. The same is true of severely subnormal children. An afternoon of creative work where the teacher's concentrated attention is on some form of art expression does not seem out of place when the children reach the upper age of this group range. Here again her provision needs to be thorough and varied and have an element of choice in it. The children will have varying levels of skill and spans of attention. Some will not remain at a guided activity for very long.

I have seen inexperienced students prepare a 'group' session of creative work. The children have remained as a group for about seven to ten minutes and then one by one have wandered off to another activity. Provided this exists all is well. Woe betide the teacher who has not arranged her classroom so that other interesting activities are easily available to the children. She might find several children sitting apathetically on the floor in a row (actually observed); she might discover a disturbed child in the group 'running' round the room and bringing chaos about within seconds.

Forewarned is forearmed and so the teacher, in thinking about an afternoon of creative art needs to have many activities and a wide range of materials available, such as painting with many colours, printing with a wide range of experimental aids, cutting out, puppet making (very simple and with quick results), clay, pencils, crayons and collage, with the teacher or alone as ability dictates. Many of these need to be there at the same time if such a period is going to be successful and the child meaningfully and gainfully interested. The number of activities and skills introduced will depend upon the teacher's willingness to use her own imagination and books for ideas. It will also depend on her ability to help the children choose, organize and control their materials.

Music. Music is an activity which the children should be exposed to every day even if for only short periods of time. For example they can:

(a) move rhythmically and imaginatively to it;
(b) listen to interesting music;
(c) listen to interesting sounds (cf. Chapter 6, page 96);
(d) listen to the teacher singing;
(e) hear/learn many simple songs;
(f) play musical games of all kinds;
(g) try to use simple instruments;
(h) go out with their teacher and tape sounds in the community to listen to;
(i) tape themselves making sounds with objects, with parts of their bodies, singing.

Provided teachers can use a record player and a tape recorder they can all take music with the children. Many of them (the 'non-musicians' as well) will find this to be true and be able to give the children wonderful musical experiences.

Cookery. The only other comment I wish to make about this particular programme is one about cookery. Cookery of one kind or another should be one of the experiences for these children at this stage in their development. Whether the teacher does it in front of them, in spontaneously-formed groups, lets them help wherever they can, or whether they make simple things themselves to eat on the spot or to take home is a matter of the kind of experiences they will have had before and their ability to imitate carefully what the teacher is doing or follow the instructions she gives. In other words what is achieved depends as in everything else upon the abilities of the particular group of children irrespective of age.

Highest ability groups

EXAMPLE PROGRAMME FOR HIGHEST ABILITY GROUP

	Jobs			
Monday	Nature table arranging	Free choice Individual work P.E.	L	Guided creative work Quiet constructional activity
Tuesday	Discussing events Preparing the 'Milk bar'	P.E. Homecraft or self care Guided creative work	U	Free choice Story/Music/Drama
Wednesday	Arranging the shop Tidying cupboards	Free choice Individual work P.E.	N C	Preparation for visit Visit all afternoon or short walk. Camping Follow-up of visit Story/Music
Thursday	Talking about events, large pictures, children's pictures	Free choice Individual work P.E.	H	Cookery Drama
Friday		Free choice Individual work Story/Music/Drama		Visit

A casual glance at this particular programme will leave the teacher with the impression that it is almost identical to the previous one. In many ways it is. The difference of course lies in the content of what is needing to be learnt and in the teacher's personal attitudes to her pupils.* She will naturally expect different behaviour and have higher expectations in the way her pupils set to work, stay at an activity and complete it, sometimes with her help and sometimes alone. Head teachers should be ensuring by careful reading of the teacher's record books that the stories, the songs, the visits and the cookery sessions have some kind of progression in them throughout the school. Heads

---

* Probably in the future the education of the physically mature, severely subnormal, young person will take place in a separate building. I should like to think that the kind of programmes carried out in such establishments will follow on the lively and individualized approach which has been suggested in this book, and which I feel young people need well into their late 'teens. I should also like to suggest that the teachers' detailed records made in previous schools should follow them.

need to discuss very much more with their members of staff than they do at the moment what is being taught. It is still too easy for unimaginative teachers to do 'the same old thing' day after day, taking the mistaken view that the children benefit from monotonous routine and repetition. At this stage too, most of these young people cannot easily report verbally their boredom or in fact report what it is they have been doing in school. This means that the teacher's integrity in her preparation has to be beyond reproach.

Before we leave the subject of the daily programme, I would like to discuss two points concerning this particular programme. As far as I can see there is little agreement about what should be done with these top groups or indeed any recognized common practice in the schools generally. The chapter on the adolescent will indicate more clearly some extra possibilities as well as describing some of the aims of education for this group.

Long free-choice period
One principle I am sure we need to examine closely is that the young people still need one long session each day when they can choose their own activities and move freely around the environment. I might remind the readers of the reasons stated for this approach in Chapters 3 and 5 for they still apply.

During these years, i.e. from thirteen plus onwards, (I am not going to state an upper age limit) the young people need more and more opportunities (not fewer) for forming relationships with their peers and for working out spontaneous group aims in their imaginative, dramatic and group activities. If we deny them these opportunities I am sure that a whole stage in their social and emotional development will have been sidetracked. Language as a form of intentional communication is also emerging more natually at this stage. They need maximum opportunity therefore to use it in this way through the situations the teacher arranges for them as part of their programme. It is so easy for the teacher of this group to keep them at sedentary tasks, usually alone, or listening to her trying to impart what she considers to be useful knowledge. It is not so easy to keep on thinking out stimulating and exciting experiences and structured activities for those with physically maturing bodies and young intellects (cf. Table games).

Another reason for keeping the long free-choice period of activities on the programme is that the young people in question are becoming increasingly able to think out beforehand what they are going to do with their time and then get on with it. In affording them this opportunity as part of their programme we are surely stimulating their thought processes and keeping them alert. We are also helping them to look ahead, to enjoy looking forward.

An important feature of this stage is that the teacher will be able to give more concentrated attention to individual children since the others in the group will be more able to plan for themselves, and organize their own time provided there are plenty of table activities, games appropriate to their stage of development, and lots of creative opportunities. It will be with this group that the teacher might find someone 'ready' to do more formal academic work such as reading. I would like to add here that only a scientific and objective approach to the subject of starting to teach reading to a severely subnormal person will enable the teacher to make her decision correctly so that she is not wasting her own time, or what is of considerably more importance, the time of the pupil concerned.* Discussion with the psychologist and a full understanding of reading readiness tests and remedial techniques will be useful guides here. I should like to feel that many more of the teachers who have started to teach 'reading' to severely subnormal children in the past five years were able to accept this principle.†

'Work maturity'

Another important principle teachers must think about most seriously is the tendency to 'prepare' in school these very intellectually young and often socially immature people for life in the Adult Training Centre. I deprecate this practice and condemn it out of hand. I would like to suggest that wherever this is happening the teachers have no

---

* The few pieces of research carried out on reading and the severely subnormal[81-84] certainly do not encourage the thoughtful teacher who understands the reading process to embark upon this process without much heart searching as to its purpose for the majority of severely subnormal children.

† I have heard recently of a group of children who can all 'read' but cannot control paint, cannot use scissors skilfully and who when the words are 'taken' from the book and matched with pictures cannot read the words. In 1952 I remember teaching a severely subnormal young person of eighteen (I.Q. 48) to read to a level of 7 years on the Burt Graded Reading Test. She could also write a sentence or two of her own composition (a diary) and refer to her own 'dictionary' of words, initially spelt out by her mother or me. It took me five years and the mother helped her daughter every day under my guidance. I compiled a weekly written description of the work I wanted her to do with her daughter. At the end of it all this same young person could not hold a conversation with me or her parents. Perhaps our time would have been better spent practising this useful social skill instead of 'barking at print,' though there can be no doubt at all that she enjoyed these lessons.

real concept of the real life experiences they need to be continuously giving their charges at this stage in their lives if the work at previous stages is to be consolidated and developed. Teachers should be developing the emerging creative and constructive skills at this stage and giving maximum opportunities for language. They must also look at the ways in which they can help the young people in feelings of responsibility by service to their community in ways other than sitting at benches carrying out contract work.

Of course we want our severely subnormal adolescent to grow up within the limits of his handicap. As far as I know no educational research has been carried out on what constitutes readiness for work on the part of the severely subnormal, though Dr. E. Whelan of the Hester Adrian Research Centre appears to be now concentrating on some of these aspects in a more objective way. We only know that many young people of sixteen and upwards are able to sit and perform monotonous work tasks and contribute to 'contract' work as a high number of the general population do. We have not yet counted the cost in terms of their all-round development. Perhaps the day is not too distant when teachers will be more concerned with genuine total development of these young people rather than with that which only looks like 'work maturity.'

11 *Planned systematic individual teaching*

Severely subnormal children need planned systematic teaching as part of their weekly programme as I emphasized in *Observing Children who are Severely Subnormal*,[22] and helped students to understand from the early 'sixties. An explanation of this phrase will help to clarify what I mean.

Individual teaching: teaching each child in the group in a one-to-one relationship:
(a) in the same room as the rest of the group (possible with most classes of ten children unless there is a really disturbed member in it);
(b) in a small room away from the group if the building and organization of the school is such as to enable the teachers to do this on some kind of regular basis.*

Planned: the teacher jots down *beforehand* what she intends to teach and her reasons for this. Cunningham has refined this idea in his analysis and evaluation of the task to be taught (reference 15, page 10). This means that the teacher will have to think out the work she wants to do with each child and prepare her teaching materials. Her plan will depend upon:
(a) the age and state of development of the child;
(b) the child's needs as revealed by her recorded observations;
(c) the child's need for a wide variety of new experiences as she sees fit to provide them;
(d) the use she can make of all the knowledge gained from various sources regarding previous work with other teachers and present achievements;
(e) the psychological profile revealing the child's strengths and weaknesses; this will mean that she must be on the receiving end of well-interpreted up-to-date test findings which she understands;
(f) an analysis of her findings on one or other of the useful growing

---

* It might mean a concerted effort throughout the school. The Head might become involved in teaching/testing the children. Large group activities could be arranged much more than they are at the moment, e.g. community singing sessions, selected TV programmes, outings with helpers and one or two teachers only. An open-plan organization throughout the school might be a possible answer.

number of check-list type of development scales being produced in this country and the States (Appendix 4, and page 47);
(g) the profile of achievement and errors in a specific area, e.g. language;
(h) the findings from her own test material;
(i) discussion at case conferences;
(j) talks with parents.

Systematic:
(A) Each child will have one, two, three sessions a week (according to the size of the group) on a strict rota basis. In this way no child will be denied his share of individual attention.
(B) After the first exploratory session with the child (and this might very well consist of giving a battery of tests) part of each succeeding session should be based upon the one preceding; the rest of the session should contain a new experience/activity. From time to time the teacher should be referring back to her notes in order to check if continuity and progression in her work with the child exists.

Expressed in such simple terms it seems a relatively easy concept to grasp. It does not seem so easy for teachers to adopt in practice. Perhaps they need to remind themselves that they are in fact employed and paid as SPECIAL educators and that this in itself should mean having the professional ability to compile and carry out individual programmes. Ted Shelley* at a recent DES/ATO In-Service Training Week described three levels of teacher-functioning he is presently (1974) observing:
(1) Teachers minding children.
(2) Teachers providing a stimulating environment and some creative education.
(3) Teachers teaching in depth.

It is with (3) that systematic individual teaching is concerned. Present teacher training needs to devise methods where students under very close skilled supervision are able to demonstrate this kind of involvement with severely subnormal child before qualifying.

Suggested reasons for possible difficulties
(1) It is a very rigorous and demanding approach if carried out well.
(2) Attitudes prevail which suggest that it might be too time-consuming in terms of the possible results which take a long time to

---

* Tutor to the Matlock College of Education Course for Teachers of the Mentally Handicapped.

achieve anyway.

(3) Student teachers do not gain the concept or the facility during training.

I know there are difficulties but I should like to place this question of individual teaching in a workable perspective. I know that the teachers themselves, if rightly placed by personality and aptitudes, will gain more satisfaction in their work because of the skills involved. The job will immediately become more interesting and intellectually challenging.

The majority of the children [though there will inevitably be children whose progress is minimal even if they do have individual attention[71, 74] (cf. page 141) unless our value system of what is worthwhile includes the evaluation of the importance of a child's happiness] will indeed benefit from increased effort on everybody's part. I have learnt from the children themselves in countless ways that they begin to know their teacher will be teaching them in a one-to-one situation. I know that they enjoy their sessions and even begin to anticipate them.

What I am suggesting is not impossible. It is not unrealistic or too idealistic but essentially practical. I have seen such an approach adopted over and over again by countless students of quality on their final teaching practice and not, I must hasten to add, always working under optimum conditions.

The approach demands:
(a) a liking for individual teaching situations;
(b) good organizing ability;
(c) quick imaginative thinking;
(d) plenty of teaching equipment (both bought and made);
(e) a continuous opportunity to discuss one's successes and failures in teaching a child with the Head and other experts;
(f) supportive attitudes from all concerned, including the parents.

I should like to make it quite clear that I am not thinking of physiotherapy and speech therapy as the individual work time, though naturally this will be part of the programme for some children when the services are fully available. The approach I am discussing concerns the particular relationship the teacher will form with the child because of the selected time she spends with each one, and because she is able to get to know the child's needs more thoroughly and supply appropriate activities.

Some reasons for individual work
(1) Developmental stage
Before the stage of solitary play is reached (14-18 months in normal children) many children will need the concentrated attention of the adult in order to develop an interest in that adult and pay attention to him in particular, i.e. form an attachment with him. Whenever the child's ability to form such an attachment is missing the teacher might do well to enquire about the environment of the child in his first months of life for, as Sheila Hewett says,[85] if 'social stimulation has been seriously lacking in these months his ability to become 'attached' later (at approximately seven months in normal babies) is seriously impaired.' Particularly does this raise questions about the effects on handicapped children when they have had to spend time in incubators (for weeks, sometimes for months) or in hospital.

(2) Attentional factor
Another important reason indeed is the attentional factor. The teacher is more likely to secure the child's attention over a longer period of time on tasks she wants him to do than if she adopts group teaching methods. She will be more likely to gain the child's concentration. She will see that perhaps with some children she must devise special aids and methods to gain the child's interest and increase his willingness to attend.*

---

* Whilst working individually with several children we devised some little games to gain the attention of some children. Other teachers might find them useful.

(1) *Equipment:* (a) large cardboard box with tracing-paper pasted over the open end and peephole in the other end; (b) torch which can flash several colours; (c) tiny toys; (d) small cardboard box.
Game: Child peeps through hole and watches light. Tell the child to put a toy in the small box when he sees the light change colour. At first move the light quickly across the tracing-paper screen with rapid colour changes so that the child realizes that something is happening. Increase length of time between colour changes.

(2) *Equipment:* (a) plank of wood 65cm. ($2\frac{1}{8}$ft.) long; (b) jumping bean or walking mechanical toy; (c) collection of shaking instruments or sweets/biscuits; (d) empty box.
Game: Place plank at slight angle so that bean will 'walk'. Encourage child to watch bean and when it jumps off the plank to shake an instrument or put a sweet in box (to eat at once or later).
Variation: Child watches bean in a mirror.

(3) *Game:* 'Stare me out' (for children who find attending particularly difficult).

(4) *Game:* Tell the child to stare at an object. Teacher guesses what it is.

(3) Adjusting language and imitation

The teacher is more likely to adjust her language to a particular child if she is with him in a one-to-one situation. In learning language skills the child has to learn to imitate gesture and the movement of the adult's lips and mouth used in the formation of words. The severely subnormal child is more likely to do this if he is near enough to his teacher's face for her facial expressions and lip movements to cause an impact on his awareness. Dorothy Jeffree* noted that the articulation of handicapped children improved when encouraged by their parents to talk about specific activities. I found similar results in my longitudinal study of George (1961-67) when I encouraged his mother to talk with him using a tape recorder. David Mosely, in presenting Talking Typewriter reading programmes (N.S.M.H.C., Barnet research project) to both E.S.N.(M) and E.S.N.(S) children, found that E.S.N.(S) children improved:

(a) their articulation score;
(b) their knowledge of small letters slightly;
(c) by a mean gain of 19 months in verbal expression; of 14 months in motor expression; of 7 months on visual closure;
(d) *the least* in skills involving sequencing;
(e) in tasks involving conceptual thought;
(f) in tasks involving eye-hand coordination.

Mosely concluded[83] that 'these improvements were probably the result of greater emphasis on communication in a one-to-one teaching situation.'

(4) Wide discrepancies in ability

In any one administrative group it is highly likely that each child is at a different level of achievement in a variety of learning areas. It is therefore impossible for the teacher to approach the learning difficulties in any structured way unless it is with individual children.

(5) Developing the teacher's skills

All children are responsible for their teacher's learning and professional development. In working with severely subnormal children this is no less true. What she learns from her time with individual children should flow into her work with the group and help her to become more efficient. The teaching aids she devises for individuals will certainly be useful both with other individual children and the group too.

(6) Increased awareness in presenting and handling teaching materials

The teacher will begin to see more clearly that she must present all

---

* Reference 15, page 293.

her teaching materials in a well-thought-out way. She will see the necessity for thinking carefully about how a child perceives an object according to whether it is at his eye level or below it, whether he is seeing it at an angle or not. She will begin to think about the possibility of confusing the child if:

(a) She is not consistent in handling materials. Particularly is this so if she wants the child to construct something in exactly the same way as she has done.

(b) She inadvertently covers a small object with her hand when pointing to it and asking the child to identify it. A gesture with the hand of one kind or another might very well alter the response of the child (cf. Dutch Research, pp. 59-61).

(c) She gives too many instructions at a time.

(d) She does not consider her seating position in relationship to the child being taught. Sometimes a teacher could usefully sit immediately in front of a child or behind him.* I usually sit at the side of a child when I am working in an individual situation. In this way one has the closeness as an added factor in the building-up of a relationship.

Planning the individual child's programme on the basis of assessment by the teacher

There are many kinds of tests for teachers to use as a guide to their work. Few are available for use by the teacher of severely subnormal children. Indeed the concept of the teacher giving any kind of test to these children as a starting point for her work is only just beginning to filter through. My own observational tests in the following pages were devised by me in the first instance to encourage young students to have an orderly approach to their individual teaching; to encourage them to see how attention could be gained from the children when real and sometimes familiar objects were used to encourage them to make up their own tests; to give them further practice in using direct observational skills. To my knowledge it was the first time such an approach had been made in training teachers. Little test material was specially published with teachers of severely subnormal children in mind until the 'seventies. Dr. Gunzburg's scales are unique in this respect.[86]

---

*One doctor we know of who is engaged in teaching handicapped children, when he wants to build up something for the child sits immediately behind him so that the child will see it from his own position. If the teacher always sits in front of the child, then he will receive only a mirror image of the activity. We have given this simple device a name. We call it 'containing the child.' We have certainly found it useful for some of the children.

It is highly unlikely that teachers in most parts of the country will have the services of educational psychologists to help them pin-point a child's learning problem. It is certain that teachers will have to rely upon their own judgements. These judgements can perhaps be made more precise if they devise test activities for themselves and use whatever becomes available as psychologists and research workers understand the teachers' needs and respond to them by devising materials. Giving the tests when they first meet their class will help the teacher begin her work in an orderly fashion. A test programme is something definite for the teacher to begin her individual sessions with. It will help her to form an initial relationship with each child in her group in a positive, confident and revealing fashion. We know that the tests are interesting to most of the children and they always bring out responses on which the teacher can build.

I have used the term 'test activities'. The examples given will perhaps beg the question 'Why the word "test"?' for this implies that there are correct responses. Teachers will see from the examples suggested for test items that there are not indeed correct answers to all. Experience with the same tests over a period of time might indicate to the teacher that there is a change in the quality of the child's response. This in itself will be found valuable because it will indicate a change of one kind or another.

Characteristics of a test activity
(1) The making or collecting together of special material which is used only periodically.
(2) The instructions to elicit responses from each child are written down and repeated in the *same* way each time a child is tested. The teacher can then refer to her own instructions and thus maintain a certain amount of standardization in the test instructions.
(3) The responses are carefully recorded and compared with the child's later performance.
(4) The test activity is presented:
   (a) in the same way
   (b) with the same instruction } to each child
   (c) just *once* and then after a period
(5) The test items are put away for use in the future and the teacher does no specific practice on them.

Most of the tests suggested in the next few pages have been tried out by us or the students. In helping students to think about the relevance of using tests and how to give them in an objective way we have been trying to demonstrate that one of the features of all education should be the readiness of the teacher to search continuously for the means to examine and evaluate the results of her teaching by increasingly objective, but nevertheless interesting, means. In so doing she will possibly be better able to serve the children in her care. Teachers of the severely subnormal could not do better than read *A Teacher's Guide to Tests* [87] for in it they will read: 'One of the most striking features in education today is a sharper awareness of individual differences, shown in the growing provision of special courses, special schools, remedial centres, diagnostic centres and the encouragement of "discovery methods". This awareness has been due in no small measure to improved techniques in measuring the social, intellectual and emotional qualities of children,' and again: 'When teachers themselves receive better briefing on the use and value of tests we might well see an increase in small but valuable studies carried out by those (the teachers) who know which problems are the most urgent and who are most likely to profit from the results.'

TEST ACTIVITIES FOR VERY YOUNG HANDICAPPED CHILDREN (ADAPT FOR THE PROFOUNDLY HANDICAPPED)

More and more provision is being made for the very young handicapped child in our special schools, i.e. those under five. It is never too early to try and make some kind of assessment of the achievements of such a child. The activities suggested will help the teacher to see individual differences in her group. The approach is exploratory.

(1) Show five brightly-coloured objects, one at a time on the palm of the hand. Note the response of the child.
(2) Have three brightly-coloured beakers (yoghurt cartons are most useful) and five small toys (two of each). Hide one of the toys under a beaker in front of the child and showing him the other matching toy. Say, 'Find me one like this.' Repeat with all toys.
(3)(a) Wipe your face with a flannel in front of the child. Say to the child, '*You* do it.'*
 (b) Put small objects in a box. Empty them and say to the child, '*You* do it.'
 (c) Run a small toy car up and down the table in front of the child and then say, '*You* do it.'
 (d) Blink at the child several times. Then say, '*You* do it.'

---

* If the word 'you' brings no response, use the child's own name.

(4) Have fifty objects that the child has experienced (soap, towel, toothbrush, toothpaste, comb, brush, mirror, knife, fork, spoon, cup, pillow, cushion, doll, bed, pan, purse, money, hat, etc.) and additionally clearly drawn pictures (or magazine cut-outs) of the first fifty words which can be so illustrated from McNally's *Keywords to Literacy* list. Number them one to fifty on the back. Putting them in groups of five, say to the child:

Show me the—
Show me the—
Show me the—

Do not remove the object/picture as it is shown but leave until the first five words are given. Score with a tick if correct. After the first five are completed place the next five and repeat. Record number of picture chosen if incorrect. An incorrect response might produce useful information for the discerning teacher.

(5) Two very useful tests, easily administered with some guided practice by any experienced teacher, are The Reynell Test of Language Comprehension and Expression and The Coral Richards Test of Language Comprehension.* Both can be used diagnostically. Both will give a teacher some idea of the comprehension of a child. They are designed to measure the language comprehension of normal children under $6\frac{1}{2}$ years so in some ways are very suitable for severely subnormal children. They will certainly provide starting points.

(6) Series III and IV of the Uzgiriz and Hunt Scale (cf. page 49) will give you a sound beginning.

Other suggested tests
Tests indicating language response—using pictures
(1) Vocabulary Test. Show the fifty pictures (see above) in order and ask, 'What is this?'† Give no help. Note correct/incorrect response.

---

* Having mentioned these tests I must add that the former for some reason or another is a closed test except to psychologists and speech therapists. That is to say the National Foundation for Educational Research will only supply it to those qualified to use such tests. However, in naming it Heads will be aware of its existence and will perhaps urge educational psychologists and speech therapists to use it on their behalf. A precise understanding of a child's comprehension of language is a useful pointer for the teacher in planning his programme. The second test is an open test and can be readily obtained.

† I find too many adults asking 'What is this?' and 'What is the colour of this?' in general conversation instead of talking with them about the objects, the colours: we need to teach before we test, i.e. as in the vocabulary test above.

Record the actual word given by the child. Given over a number of years this test will indicate the growth of a child's knowledge of and ability to use these particular words.
(2) A set of pictures depicting familiar games/sports, e.g. tennis, table tennis, netball, racing, boxing, wrestling, football, cricket, swimming, cycling.
(3) A set of pictures depicting activities in the home, various kinds of shops, objects in the home, members in the family.
(4) A set of photographs:
 (a) individual to the child's home and family;
 (b) about the children in the class and the activities which go on in it.
(5) A set of colour slides on specific topics within the child's experience; record each child's response.

Tests indicating language response—using real objects
(1) Have a handbag with a variety of contents. 'Show me the—.' 'What is this?' The instruction will vary according to whether the child has language or not. 'Show me what you do with this.' Record responses. Another way of giving this activity might be to ask the child what he thinks is in the handbag. This will afford the teacher an opportunity to collect other words in his experience and to see how far these are in fact associated with a handbag. I have used a rucksack to stimulate curiosity and language in an adolescent.
(2) Have a zipped pencil case available with the following contents: pencil, crayon, ball pen in black, red, etc., ruler, india-rubber, pair of scissors, pair of compasses. Say to the child, 'Open this and see what is inside.' Note how child goes about the task. 'Show me the—.' 'What is this?' 'Show me what you do with—,' taking each item in turn. Have pieces of paper at hand (Linda Garner, 1965).
(3) Place some everyday objects in two separate groups on the table in front of the child, for example:

Screwdriver*	Screw embedded in soft wood
Hammer	Nails and wood
Tin opener (different kinds)	Tins
Egg slicer	Unshelled hard-boiled egg
Bottle opener	Bottle with top
Funnel	Bottle and jug of water

---

* J. Ward (1970), now of Exeter University, has also recently advocated the use of criterion-referenced check lists designed to test the child's ability in real life (e.g. retrieving a hidden object, using a screwdriver).

Container for shaking dice	Dice
Bubble pipe	Bowl of water plus liquid detergent
Needle	Cotton and some material
Soap	Towel

The list can be added to by the imaginative teacher. By specific instructions the teacher will discover the child's knowledge of his everyday world.

(4) Have a shopping basket filled with twenty familiar foods/other purchases. Discover whether child can name/can describe when eaten, bought, etc. This was one of the earliest tests I designed for students to observe and discuss. It seemed so relevant in the early 'sixties because the only wall charts teachers were often making contained cut-outs of food pictures.

Tests of manipulative skill
Cutting test I. Ask child to cut along:
(i)   a very thickly drawn black line;
(ii) a thinner line;   ⎫
(iii) a pencil-thin line.   ⎬ Horizontally/vertically
                                ⎭

Ask child to cut round:
(i)   a circle;
(ii) a square;
(iii) a zig-zag line with four points;
(iv) a figure from a magazine or drawn (large/small).

Keep pieces in a folder throughout the school years to see progress due to (a) maturation, (b) specific training because the teacher feels the child should be able to use scissors but cannot.

Cutting test II. Cut string/card/cotton/etc., of varying thicknesses. In giving this test keep a special pair of scissors along with the box of materials. Be sure to give each child tested the same pair of scissors each time he is tested. In this way the conditions of the test are kept standard. Use manipulative material described in *Practical Training for the Handicapped Child* [73] (pp. 17, 21, 108) as a test. Increased skill will be reflected in the time taken to do the task. Time response with stop-watch.

Bead threading. Time how long it takes to thread five large/small beads. Poppet beads. Whilst this can be a useful test item it should rarely be a daily activity—there are so many more interesting ones to do.

Jigsaws and other puzzles
(1) Time the amount of time the child takes to do:
   A specially kept inset jigsaw puzzle.
   A set of 2-, 3-, 4-piece jigsaws which present the child with horizontal and vertical problems to solve, e.g. a mouse, a dog, a fish, a cat, a rabbit, a bird cage. These can either be obtained commercially or made by the teacher.
(2) Using old holiday cards with a prominent feature (e.g. boat, church, lighthouse, donkey, etc.) cut into 3, 4, 5 pieces. See how long it takes the child to find the picture (Jean Garston, 1966):
   (i) telling what he is making (the boat, etc.);
   (ii) just giving him the pieces and telling him to look for a picture and make it with the pieces.
   Record time. Record language response.
(3) Time how long it takes to build a tower with six nesting cups.
(4) Using a plastic (polystyrene) inset of a face or a well-known character (clown) with removable parts of the face and body, time the child's performance in replacing them. Observe increased skill in handling small pieces.

Listening tests
Child blindfolded or standing with back towards source of sound:
(1) Present child with sounds made with traditional percussion instruments. Play one at a time and allow the child to turn round to point.
(2) Present the child with sounds as above. Without turning round he must point to a picture in front of him to indicate what made the sound.
(3) As above. The child must name the instrument which made the sound. Variations on the above could then be compiled to extend the teacher's knowledge of the sounds the child knows in his environment. Child listens to nursery rhymes, folk songs, pop songs and (i) joins in; (ii) names.
(4) Perhaps the teacher could compile sound sequences of familiar sounds, e.g. making a cup of tea, using the washing machine (sound stories).

Drawing used for testing
Use the Goodenough Draw-a-Man Test.*

---

* Explained in the book *Children's Drawings as Measures of Intellectual Maturity*.[88] This test can be useful to teachers providing they do not use it to gain an I.Q. score. Children who have a global mental level of 5+ and yet do not score on this test have other difficulties which the teacher should explore with the relevant expert.

Ask the child to draw a picture and tell you all about it. Record language. File drawings.

Planning systematic teaching on the basis of a taped interview with a parent

During my six-week stay in Canada I had the opportunity of directly observing a mentally handicapped child in a well-structured teachers' assessment situation. By this I mean I assembled a host of activities and materials to use with this little girl who I was to meet just once and for whom I was expected to write out a list of suggestions for her teacher whose class she was in in the normal school. I also met her mother and taped our conversation. Some of the suggestions I made in my final long report were triggered off by the observations I made during the interview. I present the idea to indicate a possible technique in planning individual programmes. The taping was spontaneous. It was not specifically carried out with the idea, as I now present it, in mind. It was only when I was listening to a playback and making notes that I realized the value of such a technique for individual programme making. On the basis of the conversation, suggestions as follows were made to the mother in front of the teacher, who seemed to have some appreciation of the child's positive capabilities:

(1) Remain with the child when she is dressing until she has finished, then let her play. It was the mother's habit to prepare the breakfast whilst her daughter was left to dress alone. She played instead and was not dressed an hour later when mother appeared.

(2) The mother talked about her child's interests rather than her talking when asked about this. She needed to be encouraged to encourage the imaginative play of her child and to join in with her from time to time using language.

(3) Mother needs chat about child development in order to help her see that her child of ten was behaving normally relative to her handicap:
 (a) she still wanted to enjoy gross body play—swinging on a garden swing—let her;
 (b) she played alone generally;
 (c) she was imaginative in doll play; this could be extended;
 (d) she could not make a double bed; expectations too high.

(4) Try to function more slowly in certain aspects of home life so that the child could have feelings of success in things she could do if everyone was not in such a hurry, e.g. help set the table, put the dishes away.

(5) The child needs more opportunity for play in school.
(6) A different habit needed to be formed at bedtime to break the child of wanting her mother lying beside her until she fell asleep. It was suggested that mother sat in a chair rather than lying on the bed; that a chart could be shown to the child where she gained a picture of her favourite toy if she went to sleep quickly.
(7) Discussion with mother regarding her child's sleep habits when she stayed away from home with a friend—no problems—go and look at the routine in that house.

Practical training in the one-to-one situation
It took time after 1960 for the schools in which we trained students to understand that the children should have maximum opportunities to become active and to have a dynamic programme. By 1964 we felt ready to focus our attention on techniques of training which would enable students to fully understand that part of their work as a teacher consisted of working with the children individually, though I can remember outstanding students (1961-2) doing this quite spontaneously in their final teaching practice.

We did not take it for granted that theories about individual differences and suggestions about how to teach the individual child would be either understood or acted upon. We never assumed that teachers would like working in this way, though as I have said previously, it seems that to want to do so is not only an essential quality of successful teachers of the handicapped, but a necessary component in the required skills of special educators.

We began to build up positive attitudes to this aspect of teaching by giving young students plenty of opportunities for playing with and teaching individual children. Their experiences included the following:
(1) Teaching individual children in the E.S.N. schools visited for one day weekly during the first year of training. Keeping a diary and discussing their work with Tutors extended the experiences.*
(2) Working for an hour each week for a specified number of weeks with a secondary modern child needing remedial education but not necessarily receiving it. During these weeks the students talked to the child and attempted to gain his interest in learning to read, made teaching apparatus for him, and read to him at his own level of interest. Notes kept by one student were handed on to the next

---
* These well planned experiences amongst professionals run counter to the belief that some L.E.A. personnel held that these teachers rarely came into contact with teachers of other kinds of children.

so that some continuity of work was maintained. Discussion in a group of six students of the work carried out led to the sharing of ideas about the children, the teaching materials and the reading process.

(3) Playing with the babies in the families they visited fortnightly over the period of the course. Although this experience (originally introduced by my colleague Joan Fitch to students on the second two-year course) was linked in the main to the intensive Child Development part of our work and formed part of the training involved in observing children in detail, the implications for learning about teaching the very young handicapped by playing for two years with a normal child cannot be overestimated.

(4) Playing with individual children in Family Service Unit play groups held on the College* premises over a number of years.

Supervised teaching

(1) Teaching individual children in Movement sessions under the guidance of a lecturer† in both primary schools and special schools. The value in being able to compare levels of achievement was of great value.

(2) Teaching cookery to individual severely subnormal children in the schools under the supervision of a lecturer.‡

(3) Working to a planned scheme and over a set period with individual children in a Special Care Unit (a unit usually attached to the school for children with other specific handicaps, e.g. cerebral palsy, sensory defects, emotionally disturbed, autistic features) under the guidance of Tutors.**

(4) Working in teams of two or three with individual mentally handicapped children who visited us weekly, recording their activities immediately the children have left and then spending the rest of the time discussing each child in turn with Tutors who in turn were getting to know the children by working with them individually.

---

* N.A.M.H. Frances Dean House, Anson Road, Manchester.

†P. Thorley, now Head of the P.E. Department, Poundswick Comprehensive School, Manchester, 23.

‡ M. MacKay, now part-time lecturer, Didsbury College of Education, Manchester, 20.

** B. Narey, now Headteacher, Oaklands School for the Physically Handicapped, Salford.

O. Gregory, now Research Associate, Jordan Hill College of Education, Glasgow.

M. De Paulo, now Headteacher, New Fosseway School, Bristol.

(5) Working in pairs on two out of the four teaching practice periods so that a good proportion of the day could be spent by each student teaching in the one-to-one situation, recording the children's responses and planning the next session.

Observing teaching
(1) Observing the work of specialists in the Department of Education for the Deaf as they interviewed parents and helped them to help their own children.
(2) Observing me teach individual children and offering useful criticisms and suggestions for further work in the discussion which followed. These sessions were designed to encourage specific attitudes towards: forming a relationship with a child, regular educational measurement, planning such work beforehand, being spontaneous in response to the child, attending to detail in behaviour, discussing individual children with specialists.

Talking to specialists
An important feature of the teacher's role is to talk to specialists about any child she has to teach. One of the ways in which we encouraged students to learn how to do this was to arrange sessions for them with the doctor, mental welfare officers, the matron of a Home who knew the children we were teaching. They came and discussed the children when the students had also worked with the children for a short time. In this way the students were able to ask relevant questions about the children. They were also able to add their knowledge of each child gained in the teaching situation to that of the specialists.

It is highly unlikely that those training teachers always realize how difficult it is for teachers to talk to people of supposedly different disciplines. Especially is this so when these same people are considered of higher status in the eyes of the community at large. There is little wonder that teachers struggle alone with their problems or are often inclined to disregard the possible value of a specialist's advice on the grounds that 'he's not doing the practical day-to-day work with a child.' These attitudes are still common enough today and particularly where teachers with no specialized training are too much influenced by doctors and social workers.

It seemed to me that one of the ways to encourage maximum cooperation between the professions was to give students an opportunity to work with a specialist over a period of their training so that they could learn to:
(a) talk easily with him;

(b) evaluate his work and develop useful critical faculties;
(c) know the kind of questions to ask him;
(d) value more the contribution they themselves can make to the expert's thinking about a particular child;
(e) appreciate that only by successful communication amongst a group of experts (the teacher included) can a satisfactory programme be worked out for each child.

We were fortunate in our plans for training teachers in enlisting the support of a skilled psychologist and research scholar,[*] though the idea for helping students understand how to enlist the support of other specialists had been evolved by my colleague Joan Fitch and I in preparation for the 1967 Annual N.A.M.H. refresher course 'Planning for the Individual Child.' A film of this experience was made with the help of the Audio Visual Aids Department, Didsbury College of Education. Members of the Pendlebury Assessment Unit took part—Mrs. Anwys Riley and Miss I. Garvie. The sessions with Professor Mittler (1968) were designed to increase the student's positive attitudes towards any specialist they needed to consult as teachers of the future.

During these sessions the students had the opportunity (fortnightly wherever possible) of watching a skilled psychologist at work. They saw the following tests administered and were able to discuss them:

The Revised Version of the Stanford-Binet Intelligence Test.
The Wechsler Intelligence Scale for Children.
The Illinois Test of Psycholinguistic Abilities.
The Reynell Test of Language Comprehension.
The Marian Frostig Test of Perceptual Abilities.

The original plan was to encourage students by discussion, observation and comment to draw up a programme of instruction for the child based upon the findings of the tests and to design teaching aids. The arrangements we made did not enable us to do this. However we gained from the experience.

Although my immediate aim was not achieved in this particular year the students seemed to gin useful concepts from the experience—concepts which no amount of theoretical knowledge, given in lecture form, could have given them at their particular stage of learning.

(1) They gained some appreciation that an I.Q. alone or even a global mental age tells the teacher little of value about a child's abilities and disabilities. Psychologists and experienced teachers have

---

[*] Professor Peter Mittler, Hester Adrian Centre for the Study of the Learning Processes in the Handicapped, Manchester University.

always known this. Teachers in training need to gain the concept from experience and not just on the basis of being told so by their lecturers.
(2) They gained some *introductory* ideas about profiling. After all the tests had been given the test kits and the test sheets containing the information gained were given to the students to explore and 'play' with. Then they worked together as a group to plot the results in diagrammatic form. Profiles of two children tested gave ample stimuli for useful discussion with the psychologist concerned.
(3) They saw that perhaps it was of more significance to examine the actual *recorded* responses to the items failed if they were to GAIN ideas about specific teaching apparatus for the individual child concerned. In the real situation this approach places a great deal of responsibility on the educational psychologist to record, accurately, specifically and legibly all the responses made by a child 'at risk.'
(4) They saw that if the tests are to be used diagnostically the suitability of the test items for the severely subnormal child needs to be given serious thought by those designing tests.
(5) They saw the usefulness of additionally recording in detail the intermittent spontaneous language and other kinds of behaviour of the child whilst the test was being given. (Psychologists please note!)
(6) In observing and recording descriptively the skills of the psychologist they were gaining some idea of the importance of following standardized instructions and also assimilating a model for their own behaviour as teachers when they gave their own tests to the children. I am not suggesting that teachers should adopt the role of the psychologist in their teaching. What I am suggesting is that once a term they need to copy a more objective approach to each child for a relatively short time in order to sum up advances made and plan for the next stage in teaching. Perhaps such concepts are best built up by encouraging imitation of skilled and experienced workers (i.e. learning through imitation at the adult level).

In providing this experience for the students we were attempting to present an atmosphere of discovery at the adult level of learning. Perhaps Professor Mittler's words usefully sum up the approach: 'We were really helping students to think about what might be happening in the future in the realms of diagnostic techniques and encouraging attitudes towards psychologists in discovering how they might be helpful to teachers.'

Talking to parents (cf. pages 149-150)

By giving the reader such a detailed account of the methods we developed over a number of years in order to encourage students to become vitally concerned with the individual child I have emphasized the measure of importance I attribute to the teacher's work with the individual child. The rest of the book will have suggested that this can only take place against a background of purposeful activities in a richly stimulating environment and, as Tom Pascoe said[89] in 1968, 'in an atmosphere free from any undesirable emphasis upon competitive success or stress upon the shortcomings of individuals or groups. Success must be measured by individual progress in terms of increased mental, emotional and social maturity. Above all, the stigma of failure must be avoided.'

I know that the suggestions I have made once more demand a great deal of the teacher in terms of thinking and planning. I know also that conditions in the schools for the mentally handicapped, although improved in many instances since April 1971, are far from ideal. But, generally speaking, the groups are small. This being so some attempt can be made now to cater more specifically for each child's needs once the underlying prinicples as I see them are fully understood and *demanded* of teachers claiming to be 'Special' by parents who also understand them.

12 *Education after 16 plus*

A statement made by Mrs. Thatcher at a conference in Bristol in 1971 left the delegates in no doubt at all that a permissive clause exists, somewhere in the annals of educational administration, enabling young handicapped people over 16 to continue schooling until 19 years.* Some authorities, urged by parents and informed interested teachers are in fact allowing recommended individual pupils in this group to remain longer in school. Most, however, probably because of lack of space in the school, are continuing the tradition of the past and transferring these young people to adult centres at 16. They are likely to do so unless both parents and teachers in the schools and the adult training centres carefully guard their rights. Irrespective of their abilities, these young people are still too often put into the work situation at 16.

For the profoundly handicapped who cannot fit easily into a work context, even in an Adult Training Centre (and those in this group are not all grossly physically handicapped), there is often no appropriate day centre provision at all. This seems inexcusable in the mid 'seventies, for there has been provision and some form of an educational approach for this group in some Special Care Units at least in the schools for the mentally handicapped during the 'sixties. This has meant that most authorities know that they would need to plan for when these young people became adult. Lack of provision means that after 16 these young people are forced to remain at home, sometimes to the detriment of their happiness and that of their families, and the frustration of teachers who have so very often spent their energies giving them some quality of life at least, and relieving their parents sometimes of unbearable physical burdens.

Whilst most Adult Training Centres provide some form of social education programme as well as contract work for their personnel, neither the length and therefore the kind of training at present received by most of the staff (and many of them have no training in mental subnormality) afford those taking courses sufficient opportunities to study social education in any depth, nor do the centre buildings lend themselves to the kind of educational activities these young

---

* Winifred Curzon addressing [90] a Spastic Society Conference in Oxford 1967 informed delegates of this too once Education "took over."

people are needing. Of course there are bound to be adult centres that are exceptions to the rule. Few managers have written to any large extent about these, or examined the results of their particular approach to work and social education in terms of the all-round development and happiness of their charges. My impression, and it could well be I am mistaken, is that the adult training centres are still geared far too much to contract work and 'getting this done on time' rather than to the individuals* composing the working group.

They certainly do not present a picture of being in the words[91] of Davies and Gibson 'client-centred.' In their opinion a client-centred practice will be deduced from an analysis of the relationship between three interrelated elements of the social educators situation:

'(a) the society in which he operates;
 (b) the wants and needs of the young people;
 (c) his own attitudes, abilities and feelings.'

Although Davies and Gibson are referring to provision for normal adolescents their premises seem no less relevant when applied to the mentally handicapped.

During the 'sixties, Adult Training Centres were built all over the United Kingdom by local authorities and hospital management committees. The trend of activity was away from rug and basket making to contract work where trainees carried out simple repetitive, manipulative tasks following on the research of the Clarkes,[3] The National Association for Mental Health (now MIND) pioneered the first course for instructors in Adult Training Centres.† Some form of analysis of work skills is now being undertaken by research workers in the Hester Adrian Centre in Manchester.[92] The time seems ripe for examining the attitudes, abilities and feelings of the social educators (assistant managers/instructors)‡ working in the adult centres, for it is

---

* I was most interested when someone (telling me that he wished to speak to the personal instructor of a particular trainee) was told quite firmly that instructors are not allowed by the rules of that institution to come to the telephone to speak about individual trainees in their care. One can imagine the difficulties inherent in an instructor leaving some trainees in the work situation, e.g. those using tools or machines, but the impression I gained from this report was that only the 'top man' should be approached regarding any trainee in a large centre—how can he KNOW each individual well enough to discuss his needs with say his parent, hostel warden, or guardian.

† This course was held in Birmingham from 1961 to 1968 in the Martineau Teachers' Centre. Its first Tutor was Bert Flanders.

‡ Whilst those working in Adult Centres are by and large being trained by teachers [though the inclusion of certain mentally ill adults into these centres (parents please enquire) seems to have recently brought in social workers in

likely that many of them will still be forced to practise the current official training policy, i.e. of paying more attention to work output than to the needs of individuals and growing personalities.

A great deal must be happening practically all over the United Kingdom in developing a curriculum suitable for the mentally handicapped adolescent. There seems to be little sharing of ideas, however, in a form that is useful to those doing the day-to-day work with this group. There are exceptions. Eileen Baranyay's book[93] describing the excellent work that took place in Slough during 1964-8 is the only English publication in a decade dealing specifically with the adolescent living and working in a residential setting. Ann Marshall's research into the attainments and abilities of those leaving Junior Training Centres[94] also gives those interested a useful insight into the possible curriculum we might afford the mentally handicapped adolescent; it draws the teacher's attention to the possibilities of using different teaching approaches with different kinds of children, e.g. the mongol/non-mongol group. A careful study of both these publications will enable planners to understand more fully what these young people need. Constant reference to them will prevent mistakes being repeated and money wasted. Useful accumulated knowledge exists in these two publications, but we do need to be aware of them *and* consult them from time to time.

Leacroft School in Miles Platting, Manchester, has a Headteacher with a go-ahead, up-to-date, progressive attitude to the education of the mentally handicapped and the deployment of her staff. She encourages her teachers to develop their own programmes and ideas and then to write about them in concrete terms for an annual school magazine. This is then distributed to the parents, friends and governors of the school. She also encourages each class teacher to meet parents at least once a term to show them the children's work and to give them simple talks illustrated by coloured slides of the children's activities and outings.

By using these techniques, Mrs. Cathcart is giving a continuous positive feed-back to parents and involving teachers at a high professional level in things of vital interest to them both. She is also enabling her teachers to have practice in writing to communicate (and this with a wide spectrum of personalities) and in lecturing—useful

---

charge of courses] and consider themselves as teachers, their training at the present time does not seem to give them the requisite skills of a teacher (cf. page 254). A great deal of their day is still spent supervising the work efforts of their charges. Advertisements for jobs do not yet give those applying the impression that it is teaching or youth leadership qualities that are needed.

work skills whatever their future. Many of these young teachers will become the teacher trainers in the next decade even if not before.*

Housekeeping holiday in a flat
An experience described in one of these magazines by a young teacher, Sue Skelton, is about a holiday in a flat. She aptly writes that the preparation for this 'real away from home experience began several months before they all departed.' The class cooked its own lunch once a week and sometimes other children came to share it with them. A chemist's shop was set up in the classroom so that the girls could learn about relevant aspects of hygiene—it contained combs, shampoos, brushes, toothbrushes, deodorants, washing powders and liquids (the girls learnt to wash personal items of clothing too). Each girl had her hair washed in front of the group so that they could see and later discuss THE SEQUENCE† of this activity. Visits to large chemists shops in the neighbourhood and city enlarged the class shop experience.‡ Cafés were visited to practise eating out. All the household tasks necessary in the running of a flat were practised,

---

* One young and now experienced teacher in her school has been invited to become responsible for the students from a nearby college of education when they come for teaching practice. Such a teacher is gaining experience in this situation to become a future Tutor to probationary teachers when this becomes a feature in the educational system of teacher employment and education.

† A set of pictures/slides showing the sequence of such activities as dressing, hair washing, shaving, making beds could be made by the teacher to reconstruct visually the various steps in this task. This method would follow many years later the structured play activity of the young handicapped child with an adult (cf. Appendix 1). It would be sequencing in a useful, meaningful, practical life activity. Tests indicating the poor sequencing ability of the mentally handicapped are so very often abstract in nature (I.T.P.A.). [95] They inform research workers and others about some of the intellectual characteristics of the mentally handicapped. They do little to help the teacher construct activities liable to help the children over their difficulties.

A set of colour slides showing such sequences would also be useful if members of the class were photographed doing the various actions. Photographs of the familiar will certainly motivate the children to talk. If we are going to examine sequencing abilities developmentally, we perhaps need to look at the development of sequenced actions in the very early years of development.

‡ In discussing the problem about the desirability of having 'shops' in the classroom with a group of teachers from Norfolk, one small group suggested a real clothes shop in the school. If one thinks of all the opportunities for learning inherent in this suggestion one must accept its absolute relevance in the education of the mentally handicapped.

discussed where possible and mimed in movement and drama.

The experience itself, lasting for seven days, gave these young people an opportunity for a host of real relevant experiences to satisfy their needs and lives. They were encouraged to reconstruct these experiences each day in natural conversation with interested and involved adults:

(1) Learning the pattern of a day in terms of the tasks they had to do and the outings they went on.
(2) Going out in the dark.
(3) Recognizing useful signs *in the situation*. Whenever we are tempted to spend time teaching social sight words to mentally handicapped people, we need continually to reconstruct our own experiences when we visit public toilets in this country or abroad—LADIES and GENTS are certainly not always the symbols in 1974. I have variously seen ladies/gents; boots/shoes; diagrams of figures loking like a woman/man. The other day I saw a 3-D model of a Moorish-looking gentleman/a harem-type woman on the appropriate door. Gunzburg himself, who gave us this very useful concept of a social sight vocabulary (particularly for the *subnormal* with specific reading difficulties), is beginning to question the value of spending too much time teaching the mentally handicapped a social sight vocabulary. Thus he writes,[96] 'The ability to read is far less essential to survival in the community than is often assumed; it is quite easy to get through life without a reading skill. Even the teaching of a social sight vocabulary may not be as important as has always been assumed.' The interesting factor here for me as a teacher is that, in spite of the increases in the teaching of a social sight vocabulary in the past decade, no teacher or research worker has examined say a thousand severely subnormal young adults to verify the results over a period of time.
(4) Matching chairs, china, cutlery, to persons. Passing round drinks at supper time. Having a conversation in a natural setting.
(5) Handling money, writing postcards and buying presents *chosen* by themselves; going to a cinema.
(6) Buying flip-flop shoes and trying them on for size.
(7) Learning the sequence of dressing—Kathy seemed to be fully dressed but it was discovered she had forgotten to put her underclothes on (sequencing).
(8) Packing cases. Only 2/6 could do this. Fitting cases into a fixed space on the bus was an interesting experience too.

It was interesting to note the learning experiences involving the language of number, sequence and time—the skill of the teacher in making use of what was given in the living situation was naturally of major importance—it meant continual observing, linking up and using appropriate language in the experience.

'I've got three new pairs of knickers and five towels.'
'I've got four pairs and a towel to dry you on.'
'AFTER the bath?' 'Yes, you are ALL having a bath.'

The activities involving the group in household activities gave them opportunities for using and gaining concepts involving spatial relationships, size, length and shape—consider this in terms of the stove, the cupboards, the Hoover and the drawers.

Other useful learning experiences
On the bus. Full, empty, half full; up the step, down the step; next to; near the window; at the front; at the back; aisle; fitting cases into a space (making a judgement); building up cases one on top of the other; unloading and carrying cases (weight).
In the flat. Who am I sleeping with—idea of more than one. On top (bunk beds); underneath. Shape. Colour. Drinks and biscuits—one-to-one relationship. Teacher and *two* girls cooking supper—seeing, hearing a particular group of three washing up/drying—a group of three—different from those cooking supper but still three. One adult with two young people—comparing heights. If the teacher thinks this arrangement out beforehand (structures the experience) instead of allowing the groups to occur haphazardly, many useful language opportunities will present themselves.
Unpacking cases and putting away clothes. Short/shorter—comparison. Folding into two/four. So many layers of varying thicknesses to fill to the top of the drawer (number).

Adventure in the curriculum
Adventure is an aspect of life that we all enjoy in varying amounts and degrees. It is an aspect of the educational needs of the mentally handicapped adolescent still receiving the least amount of attention. Particularly is this so with teachers wanting to make them 'fit into a real school look' so very often because of their own needs and because generally speaking it is much more difficult to be always on the look-out for the learning experience in simple life situations—it is a highly developed skill. What we have to do continuously is to remind ourselves of the dull, limited, lonely and often relatively friendless lives many of these young people lead once they go home from school, whether this is to a home, a hospital ward or a hostel; to think of young, often energetic and curious people being forced without choice

to remain night after night with parents, often elderly and sometimes understandably afraid and restrictive of the activities their offspring might want to carry out. These problems will be further increased by those living in large towns.

Clubs for the mentally handicapped have increased in the past decade but there are not enough to meet the need; neither is regular transport available or friendship links established.* Parents are not always willing or able to afford to accompany their adolescent sons and daughters to clubs even if they are available.

Perhaps I tend to over-emphasize the situation because of the personal relationships I have had over the years with about twenty families having adolescent children and the countless reports of my students when they visited such families over a period of time during training. Students seeking a long essay subject in those colleges preparing them to teach the mentally handicapped could perform a useful service to the mentally handicapped by investigating the truth or otherwise of my statements. With guidance from their Tutors they could do a useful piece of survey research and thus make their investigations of practical as well as academic value. Particularly would this be so if their findings were presented quite concretely to a wider public.

Students discovering for themselves

Writing about students reminds me of two valuable pieces of work carried out by students under the guidance of my colleagues (B. Narey and O. Gregory) whilst on two-year courses of initial training (1965-71). The work was carried out over a period of nine months in the second year after initial discussions with me and my staff before the summer break in the first year.

---

* In one particular province of Canada they have what is known as the Citizens Advocacy Scheme. This involves young normal adolescents being introduced by a specially set-up bureau to a mentally handicapped adolescent and taking him/her around—ten pin bowling, swimming, walking, camping. The nearest appproach to this in England seems to be the Holiday Project—an experimental holiday for aphasic children (children often of normal and above normal intelligence with very severe receptive or expressive language difficulties)—obtainable from The Association for All Speech Impaired Children, Room 11, Nuffield and Speech Centre, Swinton Street, London WC1X 8DA. Publication *Holiday Project, 1973*, Elizabeth Browning, 15p. Normal adolescents are introduced and matched on a one-to-one basis to an adolescent who is aphasic. In a camp/holiday group setting these two spend their holiday together, get to know each other and learn how to communicate. It reminded me of the Laubach 'each one teach one' reading schemes for illiterates in the 'fifties (Unesco).

One student, Sue Hankin, looked at the following:
Opportunities for (a) mixing with the general public;
(b) keeping pets;
(c) hobbies;
(d) social activities, dances, clubs, visits;
(e) making close relationships with adults.

A comparison was made between twelve young men living in hostels and eight living at home.

Contact with the general public
In only three of the hostels did the inhabitants go out during the week to the local adult centre by bus. The other nine provided internal schooling or workshops for the residents. All eight from the homes went to school/work. With reference to going out at weekends those living in hostels visited local shops, parks, cinema, the beach and other hostels regularly. Those living at home were all able to go to the shops alone; two went to the park with their brothers or sisters. One went with his mongol friend. Four went out with their mothers more regularly than with their fathers and the remaining four more with their fathers. Even on such a small sample it is probable that more of those living in hostels have the opportunity to come into contact with the general public than those living at home.

Pets

pet	Hostel (12)	Home (8)
Birds	3 (sharing)	1
Dogs	1	3
Cat	–	1
Rabbits	–	1
Fish	–	1
Total	4	7

Hobbies
Hostel. Six only had hobbies. They were interested in:
  (a) mechanical drawings;
  (b) constructional models;
  (c) collecting and listening to records;
  (d) space;
  (e) model railways, football, cycling;
  (f) drawing, painting, acting, dancing.

Home. All eight had some form of hobby, e.g.:
  Terry liked woodwork, helped father to make models for railway layout.
  Anthony liked drawing, playing table games, cricket and cycling.
  Donald liked football, records, painting and watching wrestling.
  Leslie enjoyed playing and watching football, swimming and collecting matchboxes.
  Barry enjoyed collecting toy cars, football.
  Roger liked reading comics, making model aeroplanes, collecting stamps and cycling.
  Tony liked football, television and playing with model table-football games.
  John liked cycling around the streets near his home.

'It is interesting to see that half the hostel adolescents did not have any hobbies. All those at home did and in fact some had several. Perhaps the reason for this was that hobbies were not encouraged or financially catered for in the hostel. (Hobbies often cost money. For a young person to become interested he often has to see someone else interested—a brother/father.) Perhaps in community life such as in a hostel the young persons concerned spend more time with their peers talking, watching TV; more time going out, with the wardens of the hostels or alone.'

Opportunities for social activities
Only one hostel report showed that those in charge did not take the residents out socially. Social activities in the hostel community included film show, dances, cinema, games, plays, etc. All those living at home went to a Mencap club fortnightly (only eight were visited; it was a student's study not a full piece of research) and dances monthly. Other activities consisted of football matches, swimming, lifeboy's club. Two living at home were able to use public transport and were able to attend various functions alone. If Further Education Departments of Local Education Authorities play their part fully in the next decade, more young people will be afforded opportunities to continue the creative aspects of their education throughout a lifetime.

Take 'any ten' and do a survey
Another short but interesting, careful and conscientious study by a student* examined some aspects of the lives and achievements of ten

---

* The confidential nature of the material demands that the name of the student cannot be revealed.

adolescents currently attending an adult training centre but whom she had known as children. She visited them all in their homes too. The study was so interesting that I analysed her descriptive records and now present them here in shortened and more precise terms. The aspects chosen for study by this student seem worthy of a further survey being made on a larger scale and at regular intervals on the same group of pupils. Their inclusion in a report draw our attention to some of the characteristics found in mentally handicapped adolescents who have had a particular school approach.

ABILITIES

Name	Age	Mental Age	Intelligence Quotient	Draw-a-Man Test*	Reading test result	Social sight score	Social competence in home	Condition
Brian	18	6·9	38	6·2	0	0	3	Mongol
John	18	8·3	48	7·5	0	0	7	Brain damage
Bobby	19	8·6	50+	6·7	12·0	20	6	Mongol
James	18+	5·3	30	0	0	0	0	Mongol
Alan	19	7·0	40	4·7	0	0	0	Microcephaly
Harold	17	5·7	36	5·2	0	0	4	Undiffer.
George	18+	8·5	50	6·7	7·6	18	7	Mongol
Joan	17	5·3	32	5·0	5·3	3	5	C.p.
Angela	17	7·5	45	7·2	0	0	5	Undiff.
Andrea	19	8·3	48	6·2	5·1	5	5	Mongol

* *cf. footnote, page 181.*

WORK SITUATION

Trainee	Work attitudes expressed by supervizors	Trainee's attitude to work	Goes around neighbourhood unsupervized	Uses public transport	Task being done in work
Brian	No trouble at all; slow worker; ritualistic in arranging materials	+	−	−	Pouring grain into plastic bags; sealing when full
John	Works hard for money incentive; without this unwilling and stubborn; will upset others	Trying to make a lot of money	+	−	Sorting different sizes of cork into boxes

WORK SITUATION

Trainee	Work attitudes expressed by supervisors	Trainee's attitude to work	Goes around neighbourhood unsupervized	Uses public transport	Task being done in work
Bobby	Very good worker; works in factory 2 half-days weekly	Very willing	+	—	Weaving a bag for mother
James	Has made very good progress; works better with males	Works slowly, carefully; cannot go with peers to activities (Mother)	—	—	Rolling up sanitary towels; putting in bag
Alan	Works very well when not ill (epilepsy); is aggressive; is avoided by peers; swears	Loves record player; this used as incentive to make him work	—	—	Test weighing of parcels; sorting
Harold	Does not settle easily to work; cries; likes to work with females	Often told off by peers; wanders around from department to department	+	—	Picking up objects and watching others
George	Good worker; no trouble; goes out to factory on 2 half-days a week; factory would like to employ him	Works alone making things; Asked questions of student; asked for her address	+	+	Making paper hats
Joan	A good worker; no problems; keen to earn money; stands up for herself	Likes being at work; did not make friends; likes doing same job	—	—	Sorting and packing corks in industrial department
Angela	Will only sew; reacts badly to anything else; likes male attention; has lost 2 jobs	Told visitor she did not like ATC; neat work being done in sewing	—	—	Sewing the seam of a dress

EDUCATION AFTER 16 PLUS

Name	Material Quality of home	Attitudes in home	Special home circumstances	Position in family	Mother works	Dresses/ undresses	Washes/ baths	Helps in home	Helps unsupervized	Errands	
				HOME SITUATION			Home competencies				
Andrea						−	Works very quickly; stops often to give advice to the others; was anticipating next work task—making a knitted bag		−		Sorting a packing cork washers
Brian	Good	+	−	2/4	Part-time	+	+	+	−	−	
John	Poor	−	Single parent	1/1	Full-time	+	+	+	+	+	
Bobby	Poorish	+	−	2/5	Full-time	+	+	+	+	+	
James	Excellent	−	Overprotection against ATC	1/1	No	−	−	−	−	−	
Alan	Excellent	Realistic	Worried about aggression	2/3	No	+	+	+	−	−	
Harold	Very poor	Punished	Other S.S.N. in family	6/10	No	+	+	+	−	−	
George	Excellent	+ +	Brothers/ sisters will take him on death of parents	4/4	No	+	+	+	+	+	

Andrea: Works quickly and competently; one of the best workers: occasionally tells lies; likes to be fussed

HOME SITUATION

Name	Material Quality of home	Attitudes in home	Special home circumstances	Position in family	Mother works	Home competencies				
						Dresses/ undresses	Washes/ baths	Helps in home	Helps unsupervized	Errands
Joan	Good	+ (makes a meal)	Mother died when child 15. Father worrying about when he dies.	2/2	-	+	+ wash − bath	+	+	+
Angela	Excellent	−	Not appreciating school/ATC	3/3	No	+	+	+	+	+
Andrea	Excellent	+ +	Waits on grandmother. Very appreciative of school/ATC	2/2	No	+	+	+	+	+

KNOWLEDGE OF SPECIFIC PIECES OF INFORMATION

Time

- 10 knew the day
- 7 knew the days of the week
- 7 knew the month
- 2 knew the months in sequence
- 3 knew the year
- 1 knew the date

Telling the time

- 4 to the nearest hour
- 2 to the nearest ½ hour
- 2 to the nearest ¼ hour
- 0 to the nearest 5 minutes
- 0 to the nearest minute

Time of particular events

- 9 Getting up
- 9 dinner
- 8 tea
- 4 starting work
- 5 finishing work

Money recognition

- 5 knew ½p
- 4 knew 1p
- 2 knew 2p
- 2 knew 5p
- 2 knew 10p
- 3 knew 50p
- 10 knew £1

Prices

- 1 bread
- 1 jam
- 0 milk
- 2 chocolate bar

Personal information

- 10 knew their name and gave it
- 7 knew their home address
- 8 knew their birthday
- 1 knew the address of the centre
- 10 knew their age

Writing	Speaking in answer to a question requiring more than a one-word answer	Draw-a-man
7 could print first name	5 used complete sentences	8 drew a recognizable figure
3 could print full name	5 talked spontaneously without being questioned first	1 made an attempt
0 could do cursive writing	All used single words and phrases in conversation	1 drew lines only

*	Counting mechanically	Objects	Recognition of number symbols by matching up to
Brian	13	13	10
John	20	20	15
Bobby	100	59	100
James	11	7	7 (drew lines for a man)
Alan	9	11	11
Harold	information lost		
George	55	45	50
Joan	100	70	100
Angela	6	6	19
Andrea	28	35	1, 2, 3, 4

* This table needs to be considered warily for, though I have included it to suggest possibilities for testing, the student concerned did not describe how she gained the results as they are presented. (cf. Anne Marshall[94]).

Whilst the results presented took time to collect, the kind of information gathered by this student could easily suggest to the teacher in school and to those in th Adult Training Centre:
(a) the kind of knowledge she might be helping her own group to learn;
(b) the kind of guidance needed by the family;
(c) the kind of tests she might be presenting to the individual young person at say yearly intervals to see his advance in knowledge of his everyday world.

I have suggested elsewhere (cf. Planning systematic teaching, pages 170-189) that we might further test his knowledge of the everyday world by using specific groups/pairs of REAL objects. I see that one psychologist (J. Ward) interested in devising experimental tests using real objects is also now 'reflecting the shift from formal testing to observation[14, 86, 97, 98] either on the basis of developmental charts or towards a criterion-referenced type of observation designed to answer questions on the child's ability in real life situations, e.g. retrieve a hidden object (Piaget) or use a screwdriver.' My own list (pages 179-180) in the first edition of this book was devised many years ago to encourage students to observe the kind of activities one might provide to 'find out as much as you can about the child in half an hour using real objects.' Some of the activities described were tried out by me when I worked with children in front of students. Other activities were suggested by them.

One of the most interesting comments made by this student was that half of these young people did not know the address of their work centre or the times they started work and finished it because they had in fact not been given this information. Irrespective of mental age they ALL knew at least two songs in the current 'Top of the Pops' programme and were able to name at least two current TV programmes that appealed to them. Of course we have no way of telling whether her inference was correct or not from this short study. The point she has made however brings up a very important question in my mind. If as teachers of the mentally handicapped we think about what we have EXPLAINED to a child in any one day of our relationship with him, we shall probably find ourselves sadly lacking. It is particularly difficult to think about what to explain to a very young non-verbal handicapped child about the events and things around him, for one is always left wondering what kind of verbal information he can understand. When we consider the adolescent and mentally handicapped adult, we need to discover what he needs explaining by increased attention to what he is talking about and what he is presently doing in order to decide when information he needs is to be given. I have deliberately included this idea relating to an individual for I think that generally speaking knowledge must be imparted on an individual basis with the individual concerned physically near one. Hans Tangerud from Norway says 'their thinking will be predominantly relating themselves to life situations (*their life*—the italics are mine).[99] Their concepts are, can, and therefore *must* be developed in close relationship to such personal situations.' It seems a simple approach for the teacher to grasp, but I am not sure that the skills inherent in carrying it out are well enough developed in our teachers yet. Perhaps as Gunzburg[96] says 'the very word "teacher" carries with it such stereotyped concepts that social education in the fullest sense of the term is difficult to really get off the ground particularly when this has to take place in "schools" which have their further stereotypes.' If we delve into the educational philosophies and practices of Montessori[100], Dewey,[32] Isaacs,[39] and Neill,[101] we shall find that they saw education as something appertaining to life and all that was contained within it. If we apply these principles to the mentally handicapped we shall be taking what is obvious to us from life activities and making a lot out of these for our pupils.

Those training teachers know that students' long essays during initial training at least are designed to enable them to discover for themselves what children can/cannot do. Sometimes however their findings and their methods of work inevitably throw more light on the life of an individual child. Clearly this is so if they are trained to record carefully what *they* observe instead of trying to look for (in the first instance) other people's specific observation items. By this I mean that if we set out to check behaviour listed by others as important or telling us something, we might indeed miss what exists in the child. Checking behaviour from well tried out lists is useful once the habit and skill of observing has been firmly established. In using open-ended direct observational skills we are more likely to see and accept a child as he is and work on from that point positively. Check lists will be useful if they are used periodically as progress pointers.

The increase in observational techniques being used (initially in teacher training) in this country since the early 'sixties[14] should in fact provide us with more and more finely discriminating items of progress measurement in the mentally handicapped.

One interesting result from an academic standpoint is the apparent discrepancy between the mental age and the reading age of Bobby (19). This seems to reinforce the work of Houghton and Daniels in 1965 (cf. page 297), when they found ten children in a sample of 250 mentally handicapped children with reading ages above their global mental age scores.* In this very small sample of children it was interesting to discover one apparently similar to those ten. On reading the student's report however one finds the following:

'when she asked him to read a paragraph from a simple book familiar to him, he was unable to answer "easy" questions about the context. When he was given some Piagetian conservation tests he did not have the concept of the conservation of liquids or other materials.† Thus he would agree that a similar number of objects were alike when they were grouped in the same way, but he always said the group that was spread out to cover more area was larger than the similarly numbered group bunched together. He agreed that two balls of plasticine were the same size but when one was rolled out he said that one was now larger than the other.

I poured orange juice into two identical glasses so that the juice reached the same level in both glasses. He agreed that they were the same. However when I poured the contents of one of these glasses into two taller, much thinner glasses, he immediately said that this was more than the identical amount in the short, fat glass.'

If one looks carefully at the bits and pieces of information gathered about these ten adolescents, one is forced to the conclusion that one has to consider how one can use the particular aspects of learning that each one has achieved to date, and extend it meaningfully within the context of living—at home, in work and in leisure pursuits. Whilst the word 'sex' was never mentioned by those in the adult centre or by the parents, are they not all expressing their fears for the future by using the following expressions about the young people concerned:

'too affectionate with younger sister'
'prefers females to males' (of a male)

---

* Whenever I hear the teacher's pride in a child who is mentally handicapped and can read so that the visitor 'must hear him/her,' I am reminded of one school I visited in the South where I was asked to hear a young lady of 13 read. I listened. She enjoyed herself. Some time later she was observed trying to ride a bicycle in the school quadrangle. She persevered and finally rode round several times. When she got off the bike she bent down to pick up something. Her knickers, her legs, her body were unconsciously displayed to the observing group. I could not help feeling that time would be better spent teaching her how to bend down, so that other people would not be embarrassed, than on reading. (Of course if Houghton and Daniels are correct so many of these mentally handicapped children who have specific ability to read do not always have a great deal of 'teaching' in this skill; in other words it IS specific.)

† Some work on 'teaching' conservation to Severely Subnormals is reported in *Special Education*, November 1974.

'she is too attracted to the men' (this of a young lady of 17 years).

Some of the information in this study strongly suggests that family involvement with the adult centre is as much a part of the instructor's job as it is of the teacher's in the early years and the years spent at school. Disappointment in the family does not stop just because one gets 'used to it,' The continuity of this disappointment without an end in sight will constitute one of the major factors in mismanagement within the home as far as I can see; mismanagement that is to say that often militates against the mentally handicapped person having opportunities to continue having interesting learning experiences of all kinds.

Organized counselling of parents

Although there is a growing understanding on the part of teachers of the role that the parents might play in the education of their child, as far as I know there are no parent workshops for parents with adolescent children; the staff in adult training centres receiving adolescents at 16 have not been trained to consider their active role in helping parents understand the part they need to play in the development of their offspring. My own 13-year contact with one family and my detailed written records of this experience lead me to advocate that for the majority, educational guidance of one kind or another needs to be continued throughout life with some kind of continuity in the help given. Needs change, the family changes and support is always welcome even if direct advice is not always acted upon.

Creative adventures

Going to a place away from home for varying lengths of time is one form of adventure (and we must never underestimate the value of this to the handicapped child); building a boat—a large polystyrene model boat—to find out how to carry it with a group of friends to a lake in a park, is another. Such a project was beautifully and skilfully executed by an imaginative teacher, Crosland Ward, in another school known to me. He was responsible, throughout a large school for the mentally handicapped, for taking both girls and boys from nine onwards (if they were ready and interested) in small groups of six once a week for creative woodwork, pebble smoothing, jewellery making, modelling in cement, clay and wire and for creative cutting of polystyrene with a simple electric cutter.

What an exciting, stimulating room he has created for the children. In it he helps them to use fine motor skills, develop language about their activities, develop their imaginations and abilities in things like sharing and finishing a task. The number in the group is small, thanks to an understanding Headteacher, and this enables him to see his pupils as individuals and to develop whatever creative potential is there. Using tools successfully and seeing something that one has made oneself emerge at the end of the session—something that one has made that is accepted, however crude and imperfect it is—can be of tremendous value in the mentally retarded's emotional development.

Reference to this specific aspect of development, i.e. emotional development, reminds me of a piece of research carried out in Finland—and reported to a conference in Warsaw in 1970 by Harriet Lindgrew. The research involved a group of mentally tetarded young people living in an institution. Sixty-one were mongoloid, sixty-one were not. The research was designed (a) to discover whether the mongoloids were in fact more sociable, friendlier and easier to handle than the other group; (b) to see if their social levels would be higher than their mental levels and also higher than the social levels of the members of the control group retarded to the same degree.

The design of the research is not too important to us as teachers, but the results do have rather important implications when we are teaching non-mongol children alongside mongol groups.

For both groups the social ages were higher than the mental ages, but for the mongoloid group the difference was greater. For the total mongoloid group as well as for the profoundly and severely handicapped members of this group, the MEANS for emotional development were significantly higher than for the corresponding control group (i.e. because of being mongols and therefore looking obviously handicapped and being seen to be different, they were able to communicate successfully enough to gain a response, to contact people, to play more adequately). This finding suggests that we must be sure to afford non-mongoloid retarded individuals the responses they NEED to develop emotional stability. In thinking about integration into normal schools (classes within them with special teachers) in the next decade I think that it is highly likely that mongols will be more acceptable to the other children than the non-mongols—particularly in the middle and secondary part of education. Certainly this particular research suggests the kind of research that might be formulated for schools undertaking experiments in integration, otherwise we might find that only the adults concerned are emotionally satisfied.

To return then to creative adventure, a lovely cooperative effort with hospitalized adolescents (some who could walk and some who could not) was encouraged by the advisory teachers and the Art Adviser of Hertfordshire. The experience was illustrated to audiences by slides. These left a great impression. Whilst encouraging young primary school children to paint together as a group and produce a wall picture, collage, or mural is an accepted concept, getting hospitalized children to do the same, successfully, is not such a common feature of their education. The children were introduced to paint and all kinds of experimental brushes. The whole floor of the room in the teacher's centre to which they came was covered with a thick polythene sheet. Not one of the group painted recognizable shapes, but they were encouraged to make marks/scribbles/swirls with paint using hands or any of the items that would carry paint on to an enormous piece of paper. The finished colourful mural was framed and taken to the hospital for display. The joy of the children, noted by the teachers working in this way with them, was indescribable. Group efforts like this with something *concrete at the end* can only lead to positive effects with such young people. Of course these need to be continuous experiences throughout the person's life and not 'one off' highlights.

Other kinds of experiences considered to contain an element of adventure

These ideas have been collected from a number of sources where teachers and others have been willing to share their practices.

Sue Skelton in describing the preparations she made for the holiday in a flat scheme obviously spent a long time (a term) on this preparation. One school in Cambridgeshire told me about their method of preparing the children to have a night away from home before setting off on a camping expedition—in small groups using sleeping bags and camp beds, they stayed overnight in school on several occasions. This seems an excellent idea for, of course, if the child did not like the experience, home was nearby.

More and more schools are making arrangements for their adolescent children to attend a College of Further Education or a Technical College to join in with normal young people in practical pursuits, e.g. Alan showed me the ceramic he had made in metalwork in one such College.

Every Friday afternoon the school for the mentally handicapped in Rochdale had a disco. A room was made available for listening to self-chosen records, for dancing and for making a drink. The room lighting was red and one wall had a special 'mod' mural.

An adventure involving a group of adolescents from Ashton's Green School, St. Helens, included:
(i) a long journey by coach to St. Neots, Cambridgeshire;
(ii) being met by the warden of the hostel where they were to stay the night;
(iii) eating a cooked supper late at night in a strange place;
(iv) settling in a strange bedroom after choosing their own bed and wardrobe, unpacking and washing before going to bed. (no mishap other than a young man spraying his nose with deodorant instead of his armpits; should he have been given such an item without his teacher being informed?);
(v) displaying their dance/movement on the following day with their own teacher to an audience of 75 teachers of normal young children as well as the handicapped;
(vi) doing spontaneous drama with a strange teacher and with some of the audience wishing to become involved.

What an experience for them. How much it was enjoyed by all. What opportunities for their teachers to have conversations with them and to follow up their exciting weekend with drawings and conversations in school for the next week or two.

One family I know having an adolescent daughter gave her and her friends and neighbours a wonderful 'real' 21st birthday party. I wonder how many of the instructors in the Adult Training Centres find out if their charges have such an experience. I wonder how many of them make attempts to see that this particular experience is given to the person concerned in their centre (out of centre time).

The following is a sample of experiences constituting elements of life adventure for George who, though not an adolescent in chronological age, had nevertheless missed out on many opportunities for adventure:

1961 November. Being brought in a car by mother and brother.
Being brought in a car by brother.
1962. Sending Christmas cards to family and Maureen.
Walking to my home alone—we played dominoes.
Making tea for the two of us; making tea for visitors.
Started cooking lessons—toast, fried eggs, scrambled eggs, poached eggs.
1963. Sending more Christmas cards than 1962. Helped to copy names and addresses.
Visit to a Museum. Going on a bus. Visiting a café in town.
Buying a wedding present for a friend—his own idea.
Went with Mum and Dad to Do-it-Yourself Exhibition.
Playing dominoes, snakes and ladders.
Helped to buy his own coat—putting own money towards it.
Making bacon and eggs alone.

Reading him stories.
Meeting a student.
Tried travelling alone on a bus.
Having an identity bracelet bought for him.
1964. Sending Christmas cards—sent nine.
Labelling seed sticks for father.
Using the phone. Phoning up people we know. Using a ruler.
Visiting the Christmas lights in the city.
Began to bath himself without mother being present.
Cooking lessons continued—revising dishes—beans on toast.
Teacher bought him men's cologne for Christmas.
Visiting the motorway and riding along. Visiting exhibition.
Experiencing paying for his shirt in a shop. Mother did the ordering.
Visiting a café at night with a boy of nine.
1965. Sending Christmas cards.
Encouraging him to carry money in pocket.
Mother bought tape recorder. Making models at home.
Had a drawing board and a camera for Christmas.
Reading a story. Buying shirt.
Making fire papers for two older people and taking them to their houses.
Played with guitar which a friend had lent me—enjoyed the vibrations.
Going on a picnic with four children.
Taking the children for an ice cream. Having tea with four children.
Visiting a cave.
The Austrian dancers. Visiting restaurants and parks.
Going to town weekly several weeks before Christmas to buy presents.
Took an old lady to the country; we had a walk, gathered flowers and had tea in another kind of restaurant.
Saw bird house—he made one in wood for me.
Sent him postcards.
He obtained an old gramophone.
Visited Blackpool illuminations.
Playing table tennis with him. Listening to sounds on tape recorder.
Playing back his conversations with mother.
Meeting a physiotherapist and discussing her 'skeleton' with her.
Many car rides to different parts of the town.
Was taken to the pictures to see 'Mary Poppins' by women students.
Going to Lewis's to buy presents. Asked to go to see pictures in the basement—we did.
Singing sessions.
1966. Going to pictures several times, also News Theatre, full feature films and pantomime.
Writing (copy) a letter to me and receiving letters and postcards.
Learning how to fill a camera and how to use it.
Visiting Maureen and her baby (newborn). Visiting Joyce and her baby girl.
Going to pictures alone.
Visiting motor auctions and parks. Fish and chips in a chip shop, paying for two.
Going to town weekly to buy presents for Christmas.
Playing miniature golf with the teacher.
Buying pictures for himself.

Going to Post Office. Paying the bills—electricity, grocery.
Going for a drink of cider before the pantomime with me and old lady.
Going out to tea on his birthday—film, comedy.
Made sponge pudding to his mother's directions whilst she was ill.
Having a picture bought for him for Christmas.
Liking a girl.
Using a simple teaching machine.
Using a slide projector by himself to look at travel pictures.
Walking to his sister's from his home on his own.
Mother encouraging him much more to relate to me what happens at weekends.
Uses tape recorder.
1967. Going to the pictures alone—his own idea.
Going for a drink with one or two friends. Going to a wedding.
Playing the game of putting with a group of students and me.
Painting with poster paint.
Having a signet ring bought for him by parents. New identity bracelet with George on front and address on the inside.
Being allowed to have a bedroom containing pin-ups of pop stars, his own pictures, etc.
A record player bought for him and pop records.
Buying his own toothpaste.
Liking a particular girl.
1968. Going to a motor car auction at his own suggestion.
Tracing drawings.
Modelling in cardboard—he made a model spontaneously of the stage set in the pantomime he had seen.
Going to a football match with an adolescent boy.
Wanting a drawing-board for Christmas.
1973. Going to a Chinese restaurant on his own suggestion.
Visiting a Chinese family with me as a follow-up to this suggestion.
1974. Registering for an Art class in Further Education College helped by a friend.
Travelling home on a bus alone in the dark, using his free pass and getting off at the correct stop.

Home environment and attitudes

In my book *Observing Children who are Severely Subnormal*[22] I outlined the kind of things that teachers and other visitors to the house might look for to gain a realistic picture of the home situation for a particular child. When we think specifically of the adolescent who is severely handicapped and the environment he might be living in, we need to consider a host of other factors.

According to Kushlick[102] 75 per cent of severely subnormal children under 14 years will in fact be living at home. If we assume that the rest will live there into their early twenties at least, this means that 25 per cent will either be in a mental subnormality hospital or a local authority hostel. The hospital to the child is his home, even if we are still a very long way from achieving home-like conditions in most of our mental subnormality hospitals, even the smaller ones. The reasons are not very clear to me when I visit these places for it does not take training of any specialist nature to imagine what a home is like. Perhaps we have always to remember that there is a serious lack of care personnel and also research into the kind of comfortable, attractive, VERY hardwearing decor that might be provided for the most difficult of children one can imagine to live with.

Whilst parent workshops are becoming a regular feature of education and provision for the mentally handicapped, it is very doubtful if the concept of an *in loco parentis* (nurse) workshop with research workers/teachers has entered many people's heads. When one considers the shift system of work of these nurses in most subnormality hospitals, it is likely that the teachers never know which nurse is in fact the parent substitute to the children in their classes.

Professor Mittler[103] in a survey of hospital admissions found that out of 403 patients a large proportion were over 13, were disturbed, psychotic or suffering from psychopathic disorder. Sometimes one wonders how far the 'home' environment in which they found themselves in the hospital added to their condition—for so few hospital environments can be said to approach a normal home.

As I write I am thinking of two young men and a young lady in particular and the serious deprivation of human emotion they must be experiencing over a lifetime. One I found sitting in a ward quite alone, unoccupied, and without human contact that was meaningful to him. He had been 'expelled' from school some very long time ago. No one (as his 'parent') had felt it their responsibility to discover when he was going back again into school. The other young man had a terribly burnt face. He was ugly and frightening to the others in the group, whom he kept on wanting to kiss and hug. No one took the trouble to talk to him. To tell him how to approach his friends so that they would not run away from him. Another young person was wrapped in a very large sheet with her arms firmly bound inside. This was the immediate solution to her putting her hands down her throat and vomiting—admittedly a horrible habit to tolerate—I was on the ward the whole afternoon to observe the reactions and responses of staff to their charges. In two hours not one soul approached that child and that was when they were *being observed*. On another occasion, in this same place, I had the task of evaluating my own role as it were in offering advice to those in another profession. I did not wait to see if this particular young lady was approached or not. I took her on my knee without her sheet. She sat there quietly all afternoon and on that occasion did not vomit.

occasion did not vomit.

The steady growth of a variety of hostels is encouraging, but we need to pressurise for the setting up of an immediate inspection machinery by people knowing the mentally handicapped and their needs, lest these places too become mini-hospitals with untrained staff, with staff having a variety of qualifying diplomas but no feel for the mentally handicapped. The temptation to let those who want to be with the mentally handicapped on a daily basis, without regular informed support, and therefore to save the rest of us from the bother, needs to be resisted at all costs so that the whole community plays its part in ensuring that a satisfactory quality of life for these children is achieved and maintained. The community will do a better job if it can get away from the feeling that those devoting their working lives to the mentally handicapped are some kind of special beings. At all levels they are people with needs and, in some ways that cannot always be rationally explained, these are often satisfied when they work with the mentally handicapped.

Home visiting
Unless the teacher visits the homes of those she teaches at least once every six months and keeps regular contact with the parents, she will have an unrealistic view of the reality of their lives.* Whilst the average trend towards a lowering of the age of mothers of mongol children at birth was lower in the 'sixties (i.e. Australia, 32·44 years; [104] Argentine, 33 years [105]) than in the 'fifties, it still means that adolescent mongols will be in an 'old' home environment where the sadness of the intervening years in coming to terms with their problems may have taken their toll with respect to the mother's health and the parents' happiness. This fact seems to support my suggestion elsewhere (page 249) that we need energetic, intelligent young people directing the lives of these adolescent handicapped people—otherwise they will have no young lives of their own. Perhaps they will very often become needed companions to parents in their old age.

Whilst the concept of the older mother being more likely to have a mongol child than a younger one is generally known by teachers (and consequently must be thought about when planning their education) it is probably not thought about quite as much when we consider hydrocephalic children and *their* parents.

---

* I would like to suggest that this is one of the SPECIAL aspects of Special Education. Teachers not wanting this task should look into their motivations for being involved in this particular sphere of education.

By focusing, even if only in passing, on these two particular conditions and maternal age, I am really trying to emphasise the importance to those working with the mentally handicapped of always taking this home factor into consideration when planning their programme, for in some ways the educational process should 'make up to the pupil what he does not receive in other parts of his existence.' This is no less true now than in the 'forties (when it was written by an educator* who influenced my thinking as a young teacher) and it is certainly applicable to this group of young people.

Billy
Billy was an adolescent of 14 when I visited his home. His parents had fostered him as an abandoned baby and at the time of meeting them they were in their late sixties. Although they had provided a 'good' home for this boy, what could they understand of the needs of a young mentally handicapped person growing up through puberty. How could they understand his spontaneous erections, and explain them to him; how could they understand his nervousness at this period of his life as he grew into a gangling youth and like all other boys of his age 'broke' his voice. How could they understand that they needed to keep in contact with the school to discover why he did not talk very much in the classroom and in fact was withdrawn generally—speaking whilst there, but not when he was alone elsewhere with a group of young women students and their Tutors. His conversations over a year were very interesting and indicated an easy speech facility; indeed his progress in some language skills after a year of help was very satisfactory; his lack of progress in others was a mystery to a teacher—suggesting the need for further diagnostic tests. Working with Billy certainly highlighted one of the major problems of teachers of the mentally handicapped—do we concentrate on assets or deficits in our pupils. Clearly our experience with Billy suggested that we were 'forced' by *him* to concentrate on his assets. When we did, he made further measurable progress in those things that he could do well in the first instance.

Barry
Barry lived in a five-roomed terraced house. The toilet was in the back yard. Both his parents worked and the family owned a car. A student reporting on twelve visits to this home gives us a very clear descriptive picture of this adolescent in his early twenties and his life with his ageing parents. The family regards itself as a happy family. They go into the country every week; visit relatives in Southampton; and go on

---

* Nancy Catty.

holiday every year.

Barry can wash, shave and bath himself; make himself a sandwich; keep sweet papers in his pocket until he arrives home to throw them away (family good habit); help mother to make tea; can answer the telephone with an appropriate phrase; can wash dishes; woke parents after hearing a noise some time after their house had been broken into; can show a visitor his photograph album; can use three word sentences (needs help to extend the use of passive language).

Hobbies. TV (out of 12 visits, family watching TV 8 times), football on the TV, playing football WITH DAD; 'playing' his guitar; having a pint with his dad/cousins; using the family record collection; looking at TV pictures of footballers; looking at football comics.

Barry's problems. Overweight. Takes the butter from the kitchen to eat. Eats alone! Needs much more exercise (and yet this young man will no doubt be sedentary for the greater part of each day at the centre where he works and then again at home). Has no friends living near to him. Has alopaecia (I often wonder when I see these young people with bald/balding heads why no one in charge of them has suggested a toupé). Cannot wear a tie because he always feels uncomfortable in one. Afraid to sleep in a darkened room, so has a dim light on all night. Has ear trouble so cannot go swimming. When his very sensible mother saw him squinting she took him for an eye test. He now wears glasses.

Problems of Barry's parents. Worrying about the future for their son when they were dead.* No one to leave Barry with even for an evening. Inconsistent attitudes between parents. Father allowing something mother had forbidden. Mother having to make all her son's shirts because she cannot get a size/shape to fit him so that he is comfortable. Mother will not go away and leave Barry and father alone even for a short time. Barry is an only child for they did not 'try' for any other children when they knew Barry was handicapped. *Being hurt by people's attitudes.* Father used to take Barry to the football match until a spectator was rude about him. The embarrassment he felt was enough for him to stop the visits. When Barry touched a baby

---

* I was impressed by the fact that when George was taken on holiday by the staff of the adult training centre he attends, they visited a 'girl' they all knew in a 'hostel.' This was a useful experience because it gave the staff an opportunity to talk about the future homes of the mentally handicapped people they were with. When George told me about it, it certainly gave me an opportunity to talk to him about where he would live when his father died. In actual fact he knows already where the hostel is, knows someone who lives there and knows someone too who has a flat—he would like one.

a neighbour said, 'Don't let him touch her as he's very strong. THEY always are.' Although hurt, his parents were constantly trying to ignore such remarks. Wishing they had more friends *without* a mentally handicapped child. Barry often wakes up in the middle of the night and goes into parents' room. Difficulties in expressive communication because this is not yet developed.

There was no mention in the report that Barry went out other than with his parents. He did not attend a club.

THE ADOLESCENT AS A WHOLE PERSON

When I am contemplating the research, the recorded descriptions, thoughts and experiences of those concerned with the adolescent subnormal as a whole person, a few persons only spring to mind— Maria Egg in Switzerland,[106] Marie Neale in Australia,[80] H. C. Gunzberg,[96] E. Baranyay,[93] C. Cortazzi,[107] and T. Whalley[108] in England have written about their experiences. Others have trained students to be concerned, including B. Flanders, T. Pascoe, T. Fechnie. Names representing the positive attitudes of a host of people in Denmark, Mickelson[109] and Henning Sletved,[110] and quite recently (1974) six women studying and meeting the needs of severely and profoundly handicapped adolescents in Poland[33] might be added to this group.

I suppose what I am trying to say here is that these are the people I know whose work I have read; whose lectures I have listened to. They are the ones who have influenced my thinking and supported my own teaching experience with adolescents. Acquaintance with their work has been salutary for my teaching.

'The Slough Project,' the mentally handicapped adolescent [93]

This project (N.S.M.H.C.-funded) was intended as a demonstration model relating to the community care of the severely subnormal adolescent. It was the first experiment of its kind in England in 1962:

(a) to show in the words of C. C. Earl 'that we need to regard the severely subnormal person as a person not merely as someone representing cognitive deficiency;'
(b) to illustrate in action the thoughts of Gunzburg concerning social education in that the role of education is to promote the personality in general and to mitigate social deprivation in particular.

Flanders was the first Director of this project. His planning and example as an educationist were important from the outset and continued to influence the work of colleagues succeeding him.

Eileen Baranyay has performed a useful service to all the people concerned for she describes the project in very great detail and evaluates it most ably. She draws our attention to the results in terms of young people going out into open employment and therefore being considered 'successful' participants of the experiment; she describes real adolescents and, in commenting on their responses to the experiment and to their return home, gives us a practical guide to their personalities and about how their future needs might be satisfied if we will only take heed.*

Sex and the mentally handicapped adolescent
Maria Egg (Switzerland) in her book *The Different Child Grows Up* reminds us [106] that for this group it is not their need for a full sexual experience that is the question, but their need for expressed affection; but she writes (1970) 'The tragedy of the retarded is not his handicap as such but the fact that there are so many people unable to accept him, who reject him, and deny him the respect which is the right of every human being. Although he cannot express his feelings in words he inwardly reacts to his encounters with a rich range of feelings.'

Eileen Baranyay in her book states 'at no time was sex a problem.' Baranyay describes the fears of sex behaviour in the minds of others when two-bedded rooms were provided—a daring feature of Slough at the time—they would do mischief or just lie down together.' In fact 'in spite of the integration of the sexes a complete absence of any serious sex behaviour throughout the whole of the experiment proved the fears to be groundless and unfounded.'

I can remember the distress of a student who found two mentally handicapped adolescents kissing each other. She said of the boy, 'he is sexy.' I reminded her of the time when she was six and had a sweetheart and played at weddings, and suggested that she provided the necessary dressing-up clothes for the 'couple' in her class and saw what happened. Dramatic play at weddings followed as I suspected. George was kissed by his girl friend at work. He told me in a whisper, though we were alone. He then wanted to show me how she had done it for, as it seemed to me, he could not envisage that I too knew what a

---

* It has always been far easier in education generally and less painful in the sphere of subnormality in particular, to spend time and money exploring and describing needs (children's needs, teachers' needs, parents' needs) than it is to explore those reasons inherent in the system and in society's attitudes and own needs preventing these needs being fully met. The latter is more difficult because it cuts across personalities, economics, politics and unfortunately sometimes personal ambitions.

kiss was—was he just seeing the experience from his own point of view (i.e. preoperational thinking).

To return to the work of Maria Egg then, she writes 'In spite of careful training only one-third of the mentally handicapped can find employment on the open market.' This is an interesting comparison with the eleven out of sixty-eight from the Slough project. By far the most important idea contained in Maria Egg's work, for me at any rate, is her emphasis on their emotional/social existence. She makes the point that as it is difficult for the normal youth to be tolerant towards the mentally weak they, the mentally handicapped, therefore have to be trained to be accommodating. Unfortunately she does not elaborate in her paper how this is to be achieved but the idea seems worthy of our attention.

For those concerned with the adolescent mentally handicapped person Maria Egg's book is a must for the hopefulness it radiates in terms of human growth.

Problems in formulating their education
One of the difficulties facing those considering the educational needs of the mentally handicapped adolescent is the enormity of some of the problems presented. The immediate and obvious problem for the planners and the teachers is once again their 'individualness' in terms of their clinical/medical conditions [their physical development which, if this is normal and they fit into the group looking like 'normal' people, seems an added hazard because it is difficult then to keep on remembering their handicaps in comprehension, the range of their mental ages (cf. Appendix 5)—say from under one to about $8\frac{1}{2}$ years—the varying rates of their development, the range of their social maturity (Baranyay), their possible deprivation of experience, their varied home backgrounds and family attitudes].

Several adolescents (11/68) learning to live away from home in the hostel/work training scheme at Slough were finally employed in the open community. They had variously increased their social age scores by one to six years during training lasting between a year and $2\frac{1}{2}$ years. Their I.Q.'s on entry ranged between 34 and 48 with a preponderance of test scores in the 40's.

Raymond living in a mental subnormality hospital has an intellectual age under one year at 18 years of age. He will obviously never live and work in the open community. An examination of the personalities of individuals in this 'stage' group will highlight the difficulties in planning; it will also force us to examine the definition of 'adolescence' in the normal population and to consider whether this 'stage' has been designed over the years by adults to solve *their* problems, to satisfy *their* needs rather than those of the young people concerned.[91]

If we look at the clinical/medical conditions of these young people we are likely to find a high proportion of mongols in the age group in question. Anne Marshall, a research worker looking in the mid-sixties at the achievements of 165 pupils leaving Junior Training Centres, found that 45 per cent had Down's syndrome, 10 per cent fell into what is frequently referred to as the undifferentiated group, i.e. do not look handicapped; 10 per cent were mentally handicapped because of some birth injury, 10 per cent were handicapped for a variety of miscellaneous reasons; and 25 per cent were handicapped from no known cause. If we look into a mental subnormality hospital, Spastic Society Unit/School, Special Care Unit, we shall certainly be overwhelmed by young people having a range of rare conditions some of which might mean those having them will be grossly affected in their physical appearance—I am thinking here of conditions such as microcephaly, hydrocephaly, tuberous sclerosis, quadriplegia, as well as conditions including severe sensory or psychological defects.

We might have to take into account that some young people might become mentally retarded as they near adolescence because of conditions such as Wilson's disease,[78] a disease showing itself in the second decade of life, and adolescents becoming mentally handicapped because of brain damage through accidents.

Jack aged 19 years, very tall and able to walk, is profoundly handicapped because of serious intellectual impairment and epilepsy. He lives with his elderly parents and brothers and sisters in the country. He has a few words which could be usefully extended. His parents are devoted to him and are trying to cope positively with his tendency to hug them very hard. He is so strong that when he does this he can hurt. He has only been on holiday away from his parents once in his life. Such young people and their parents have a very difficult social problem because of the geographical position of their homes.

Leslie, who has attended a lively progressive school where his interests have been fostered over a good half of his school life, when asked as a little boy of eleven to sing me a song sang 'Three blind mice' very sweetly with a good sense of pitch and rhythm. He also sang 'Hush-a-bye, baby.' He did not know the words very well and those he sang were poorly articulated but he 'filled in' with rhythmic sounds. I was also interested to note (on my tape) that when I sang him a phrase of 'Hush-a-bye, baby,' to imitate he *continued* with the tune perfectly correctly even though he did not follow my instruction to 'sing this, Leslie.'

When he was fourteen and a year later at 15 he sang for me again (he always came to me over the years when I was visiting students on teaching practice). Immediately he began to sing a pop song of the day—songs on both occasions relevant to his adolescent years—'I want to teach the world to sing' and 'Lieutenant Pidgeon.' After singing to me we had a conversation. Leslie had poor articulation but constant practice in listening on my part meant that all the conversation on the tape was comprehended.

Leslie (aged 14 years). Sings 'I'd like to teach the world to sing.'
Me. Good. Now, Leslie, tell me where you're going when you leave this school.
Leslie. I'm going to the Training Centre in Widnes.
Me. And what are you going to do?
Leslie. I don't know when I'm going though.
Me. You don't know *when* you're going?
Leslie. I'll be going when I leave here but— —
Leslie. I don't know what's the place of the name called.
Me. I see.
Me. What will you do when you get there?
Leslie. I'll be able to start work and get paid.
Me. Yes. Are you looking forward to going?
Leslie. Yes.
Me. Can you tell me why?
Leslie. Because I want to pay my mum. I want to give my mum a pound note. Then I can have the rest to get some food.
Me. I see.
Me. Why, don't you get enough food from your mam?
Leslie. Yes. She goes to the Astor, over Lloyds Bank. That's where we go shopping.
Me. Can you tell me about your family?
Leslie. You — —
Leslie. Three at home—lives at Penketh.
Me. Oh.
Leslie. Brian's at home. He goes to another school. Our Andrew's off school.
Me. Why?
Leslie. Because he had a gumboil right on the inside of his mouth, there.
Me. I see.
Leslie. So he was off all week.
Me. Can you tell me how old they are Leslie?
Leslie. Our Andrew is about 10. Our Brian is about 11.
Me. Yes.
Leslie. I think our Andrew's 8.
Me. How old are you?
Leslie. I'm 9. Andrew's 9 I think.
Me. How old are you?
Leslie. I'm 14.

Me. Oh, you're 14 are you? I see. You're not 16. You've got a long time to go before— —
Leslie. (interrupts) I'm 15 in June.
Me. You're 15 in June, are you?
Leslie. On Sunday the 11th.
Me. You've got a long time to go before you leave school.
Leslie. Yes. Sunday the 11th my birthday.
Me. Tell me what you like doing in school.
Leslie. I like *playing* buses and cars and lorries and trains.
Me. I see. Yes, yes.
Leslie. And I like doing some writing.
Me. And I know you like drawing. Tell me about what you've been drawing this morning.
Leslie. I've been drawing tulips about spring.
Me. What other flowers grow in spring?
Leslie. Daffodils. Trees and leaves. The leaves fall in winter. They come back on the trees and but they don't the leaves fall off the tree in winters don't they?
Me. They do. You're absolutely right. Well, thank you, Leslie. Would you like to hear yourself now?
Leslie (15 years). Improved articulation. Had played simple tunes on a xylophone in the concert.
Me. I enjoyed listening to you this morning, Leslie, when you were playing the xylophone.
Leslie. Yes. It.
Me. How long did it take you to learn that?
Leslie. Well, I just learnt and that's all.
Me. You just learnt it?
Me. How?
Me. How did you learn it?
Me. Can you tell me how you learnt it?
Leslie. I done it on' piano.
Me. Oh, I see.
Leslie. You know when the 'Top of the Pops' comes on a Thursday.
Me. Mm.
Leslie. Well I always learn it off there.
Me. I see. So you go and pick the notes out do you, yourself, by yourself, and then you play it on the xylophone? Mm. Very nice. You told me that you're going to work now. Last time I met you you told me that you were going to the Adult Training Centre. But are you going to work now? Tell me about it.
Leslie. I'm going to work on. I'm going to work at the Training Centre.
Me. Oh.
Leslie. And—er, mind you its not too far. It's only up Chester Lodge. You can either— You can either go on yer bike or walk it.
Me. Oh I see, you can ride a bicycle can you?
Leslie. I don't ride a bike. My mum can't get me one so— —
Me. No.
Leslie. So I won't get one.
Me. But you'll walk will you?
Leslie. It's not that far (superimposed on my words).

Me. Do you know how long it will take you to walk?
Leslie. It only takes about an hour.
Me. Oh, that's a long way.
Leslie. It's only up Chester Lodge, Springfield. Near Springfield.
Me. I see and what's Springfield?
Leslie. It's our Steve's school where our Steve goes. Springfield. That's what it's called.
Me. Oh, it's a school is it? Mm. Mm and have you been over to that—
Leslie. (Intervening) Yes.
Me. Adult Training Centre?
Leslie. I've not been to the A.T.C. yet, no, only Miss Cooke says she'll take me one day. I don't know when.
Me. To see what you'll do and you've no idea what kind of job you're going to do?
Leslie. No.
Me. What would you like to do?
Leslie. I don't know yet so I can't think of any.
Me. Can you tell me some jobs?
Leslie. I can't think what jobs they are.
Me. Well, can you tell me any job that anybody does?
Leslie. I can either do cleaning up and that you know. I'd rather do cleaning up and—
Me. Cleaning up. You'd like to clean up would you? What would you use to clean?
Leslie. A brush, a mop, a mop bucket.
Me. Yes. And you'd like that would you?
Leslie. Yes.
Me. What other jobs?
Leslie. I always help the domestics over there, you know, on a Satday when Hilda's on her own. Mrs. Johnson over there. But I always help Mrs. Johnson every Satday when she's on her own or—on a Sunday.
Me. In the hostel do you mean? Oh, do you? That's useful isn't it?
Leslie. So I always do it on a Satday when I'm off school.
Me. Well, what do you do for her? Tell me what.
Leslie. Well, she does the sinks with the cloth—She gets you know she gets what she wants. Vim, er, that other stuff for the toilets. I don't know what it's called. Mm, mm. She has a brush an all to do the toilets out. Anyway. So. I do it every Saturday. So you know. Then next minute I get the mop bucket and er you know mop up and that but mop the bath. Mop the floor, mop the toilets and the toilets an' all.
Me. Yes, Good, Mm, mm. — What other jobs do people do in the kitchen?
Leslie. They cook the food and that.
Me. Can you make your own cup of tea?
Leslie. No. You can over here (School), but they won't let you there (Hostel).
Me. No— —
Leslie. I don't—Yes—Ah but it's up to Mr. Heavey though.
Me. Well, yes, that's what I said. You'll have to ask him if you can learn to make a cup of tea, a pot of tea.
Leslie. I always do a pot of tea at home for my mum though at night and that. I always have a sit down and I've got nice reords at home.
Me. Have you?

Leslie. I always listen to them.
Me. Do you buy the records yourself?
Leslie. Yes.
Me. Oh yes.
Leslie. You know—My mum buys them when I come back here my mum buys them. When I'm at home I buy them myself.
Me. Yes.
Me. Can you tell which records you're going to put on.
Leslie. I've got Lieutenant Pidgeon. I've got an L.P. of Top of the Pops. You know. The part—of the Union.
Me. How do you tell, Leslie, which tune's going to come when you put a record on?
Me. You don't read the name do you?
Leslie. I can read the name, it says Lieutenant P.— If it's got L.P. on it can——
Me. Can you recognize L.P.?
Leslie. Yes.
Me. How? How?—Tell me how you recognize it? Tell me how you know.
Leslie. I bought them off the market.
Me. Yes, I know, but when you look at that record how do you know that it's going to be L.P.?
Leslie. 'Cos it goes like this (he sings).
Me. Yes, that is L. Pidgeon is it (interjecting).
Leslie does not stop but goes on singing.

Further problems in considering their education

The adults

Adults who will not always let them learn 'to be' in their own time and at their own rate. Adults who will not give them an opportunity to gain a self concept in socially secure peer groups in conditions that have been planned so that such growth can take place.

Sletved (Denmark) in 1970 wrote 'The objective of the education of severely and profoundly mentally handicapped pupils is to provide them with such social accomplishments that they, like other people, are enabled to develop their identity.' [110] Some of their problems are indeed increased by the attitudes of some of the adults around them. Parents often fail to understand the developmental process in human growth. How can we expect more of them unless we make special provision to enable them to understand a rather difficult theoretical concept. This should not surprise us for if we examine Anne Marshall's figures we shall see that although mental handicap can strike at all social classes, the majority of those affected live in social classes 3 and 4, i.e. skilled and semi-skilled workers. How can we expect these parents to listen to a young person's conversation, analyse the content of their language and adapt their own language to help their child unless they have a great deal of practical *demonstrated* help.*

Normalization

Another problem is the mistaken concept underlying the present focus on normalization programmes—a phrase brought into this country from Scandinavia and taken up by parents and teachers of the young people in question, without questioning very seriously the kind of society in these countries in terms of economic stability, population size and, comparing these factors with densely populated cities, the population generally and geographical features, etc. Bank Mikkelson in his paper [109] on the quality of the services in Denmark explained 'normalization' not as meaning that we are trying to make the mentally handicapped normal but *that their living conditions are normalized.* He goes on to state that whilst offering living conditions which are normal to the mentally handicapped (and this when they are adult might mean living in a block of flats amongst normal adults but having a central meeting place to eat and 'play' with the other handicapped members living in the flats) they are not oblivious of their duties to offer special care, support and treatment.

Conflicting attitudes

Here I am thinking of those professionals who are always wanting to see something especially good for this particular group of adolescents. Does anyone know what is good? Is anyone measuring the progress of all aspects of their personalities? How and who should evaluate whether what is happening is good or not. What are the criteria? Later on in this chapter I have attempted to formulate some principles and describe a philosophy as it were, regarding the kind of education that might fulfil the needs of the mentally handicapped adolescent and be considered 'especially good.'

Teachers/parents

To return briefly to conflicting attitudes amongst the adults concerned—consider the complexity of the situation where the teachers encourage some measure of independence in their charges and their parents for a variety of reasons will not allow their offspring to practise this.

---

*Many of them clearly will find less difficulty in communicating simply than will parents using language with complex structures.

Other possible problems in considering the education of the adolescent

(1) Lack of specially trained Youth Leaders.
(2) Lack of male members of staff in this particular field of education [though since the passing of the Education Act, 1971 (Handicapped Children), more men teachers have entered the ranks of teachers of the mentally handicapped, many of these are in organizing, lecturing and administration posts and not in day-to-day contact with these young people].
(3) Lack of suitable buildings. Many of these young people have to be in buildings planned to take children from two years of age. There seems to be some evidence that this will be changed in the future as those nationally now responsible for looking at needs of the handicapped* make recommendations based upon present experience and a critical evaluation (with positive outcome) of other people's mistakes.

Gunzburg as a leading applied and practical psychologist in the field of mental subnormality, in attempting to formulate a philosophy, gives us a fund of common sense suggestions, for he writes 'The syllabus *must* centre round social skills which might be required in the community and particularly communication skills of various types which will be necessary for a mentally handicapped person who is to function in the community. Priority in an educational scheme of this kind will be given to language skills which must be systematically developed.' He points out the lack of virtue in giving the mentally handicapped such a variety of experiences that they become confused and disturbed but 'to give them a feeling of security and confidence by letting them experience familiar situations with small variations and varying levels of difficulty will be of great benefit.' The question of what particular experiences mean to the mentally handicapped and how much emphasis needs to be laid upon giving them experiences of all kinds will only be ultimately decided upon by teachers with philosophies of their own brought sometimes from their own experience with other groups of pupils.

The problem of how to ensure that developing educational schemes become in fact a reality is perhaps of even greater importance than considering the content of the education given at the present time. Too much theoretical concentration on the content of a syllabus can never be generalized—indeed it might be too successful and therefore deflect our attention from critically analysing those factors preventing the reality (education at least to 19 years) for those needing it.

---

* The Warnock Committee.

Another problem: lack of definition of the term 'adolescence' in mental subnormality

(a) the lack of definition by 'growth' psychologists regarding the meaning of adolescence in terms of the mentally handicapped;
(b) the paucity of educational research and useful literature;*
(c) the necessity of seeing the adolescent mentally handicapped person against the background of the contemporary and future scene of our particular society—highly populated, highly pressurized and ultimately almost reaching its peak in materialistic terms with the promise of a trend to a more caring outlook. [111]

Discussions about normal adolescence seem to range round the following points and if we take each point in turn some order might emerge in our thinking about adolescence in the mentally handicapped:

(1) The state of the mind and the physiology of the body—the teens and the early twenties being generally accepted as the years in question.
(2) The uncertainty of the individual on the threshold of independence.
(3) The crisis of identity which this intended independence brings.
(4) Experimentation in different types of conduct and dressing.
(5) Greater awareness of others and an increased sensitivity towards them.
(6) A corresponding concern for what others think of him (along with 5).
(7) Reappraisal of himself.
(8) The period as one of great psychological adjustment—behaviour swings from one extreme to the other—essence of unselfishness, vowing dedication to noble causes on the one hand, to pleasure-seeking and headstrong egoistic behaviour on the other.

The above points (1–8) have been compiled from the study of adolescents by the writers Davies and Gibson.[91] A further point regarding the adolescent's personality is emphasized by Marie Neale in her book *Education for the Intellectually Limited Child and Adolescent*[80] when she writes 'Adolescence is a period of growth in

---

* A personal definition of useful literature is that which describes positive, concrete and real experiences so that the adult assimilating such descriptions can bring his own mind to bear at whatever level he is capable of—this might mean imitating the original suggestion and if this is sound it cannot be harmful; it might mean extending the original idea to such a degree that the source is lost; it might mean formulating a research hypothesis the results of which reinforce the intuition of skilled workers but add to recognized academic knowledge and supply a new theoretical vocabulary.

which the individual achieves an integrated image of what he is and what his future will be.

Little reference to the 'norm'
It is not uncommon for a handicapped person to be thought about and planned for (particularly at this stage) without constant reference to the norm. Youth leaders and teachers accustomed to the normal adolescent would probably plan in ways that are different from those knowing mental handicap but not the normal in any depth.

The points formulated by skilled observers over a period of time about normal adolescence do not seem to correspond on most counts with the 'known' personalities of mentally handicapped adolescents. The 'known' is in inverted commas because those working with them by and large have made no detailed academic observational studies of their personalities in educational settings and therefore we have no recognized authoritative body of accumulated knowledge to refer to even though we 'know' them as people.

In my work with George, now in his forties, I have plenty of written recorded evidence of his verbalized strivings towards independence and some greater awareness of others. He spontaneously refers to the bus for the 'handicapped' but when questioned about handicap he has no real concept—he has not yet gained the image of himself as handicapped. I know from his mother's comments that he was very afraid at 16, when he became aware of his penis because of spontaneous erections, that he was going to lose it as it deflated after urinating. I have plenty of records of his awareness of girls and of his desire to have a girl friend. As yet there has been no 'experimentation in his conduct' towards them unless asking them to dance with him can be included in this feature of adolescent behaviour.

What I am trying to question here is the whole concept of adolescence in the severely subnormal if we adhere to the norms. What does adolescence consist of indeed? Does it in fact begin as with normal teenagers with physiological changes? Does it ever end in the mentally handicapped? Does this questioning lead us to the same conclusions as those of Davies and Gibson that adolescence is a named period of use to the adults in society—that adults have in fact 'artificially created adolescence for their own ends.' Perhaps future personality studies in the field of mental subnormality will throw new light on these concepts of adolescence in the normal growth too; will examine the varying qualitative differences between groups; will emphasize the importance of the possibility of continued growth in a number of life areas as for all members of society even if the intellectual aspects *are* permanently impaired or limited. The community's responsibilities surely lie in providing the opportunities for such growth to take place and we have a long way to travel before this may be judged satisfactory.

If we look at the supernormal youth's opportunities for an extended adolescence in contemporary middle class society particularly—by this I mean that many in this group train for a career, qualify and then do not follow it up immediately in responsible work but are silently condoned by the adults to leave responsibility until later in the mid-twenties until 'they really know what they want to do'—I think a very good case can be made for the subnormal to have an extended adolescence too and a programme which maximizes on further education. If they do not, we are surely placing upon them a burden of work responsibility at too early an age and thus depriving them of the opportunities given to those with higher intelligence, opportunities they perhaps need even more. If we believe in the dignity of 'work' (a phrase bandied about in the field of the mentally handicapped in the 'sixties) it should surely be for all groups of youth: if we believe in Further Education then this too should not only be considered for all but become a reality—for the mentally handicapped. I should like to substitute the word 'Further' in Further Education by 'Continuous'.

Some special educational aims and principles for the 14-plus group

Those who know me well and those who have worked with me know that the suggestions I make have usually been formulated from first-hand experience in the first instance. The aims and principles I am now going to discuss have indeed been formulated from constant contact with mentally handicapped adolescents and adults in a wide variety of contexts. Some of these include:

(i) A teaching/assessing job in a Classifying School for delinquent girls, some of whom were admitted to mental subnormality hospitals.

(ii) An ongoing relationship with two families having a member who was mentally handicapped; a woman of 18 (for five years teaching her on one evening a week and writing notes for her mother to work with her during the intervening period 1954-9); a man 28-41 years (teaching him for one evening a week 1961-7, keeping contact since then in a variety of ways).

(iii) Working with a class of 14 profoundly and severely handicapped men in a mental subnormality hospital on one evening a week over a two-year period. This included two physically handicapped men.

(iv) Helping students to understand language stimulation processes during training by having young teenage people visit our course on one day a week to cook their own lunch, to go for walks, to listen to stories, to talk on the tape recorder, to choose their own play activities (page 127), to work with me individually. Whilst the premises in which these student teacher training activities took place were substandard by any present teacher training establishment standards, the quality of the work that went on did not detract from the usefulness of the findings based on intensive observations which have clearly continued to influence teachers and others working with the mentally handicapped.

Aims
(1) To help them to have *fun* in living and feel that each day is well spent.
(2) To continue to stimulate their thought processes.
(3) To continue to promote the acquisition of language including comprehension and facility in expressive language.
(4) To encourage them to express THEIR OWN IDEAS, FEELINGS, NEEDS.
(5) To enable them to reconstruct THEIR life experiences in art, drama, movement.
(6) To introduce them to a very wide variety of worthwhile life experiences and to give them opportunities to relate to an ever-increasing number and variety of people.
(7) To help them grow in confidence by providing activities where they can *immediately* see the results of their efforts where activities and situations are provided to enable them to succeed in however simple a way. Thus *Brian* was a profoundly institutionalized handicapped mongol man in his mid-twenties. The highlight of his week was being allowed to fill the kettle with water and plug in the lead to boil the water for tea-making. At the moment of knowing him he was not able to carry out the full sequence of making tea but he was able to do the two activities mentioned above. *Mary,* an athetoid woman, was delighted when pieces of cloth saturated with paint and attached to the sleeves of her dress made 'attractive' marks on the paper put before her by an interested teacher. Maria Siejko writing [112] in the book *Studies in the Socialization of the Severely and Profoundly Handicapped Child* describes the situation of children helping each other and thus gaining from this. *Ted* likes babies. He approaches them, looks at them as if at a toy, and touches them gently with his finger tips. Today after watching a small child he asked for money. When asked what for, he smiled

ever so sweetly and said 'Buy'. *Johnnie* is a big strapping fellow. He played ball today with a little boy he met in the park. Johnnie is temperamental and highly excitable but he handed the ball to the little boy knowing full well that he was playing with a younger and weaker child. This required controlling his strength and normal energy. The two played together this way for about 10 minutes.

(8) To help them develop a number of skills so that each in his own time becomes an accepted and useful member of society within the limits of his handicap, his family attitudes and immediate neighbourhood.

(9) To consider a programme (see below) of special education rather than education (W. Brennan, in a lecture, 1971) and a life of 'planned dependence'[113] rather than one that strives after independent social competence. We do not really need to spend countless thousands of pounds on research in the future on this aspect of the mentally handicapped—figures are available both in this country and the States to indicate that the vast majority will be dependent even though more and more will probably become independent because of increased educational opportunities. This is not intended to be a pessimistic attitude but rather a realistic one.

The curriculum might be developed according to principles suggesting that:

(1) The teacher looks at the young people as they are and tries to fulfil THEIR needs rather than her own needs, the needs of parents and those who might not fully accept them and show this by often giving them inappropriate activities.

(2) There should be periods of time daily when the pupils can choose their own activity in a well-structured learning environment because they need:

(a) far more opportunities (not fewer) at this stage of development to form friendships and relationships with their own age group and others around them;

(b) to work out spontaneous aims of their own in imaginative and dramatic activity;*

(c) maximum opportunities for USING receptive and expressive language;

---

* Janet, Rosie and Robert were all aged twenty or thereabouts. They attended a club one evening a week organized by students. While they joined in with the other activities such as cards, dancing, cooking, listening to music, etc., I saw them on one occasion walk into a room and begin to dramatize (play) a visit to the dentist. Rosie told the others what to do. Janet was the receptionist and Robert was the patient.

(d) opportunities for thinking out beforehand what they are going to do with their time and then getting on with it—keeping them alert, stimulating thinking, encouraging them to look ahead.
(3) There is a continuation of all the creative and concept-building activities, i.e. carefully planned art, woodwork, drama, music, physical activity, table games in order to:
(a) stimulate imagination;
(b) stimulate language and increase vocabulary;
(c) give those around them an opportunity to learn what they need explaining;
(d) possibilities for practising sequencing of experiences and ideas in drama, creative dance and cookery;
(e) encourage concentration, cooperation and gain emotional satisfaction in music;
(f) enable them to communicate their ideas and experiences in graphic and three dimensional (model) forms.
(4) There is continued assessment and consideration of each individual in a one-to-one situation (this might mean just on a once a week or fortnightly basis).
(5) The greater part of the educational programme should perhaps be carried out:
(a) out of school and the adult centre and in the community;
(b) in specially planned 'workshop activity' areas not classrooms, e.g.:
   (i)   home areas for the practice of useful home skills;
   (ii) areas for learning how to care for the self;
   (iii) art studios.
(6) The teacher has expectations for these young people.
(7) There is teacher/parent involvement to ensure that:
(a) they can be given ecouragement and support;
(b) they can be encouraged to give maximum encouragement to the handicapped offspring and maximum opportunities for increased enjoyment of life;
(c) there is consistence of behaviour in home, work and school by counselling parents.
Such counselling needs to help parents in the following:
   (i)   how to talk with their mentally handicapped son or daughter (direct demonstration might possibly be of the greatest help particularly to non-academic parents);
   (ii) what to do with them in the form of outings, activities in the home and how to follow them up;
   (iii) to ensure that their offspring have regular health check-

ups particularly when they are nearing middle age. This is a very difficult problem because of course so many of the parents will then often be in their late sixties/early seventies/dead;
(iv) allowing independence of some measure;
(v) encouraging them to make friends and to invite them into the home;
(vi) getting them to think about and talk to their 'children' about where they will live when they die; making arrangements with the social services departments where they live for their children's lives after their death; taking them to see the place, to meet the staff;
(vii) to encourage appropriate dress; regular changing of socks;
(viii) the possibilities for fun/learning when the family eat together;
(ix) about the ways in which the normal brothers and sisters might support the mother and father in later life without becoming totally absorbed in the problem to the extent that their lives are considered spoiled;
(x) how to cope with the general attitudes of the immediate community towards one because one obviously or not so obviously has a handicapped child. Are there strategies that could usefully be taught?
(xi) how to use the Attendance Allowance.
(8) There are regular health check-ups throughout life.

AN EDUCATIONAL PROGRAMME

It might consist of:
(a) skills;
(b) creative education;
(c) prescriptive education after assessment of specific needs;
(d) preparation for work where applicable.

Skills
Activities needing to be broken down into small steps and practised until they are well learned.

Home skills
Bedmaking, putting clothes on hangers, folding and putting clothes away in drawers, washing own clothes, setting a table, making a really simple meal, dusting, using a carpet sweeper and a vacuum cleaner,

using an electric toaster, washing own hair (practising combing and washing someone else's hair first so that they can see what they are doing outside of themselves), shaving with an electric shaver, washing the dishes and drying them.

Community skills under supervision
Going to a shop, buying for themselves, buying for the family, buying for others, using a supermarket, using other kinds of large shops, going on a bus/train accompanied (not the school bus, that is a very sheltered experience), going into a cafe/cafeteria/snack bar sometimes having high stools, going to a party, having a friend to tea (a great deal of parent cooperation and involvement is needed here), preparing a simple meal for a friend, adopting an old person as a group activity—a community involvement—visiting the old person (I can see Leslie being able to sing to an old person, why not other handicapped young people?), bringing in the coal, dusting, making firelighting papers, washing up their dishes, doing the shopping for them (a much needed service for old people), making a meal in school and taking it to an old person.

Conversational skills
This is perhaps one of the most important skills to be practised. Teachers need to be trained to sit down (as with a friend) and talk with these young people both individually and in groups. Drawing out their experiences and talking about them is not easy unless *both the teacher and the pupil* have something interesting to talk about. The teachers need to tell their pupils about their lives too. Extensions of thought may be elicited by asking 'why'. Teachers have to remember here that they are not seeking correct answers but encouraging their pupils' expression of their ideas even if these are often immature. Communication is the all-important feature of such a skill.

I should like to add a word of warning here that I am not envisaging a group of young people sitting round the teacher having a formal question and answer session or a news session. I am referring to the fact that to have the concept of what a conversation is, it should be carried out in as natural a conversation situation as possible. In the first instance this will have to be engineered by the teachers/adults. This seems to be an important skill, for so very often when one meets a mentally handicapped child with his parents, however old he is, it is the parents who speak on their offspring's behalf, though it is also quite feasible that the adult talking with the family will often assume that the handicapped person will have nothing of interest to speak about—of course this will depend upon the visitor's interest in other people's conversations. Sometimes we can be at fault and address the parent on behalf of the child.

Observational skills

Taking these young people out and about and then following their experiences up by letting them make drawing diaries of their experiences (scrap books of pictures where the nature of the condition might mean that they are unable to express themselves graphically) will increase their ability to take notice of things around them. Such diaries will also act as a measure of their increasing understanding of what they see. Carried out over a long enough period of time this method might provide them with a hobby that can be carried out quite spontaneously and independently at home (cf. page 22).

Leisure skills

Putting on a record player, riding a bicycle, playing simple table games (and these might have to be specially devised/adapted), roller skating (first seen in a school in Salford in the mid-sixties), bowling, dancing, using a camera, going to the cinema to give the family a rest, attending a club, playing putting, collecting.

The whole problem of leisure and the mentally handicapped needs to be given a great deal of thought within each Local Authority. The National Federation of Gateway Clubs' Handbook leaves one with the impression that the mentally handicapped members of our community are well catered for. Thirty-one activities are described in a handout from this group* as being offered in some clubs. The booklet is well worth reading though we should perhaps criticize its use of the word 'children' in its pages. If we use the word, we shall tend to think of them as children or girls or boys. It is obvious that in the 1960's there was a steady increase in the growth of clubs due to the major efforts of the National Society for Mentally Handicapped Children. Not as much effort has been expended into describing the methods being used throughout the country to ensure that EVERY known mentally handicapped person has the same opportunity to attend a club at least once or twice a week; nor has there been any evidence that the young people running these clubs have had any special courses (perhaps we might be wrong to suggest it is necessary, for young people often find their own way through); I suspect that too many clubs are being run by parents of the handicapped for lack of other kind of community help.

---

* Gateway Clubs, National Organizing Officer, N.S.M.H.C., London.

The following points may stimulate discussion about this question of leisure and the mentally handicapped adolescent:

(1) Do we spend part of each school/work day introducing them to leisure pursuits which often then have no channel for expression once they return home at 4.30 p.m.? Do we persuade others to organize leisure pursuits in the evenings as well as allowing for the common-sense fact that we all need a rest from our work?

(2) What kind of leisure pursuits should be available—hobbies of all kinds including model-making, collecting things, pottery, pet keeping, rambling clubs, camping, playing team games?

(3) Considering the kind of activity that is possible if the adults come forward to organize these:

   (a) Are the club premises usually available/suitable/purpose-built?
   (b) Have the services always to be given by untrained volunteers?
   (c) Should all Further Education Departments be approached and persuaded to set up special classes in art, music, drama, sport? Members of these classes will have to pay a small fee, but then so do all normal members attending such classes. Should it be free?
   (d) Should all Principals of Evening Institutes be approached and asked to institute such leisure groups or encourage those teaching in the classes to take in a certain percentage of handicapped members where this is appropriate?
   (e) Should the whole question of *the difficulties* of getting the young person to the club be widely publicized in the mass media?

My students ran a club for the mentally handicapped adolescent and adult for almost six years. The majority of the members were brought by their parents (some quite a distance), others walked to the club or came by public transport (two or three). Some of the parents then left their offspring for the period of time the club was open (two hours) and went for a drink. Most of the others (mothers) sat in a room apart from the club, and over a cup of tea talked with each other. Television was not available quite deliberately. The same group of mothers, about 6–8, came weekly over the period that the club was available. The only time they joined in the club's activities was at the end-of-term parties.

Whilst organizing clubs for the mentally handicapped is laudable, those running them get as much satisfaction if not more than the handicapped members attending. We have no way of knowing whether the needs of the handicapped themselves are indeed satisfied.

Clubs where groups meet together and have periods of enjoyment are one way of organizing leisure for the mentally handicapped. The idea from Canada called Citizen's Advocacy might extend the services that already exist (cf. page 195).

Clearly the Holiday Project of the Association for All Speech Impaired Children (page 195) where a normal speaking youngster is paired with a non-communicating youngster during a camping holiday has possibilities too in the field of mental handicap. Ideas of all kinds are being worked out all over the country. If only there was a platform for the immediate dissemination of ideas *and how to put them into practice*, the mentally handicapped would surely be better served as would those working on their behalf.

Further Education evening classes
Whilst it is well known that some authorities and parent groups are well ahead in their plans for the mentally handicapped to attend Further Education classes, this will only refer to the minority of those really needing this experience. Perhaps I should remind the reader of one of my footnotes—35 trainees only from a centre of 200 were able to attend evening classes—the criterion for attending was that they were able to go home alone or be brought home. The fact that this experience has even been organized is creditable but the real numbers taking advantage of the scheme do indicate the limits.

If we believe that there should be opportunities for the mentally handicapped adolescent to continue his education right into his twenties if not indeed into adulthood as well, we need authorities willing to offer classes in music, drama, physical education activities, hobby group and perhaps camping craft, cookery and creative woodwork. There might even be classes in 'taking care of ourselves' and in view of the existence of classes for illiterates in Evening Institutes, it is reasonable to suggest that there might be language classes particularly for those not having attained language facility (sometimes fluency) by the end of their school years at 16/19 years.

The opportunity of these young people attending such classes with a teacher wanting to gain some knowledge of mental handicap as well as introducing her/his subject to them is a dream of the future for those wanting the best care for this handicapped group in our population. Sometimes the classes will be composed entirely of mentally handicapped people; on other occasions they could clearly be classes where the handicapped are integrated with normal members of the institute. It is an obvious fact that if such classes and teachers were available the authorities concerned would have the added burden of extra finance and the organization of special evening transport. Perhaps a special post could be created in the Further

Education Department of all L.E.A's to pay particular attention to improving the quality of leisure life for the more handicapped members of our society.

One of the undoubted and obvious reasons for the lack of organized provision for the further education and leisure of the handicapped is a lack of money and our reliance by and large on largely unorganized voluntary effort. No national scheme exists, as in Denmark, by which a sum of money is put aside to develop appropriate schemes for the mentally handicapped adolescents and adults of our society to ensure they do not suffer loneliness and deprivation of experiences.

Ann Marshall's research into the attainments and abilities of children leaving Junior Training Centres [94] indicated that 10 per cent of her 165 sample only used public transport. 64 per cent of those attending schools before going to these centres were *able* to go about the streets alone but did not cross the roads of these streets. Surveys in adult centres (and the collection of data could be done by the Managers at no extra cost to anyone—only time) would give local authorities the information they need regarding the necessity and amount of provision of special transport—and I might add here that the lack of this on a regular consistent basis very often constitutes one of the gravest drawbacks in getting the handicapped OUT of their homes during the week for an evening or two. Organizing transport in a large city for say 500/600 mentally handicapped members seems to warrant a post of special evening responsibility within an Adult Training Centre being available.

At the moment there is no national conscience that this is necessary. Perhaps we should follow the example of Holland in the 'sixties and make sure soon that the period of material prosperity (in spite of inflation) should be shared in the immediate future by those less fortunate.

Preparing to receive the S.S.N. school leaver in the adult centre
An interesting aspect of working in the field of the mentally handicapped is the opportunity one is sometimes afforded to look at what is happening in a place where the legislation for their care differs from that used in England and Wales. I am referring immediately to the system existing in Northern Ireland.

Most of the schools in this country have adult centres attached to them and the Headteacher of the school is the 'manager' of the Adult Training Centre as well. The total population of both departments is usually small and therefore rather personal in approach. One of the most interesting centres I visited, not attached to a school, contained adolescents and adults who were currently not ready for a work situation; some of them never will be, and this was sensibly accepted. A lively, relevant, educational experience was being given to these young people, as far as I could assess from a very hasty visit, and there was no pretence that work was being done by those attending this particular centre or that there ever would be.

The experience reminded me too of a similar one in Holland where a special building designed, if one took an aerial view, to look like a star in its arrangement of rooms of educationally-oriented activities. During the past five years, profoundly handicapped adults, mostly ambulant, who had been living at home after leaving 'school' (some of them in their thirties or forties) had been encouraged to attend this educational centre for adults. The physical education I observed given to individuals by specially trained physical education teachers was most impressive as were the evident possibilities for a wide number of creative activities.

To my knowledge there does not exist a separate building educationally oriented in such a way in England or Wales administered by a local authority. Rooms there may be within the Adult Training Centre work setting, but no purpose-built place for the profoundly handicapped and those who will not be able to join in with a work concept of life; no place where specially trained educational staff concern themselves with this kind of mentally handicapped adolescent and adult.

To return then to Northern Ireland, I was invited by the newly-formed Association of Teachers of the Mentally Handicapped to talk about how the school could prepare the S.S.N. school leaver for work. I decided to look at the problem from the position of the adult centre rather than the school, though the points I will present briefly to you clearly involved both the school and work centre.

A general principle of considerable importance is that there should be systematic movement of staff between the school and the centre—not a problem in the organization of these institutions in Northern Ireland but apparently causing some disquiet in this country—not only because of geographical distance but sometimes because of the gulf that very often exists between the members of staff in the separate establishments.

From the adult centre
Over a period of time, say two or three months, before a group of young people are ready to enter the adult centre:
(1) Visits of observation are made to the school so that:

(a) the young person would be seen in the school situation;
(b) the skills and interests of the future trainee would be assessed from direct observation in a familiar setting against the knowledge of what is available in terms of staff and work tasks in the receiving centre;
(c) the individual records can be read and discussed with the Head AND the teacher;
(d) the parents can be consulted with the teacher/instructor present and the parents invited to see the adult centre and meet the staff as individuals (and not as part of a group in some organized social group occasion).

(2) The visitor from the adult centre (a member of staff perhaps with special responsibility for new admissions) could show on two or three occasions, specially prepared slides of the centre building, its people doing jobs, its programme over a week and throughout a particular day to the young people concerned. This would mean that the daily programme, the idea of what work is and the renewing of relationships (for the pupils would see their friends on the slides but in unfamiliar situations) would be gradually absorbed with opportunities for the visitor to talk about what was happening in very simple terms. It would be essential for the teacher to be present in order to continue the conversation when the visitor had gone.

(3) Enlarged pictures of some of the slides of the Adult Training Centre could be placed on view in the school (a local photography club or the educational technology section of a college might be willing to help here if there is no finance available in the annual estimates). These would change from time to time. The pictures would be a focal point for discussion between the pupils and the teacher. They would form a link with the visitor on his second visit, particularly if he appeared in the pictures.

(4) A creative table games area might be set up in the centre similar to those found in classrooms in the school to form a familiar link with what is known by the trainees.

The school's task vis-a-vis *the adult training centre and work*
(1) Extending the visits in the community to places where work is taking place with follow-ups (cf. page 236).
(2) Prepare a comprehensive report on a pupil ready to leave school, consulting all the past records on the child and aiming to give as detailed a descriptive picture of the personality, achievements, personal difficulties, interests and needs, etc., as is possible. And by

this I do not mean just fill in a Progress Assessment Chart. Such a task might be carried out by a teacher specially interested in accurate, sensitive report-making, a teacher perhaps with a special post of responsibility.

(3) The above teacher might visit the Adult Training Centre alone to see what the work tasks consist of, what difficulties the pupil (he should know well after studying his records) will likely have.

(4) Take the leavers to the Adult Training Centre for half a day a week over a period of time. Comprehensive school leavers could be involved too in the actual travel that is sometimes involved in such a trip.

(5) The school could invite some of their pupils back to lunch six months and a year after leaving. These would be the friends of the pupils ready for leaving school.

(6) Give photographs of the school's activities and the children to the Adult Training Centre.

These general suggestions have been made particularly in the present climate of the school leavers' situation. Since the Education Act of 1971, the general cry of the teachers at any rate is that they no longer seem to have any contact with the Adult Training Centres. Inequality in the recognized status, conditions and the pay of the different staff involved no doubt is part of the 'scene' the young person is in the midst of—both groups indeed have a great responsibility towards each other and those they are spending their working lives with—no doubt their genuine mutual concern will iron out the present difficulties that exist, but getting together systematically and regularly will certainly help.

13 *Specially trained teachers*

There seems little point in pretending that we do not know the skills and strategies that should be practised by teachers of the mentally handicapped. Many people in England* applied their minds in a very serious committed fashion to the problem for nearly fifteen years. Indeed some of them formulated and propagated ideas about these in a number of ways. Have they been wasting their own time? Have they been wasting the time of students and the money of health authorities seconding students? Were not some of them seeing the positive results of such training around them as they went into the schools for the mentally handicapped over these years?

If we pretend that these ideas were not sound, then a great many paid professionals from a variety of disciplines condoned them over the years. These must perforce accept some responsibility for the new psychologists and educationists coming to the fore in the 'seventies spending time and perhaps other people's money discussing what is needed in training teachers, instead of discussing new means for gaining sufficient TIME in one way or another in the present teacher training programmes for helping teachers gain the requisite skills already supported by these experienced people.

A survey of recent published literature gives me the impression that the positive aspects of the long pioneering of special training for teachers of the mentally handicapped in this country is already deliberately ignored and forgotten. It certainly is rare to see it mentioned. When one has experience of the international as well as the national scene, one can perhaps excuse the ignorance about this matter; can excuse newcomers to training and even researchers for not knowing that if the former two-year training had really been extended to three years in a special way† instead of it being considered by some

---

* All Tutors organizing courses, those supporting them professionally from relevant training committees, the visiting lecturers from Colleges of Education, University Departments and schools and those externally examining the written and practical aspects of the courses in order for students to gain the recognized qualifying Diploma.

† So that students would have the opportunity to experience the *special* part of a special teacher's education programme:
(a) assessment of an individual child's needs and compilation of teaching

unhealthy to allow young people the right to 'go in for teaching the mentally handicapped without pressure, that this might initially be wrong for them'†) then we might have led the positive thinking of the world in special teacher training projects.

Special education too generally might have been better served, for I know that the best teachers we trained would have benefitted children with any handicap needing individual help. Mrs. Forrest wrote in the foreword to the first edition of this book 'many of the ideas and methods (described) may be found to illuminate the field of normal education.' and again Professor Mittler [114] wrote 'it is also just possible that the kind of detailed analysis of teaching and learning processes which may come out from a study of severely subnormal children will in the long term benefit the teaching of the less handicapped and even normal children.' I expressed this sentiment too (in my previous preface) when I stated that teachers of normal children 'might realize the possibilities for deepening their own thinking about the meaning of education and the learning processes through contact with them.' Of course I was using my own experience and understanding here, for I had been a teacher of normal and handicapped children and I knew what my new experience with the mentally handicapped had meant.

During the years 1960–70 educationists* principally responsible for training the teachers of these children had the freedom to innovate and develop: (cf. ref. 25)

(1) Appropriate forms of training to achieve a degree of professionalism.
(2) Important attributes in their students which undoubtedly enabled them to demonstrate the educability of these children in developing the curriculum for physical education, creative dance, music, art, drama, woodwork, home economics, language, play and the social aspects of education.
(3) Opportunities for students to meet and work professionally over

---

† We might just as well say that teachers/lecturers wishing to teach Latin, Greek or Chemistry all their lives because they love to do so is unhealthy too.

* Miss W. Willis (London), Mrs. M. Forrest (Bristol), Mrs. M. Stevens (Manchester), Mrs. M. Lettie (Sheffield), Mr. B. Flanders (Leeds), Mr. A. Hardman (Preston), Mrs. B. Cannon (Nottingham) and Mr. T. Pascoe (Cardiff).

---

programmes.
(b) parent support;
(c) design and evaluation of teaching aids.

varying lengths of time* with teachers from other fields of education including normal, remedial and special education.
(4) Opportunities to have programmes where they could meet professionals from a number of allied disciplines and on some occasions work with them or see them at work (cf. Chapter 11).
(5) Methods allowing students to study in some depth and with some measure of practical understanding the development of the normal child and to examine in well-supervised situations, sometimes with involved Tutors, the relevance of this to the severely subnormal child. Whenever students visited children they were given detailed notes in order to help them know what to look for. A week's experience in a normal nursery in their first and second year with a programme including direct observation and recording of the behaviour of the same individual child and the same group of children gave them an interesting comparative insight into a year of development, as it were, in a normal child. Two years studying a baby from two months up to two years of age gave students knowledge from first hand of an experience that they could not have gained from books, films, or lectures, however interesting. All these visits to children whether normal or handicapped had to be reported in full and all reports were closely and carefully marked and commented upon by the relevant staff. A spin-off from such an experience was the sharing of experiences about homes covering all social classes—a sound basis indeed for understanding the sociological aspects of education in a very practical sense.
(6) Highly structured presentation of course material to meet the current learning needs of the students and the developing curricula needs of the schools in the areas in which courses were sited. As far as was possible students experienced something at first hand *before* they had lectures on the topic. The number of academic lectures in the first year of training were in some courses deliberately minimal, and a programme of stimulating experiences with children of all kinds and people from a variety of disciplines and backgrounds was arranged to give the experience against which the theory could then be given more meaningfully.
(7) A deliberate policy of guidance and counselling of all students in small groups and individually so that they personally experienced a similar one-to-one learning relationship that they would be applying from time to time in their work with handicapped children. On

---

* Students on some courses taught children in a school for Educationally Subnormal (M) children on one day a week over a year (cf. Appendix 6, page 278).

some occasions this meant directive counselling (when a mother was persuaded to allow her daughter to live in a flat instead of at home), remedial education to strengthen a student's belief in her own ability, seeking the possibilities for non-directive counselling from a youth counsellor/psychiatrist and individual sessions with the art lecturer, Mrs. Pat Simpson,* for students needing extra help in using their imaginations in creative work.

(8) Situations where students came into continuous, caring, effectual contact with a very wide variety of handicapped people—for as Jordan states [115] 'positive attitudes towards the mentally handicapped have an *affectual*/contactual base rather than a cognitive/knowledge one.'

(9) Possibilities for being highly selective in the lecturers they invited to participate in these two-year courses (such independent selection by Tutors was indeed one of the strengths of the courses) for it meant that these Tutors could retain a degree of influence necessary in helping them maintain a measure of consistency in encouraging positive yet unsentimental attitudes towards these children. What I am suggesting in this section is that one cannot be entirely sure in the present teacher training 'set up' for teachers of the mentally handicapped, that all members of staff in the College have an equally consistent caring approach to this group of children and to those wishing to teach them. I have not heard of any special courses being organized since 1971 within the Colleges to enable staff (other than those immediately concerned with mental handicap) to become informed about the problems in mental subnormality.

(10) A measure of guided In-Service training given to full- and part-time colleagues entering the field for the first time (and therefore needing the time to sit in on some of the lectures; to visit a large number and variety of schools and other establishments; to participate with students in their work; to consult with more experienced colleagues).

As a teacher experienced over a lifetime in diagnostic and active experiential methods of education, [116] the kinds of courses that were evolved because of the opportunities afforded to those organizing

---

* A dedicated lecturer to the Manchester N.A.M.H. Course responsible (over 11 years) for a constant flow of creative ideas; for awakening a student's interest in the possibilities for using waste materials. She was an art therapist in some Manchester hospitals. During the 'forties she introduced a picture loan scheme and in the 'sixties and 'seventies was still working creatively with geriatric patients in a local Manchester hospital.

them equated in my mind at least to an informal but well-structured approach at an adult level for* 'the best kind of teaching is . . . teaching geared to problems that are discovered in the ongoing situation.'[117] The problems we constantly met in the ongoing situations on the old training courses certainly meant that imagination had to be used in order to solve some of them satisfactorily; to solve others rather tentatively; that the teaching was indeed geared to problems that existed.

It was into rather formal rigid educational climates, in some colleges at any rate, that these courses were FORCED to fit after 1971—whatever the outcome for those who to a large extent had been personally responsible for bringing about much needed change in the day-to-day management of these children and whatever the outcome for the children in terms of their having enough specially trained, dedicated and committed† teachers. Fifteen years of thought regarding the special education of these teachers, was almost completely destroyed overnight by those more concerned perhaps with current regulations, the politics, the economics and the whole future of teacher unemployment than with mentally handicapped children.

Some Tutors were completely demoralized by the methods used to make them 'fit in'; to make them 'admit' that the old courses led to narrowness of outlook, the 'mother hen' complex with students; that teachers trained to teach normal children first must obviously be better than those beginning with the severely subnormal; that if we insisted on specialized professional training we were condemning our young teachers to teach the mentally handicapped all their teaching lives.‡

Others were concerned that the official demand that students should train within the same three years to teach normal children as

---

* Dr. Ravenette was describing the philosophy underlying an approach he is currently making, with a group of teachers (1972) on In-Service courses to encourage them to observe systematically teacher/child interaction, to a study group of psychologists brought together by Professor P. Mittler.

† It was reported to me the other week that one student on teaching practice in a school for the mentally handicapped was heard to be calling the children 'dim wits'. Needless to say there seemed to be some kind of inquest into this matter by the Head concerned. I hope he sent that student back to college. A few weeks later I came across a College where students gave up their free sports afternoon to work in a school for the mentally handicapped throughout the duration of their three-year course.

‡ I hope my present edition has indicated what a lovely, varied, interesting teaching career this can indeed be with plenty of opportunities for a successful, varied career structure.

well as the severely subnormal seemed to indicate that:

(a) teaching the subnormal was not yet fully accepted in this country, or that good teachers trained to teach these children would be equally able to transfer their teaching skills to other kinds of children as say those who had trained to teach normal adolescents and who then wished to teach infants or the E.S.N.(M). Bert Flanders, Principal Tutor to training teachers of the mentally handicapped in Leeds, found [118] that (during the temporary one-year conversion courses devised to enable two-year trained teachers to gain a full teaching certificate within three years instead of waiting for five post-diploma years) 'in every case the good teacher of the mentally handicapped showed herself to be a good teacher of normal children in spite of the difference in class size, organization, presentation and so on;

(b) preconceived notions about the desirability of teachers working in the first instance with normal children before experiencing the subnormal were rigidly adhered to by those responsible for the new organization and by those who were uninformed because of their own lack of experience, without any examination or research being undertaken about the possible contribution that could be made to normal education by those trained in a differently conceived structure—a structure constructed experimentally and imaginatively by educational enthusiasts in an 'ongoing challenging situation.'

(c) preconceived notions following the British system of teacher training* that students may not become educated 'if they study subnormality in depth and with intellectual rigour rather than say English Literature or History' [118] would mean that students did not have time to gain much more than a superficial cognitive understanding of mental subnormality.

Educational changes do not occur of their own accord, [23] and in my considered opinion, because I was completely involved, many of the changes that took place from 1960 onwards (though changes had been striven for by other devoted women long before this) were due to rather practical reasons, e.g.:

(1) The appointment of educationists by the National Association for Mental Health to be responsible for their courses from 1960 onwards.

(2) The appointment of an Honorary Educational Advisor, Miss Mary Lindsay (an ex-H.M.I.) to the above body, to whom the

---

* Which until now insists that every student studies a subject (some Colleges study two) in addition to those related to her future career as a teacher.

tutors could go to discuss their problems and their plans with some measure of confidence that someone knew what they were talking about.
(3) The increase in the number of courses approved by the Training Council (including the above) after 1964.
(4) The improved material conditions of the new and beautiful schools (however initially much criticized by educational administrators themselves still having inadequate buildings for normal children and adults in Further Education establishments after over half a century of public education for all) built by forward-looking health authorities.
(5) The influx into the work of YOUNG, intelligent, HEALTHY, energetic teachers trained to have positive attitudes towards the problems existing; to provide a wide variety of educational activities and to have higher expectations for the children; to look at children's needs rather than at clinical conditions.
(6) Techniques of training enabling students to learn that the ultimate aim of their training was to understand that the individual child needs systematic structured teaching, individual teaching (sometimes, but by no means always, with special teaching machines/aids), alongside a balanced, planned programme of stimulating, educational activities appropriate to the levels of the children and designed to arouse and maintain learning readiness.

Much of the training in England between 1960 and 1964 had initially to concern itself with promoting changes of attitudes towards the educational possibilities for these children, i.e. in demonstrating what they could do* and in helping teachers organize schools and classrooms for more active learning.

Direct observational techniques were also introduced into this form of teaching for the first time (cf. pages 127-129). It was a logical approach too, for no one could begin to consider training teachers to work systematically with individual children until the schools were freed of the rigid practices of the past,† patterns we can be sure reinforced apathy, behaviour problems and rigidity in the children for whom they were designed, often because of lack of opportunities to become otherwise.

Apart from those Tutors employed by the National Association for

---

* I have some slides in my possession showing how the children 'did drill.' They imitated the formal stereotyped drill movements of a 'teacher' as she stood in front of the class in the 'school' yard.

† In a little book called *Serving the Mentally Handicapped* the reader can gain some idea about how these practices came about.

Mental Health, the methods used by other Tutors in the country to train their teachers and to bring about changes in attitudes in the areas where they happened to function are largely unknown. This has led some to postulate that the methods were indeed not 'well thought out' or evaluated. In the next page or two I will try to describe some of the very broad techniques I deliberately used (even though some of them were most unpopular at the time) to change what I saw as a teacher entering 'this new world of different children' for the first time in the early 'sixties—what I saw, indeed, horrified me.* Was it the methods? Was it the impact of mental subnormality? I shall never know now for I have become accustomed to being with those who are severely subnormal and appreciative of those who work WITH them day by day.

Broad communication techniques [23]

(1) The creative work of severely subnormal children was exhibited by the students after each teaching practice for each other and for all the staff of the schools known to us. In this way teachers gained the concept that *everything* the child presented was valuable if looked at developmentally and that scribbles were of equal value to more recognizable representations. These exhibitions from 1962 onwards constituted the first attempts in this country to appreciate the spontaneous work of the children; to encourage mounting and display of children's work in the 'schools' in spite of shortage of materials. The exhibitions were carried all over the country to refresher courses until it was obvious that 'schools' had their own.

(2) Certain group activities, for example 'band', 'speech' (a period of ten minutes), 'rest' (for children up to nine), were compulsorily banned from the programme when our particular students were teaching. In this way we did *not* reinforce what we considered to be undesirable, rictualistic, meaningless activities.

(3) Students were encouraged to collect, and were shown how to use, waste materials for all kinds of creative work by my friend and colleague, Mrs. Pat Simpson, and how to make teaching aids by all concerned in order to make *some* kind of provision for the children in 'schools' where £40 per annum (sometimes a little more) was generally allowed for all educational equipment; where only £150 a year was available for equipment on the N.A.M.H. courses.

(4) Different groups of students practised in the same schools year

---

* And still does when these children are denied an experiential approach by teachers finding it easier to encourage the children to sit at tables with books/cardboard/wooden equipment like 'normal' children. These children cannot 'report' their boredom and may indeed be labelled "maladjusted" if they "rebel".

after year. The Headteachers themselves were then experiencing the wider range of activities considered appropriate (by skilled teachers willing to learn from the children) and the children's responses to these activities. Heads also began to discover that our particular approach to training teachers was dynamic in essence. As *their* attitudes became increasingly flexible and our experience grew, further ideas for the curriculum were introduced into the programme through our students.

(5) A request was made that the teacher of the class should not be present whilst a student was teaching. This meant a student had full responsibility for a class on the second day of her practice. It also meant that teachers (mostly untrained at this time) were prevented from discouraging students by negative intervention when they explored new methods with the children. It was our method of showing the students we had confidence in them. We supported them by presenting them and the Headteachers with detailed teaching practice notes (Appendix 6) on each occasion. These were developed as our students' understanding developed. We also supported them by *regular, long,* supervisory visits which they began to look forward to as they realized that we were there to help them to do a more competent job with the children they wished to teach. We did not go to assess teaching ability until students had had plenty of time to make mistakes, to practise their skills and until we had time *too* to get to know some of the problems they were faced with in the particular class they had in the final teaching practice.

(6) Heads of schools were finally invited to inspect the students' notebooks. In this way we were intending to involve them fully and actively in the teacher training process. In reading these notebooks they were assimilating and learning about the expectations we had for our teachers in terms of daily preparation and observational skills. They were also learning about the *reasons* for the particular curricula we introduced.

(7) Exhibitions of teaching materials and teaching aids made and provided by the students were held after each teaching practice. In this way useful ideas were continually shared and the viewers' imagination triggered off. These exhibitions were open to the teachers and Headteachers of all the schools for the handicapped and also to all the other workers in mental handicap in the area of our course.

(8) Each group of students on successfully completing and gaining their diploma was invited in structured, standardized, *individual* tutorials to criticize any aspects of their training and to make

suggestions for its improvement. In this way we added a new dimension every year to our training techniques based upon the students' evaluations. In this way the course was dynamic; we wanted students to feel that they had contributed positively to the growth of the course. It was a method for us of evaluating what had been offered to them over a period of time.

From 1964 onwards ideas were increasingly developed regarding the curriculum for the children. I must remind the reader that whatever was developed cost money and this was not always officially available. In introducing home economics for example, students in the first instance had to pay for the ingredients themselves; hence a student would buy one jelly for a whole class—it was her contribution for the week's experience of 'cookery.' As the Headteachers saw how much the children enjoyed these simple but necessary experiences, they themselves found ways and means to help students and then their own teachers obtain money to carry out the programmes we suggested. We also developed techniques aimed at encouraging students to want to work with individual children, and give students ideas about what to do with individual children (cf. pages 84–93).

The reader will have gained the impression from the previous paragraphs that contrary to the belief of some, some Tutors were in fact considering *most* seriously the kind of training teachers of the mentally handicapped should in fact be receiving. I have already said elsewhere (page 3) why the results of this training might not have been as successful as it should have been, or as we thought it was, though I have it on the best authority quite recently that some teachers with only normal training have been saying that they wished they'd had the kind of training we gave to our teachers. My students were always telling me this.

As far as one can judge from an informed position, teachers of the mentally handicapped need[25]

(A) Programmes that build up concepts of special education and promote positive attitudes.
(B) Training in particular skills.
(C) Specific knowledge about mental subnormality.

The following ideas are suggested for the way in which they build up concepts of special education and positive, caring, professional attitudes:

(1) *Informal and structured field work*
   (i) To have the serious problems of mental handicap in all its facets (home, school and society) ever present during the training period by ongoing contact with the mentally handicapped:

(a) in college;
(b) in schools, mental subnormality institutions, special care units for the profoundly handicapped;
(c) in their own homes and hostels; and
(d) through tape recorded question/answer type sessions with parents.

It is too easy to forget the real problems if the regular contact is omitted. It is too easy to think that these children are like the E.S.N.(M) child, or like infants attending first school, particularly if the kind and quality of their education is such that one tends to forget the lifelong nature of the *family* problem and the necessity for understanding mental health.

(ii) To have opportunities for supervised comparative exercises in child observation by visiting schools for normal children, residential schools, community homes, opportunity playgroups so that:
   (a) independent judgements may be formulated;
   (b) society's achievements and provision for children generally can be critically assessed;
   (c) they can make decisions about their own future role as adults in relationship to children;
   (d) intellectual curiosity in the problems surrounding the variable standards of care of children in society shall be aroused.

(iii) To gain knowledge about the skills of other workers in a practical way in order to make informed critical evaluations and to learn *the kind* of questions they need to ask (and the particular jargon to use) if children are to gain from the knowledge received by their teachers, e.g. the testing procedures of the psychologist, the case loads of social workers, the skills of the speech therapist and physiotherapist.

(2) *Involved and committed Tutors/Organizers/Advisory Teachers*

(i) To have lecturers who *make* the opportunities and *see* the possibilities in having personal contact with mentally handicapped children and their parents in a learning situation alongside their students and other workers. Such lecturers might more successfully be able to provide more than a conceptual approach and be able to link theory with practice in a realistic fashion; be able to demonstrate enthusiasm and warmth in their relationships with the handicapped; be able to share and receive ideas.

(ii) To have lecturers able to relate the main theories of child centred education and normal child development to the practice of the education of the mentally handicapped.

(3) Personal enrichment programme
  (i) To have programmes in creative subjects—drama, art, music, woodwork, home economics, outdoor pursuits, storytelling—to encourage inventiveness, imagination and spontaneity.
  (ii) To study in some depth all relevant aspects of physical education. This is considered to be one of the most important activities in the curriculum for the mentally handicapped. It therefore seems important that all their teachers should have an extensive knowledge and experience of the various aspects involved and the opportunities *to practise* the various aspects with people knowing *the mentally handicapped.*

(4) Self awareness
To have opportunities:
  (i) During training in small groups and individual tutorials to discuss their own needs and motivation to work with the mentally handicapped.
  (ii) To discover if they enjoy working with individual children in a one-to-one situation.
  (iii) For discovering their ability to work persistently and systematically with individual children over a long period of time *without becoming discouraged by the slowness* of progress or on some occasions the lack of any visible sign of progress.
  (iv) For examining the effect of the course on their own personal development.
  (v) For discovering that they can introduce new ideas that will with some kind of certainty be acted upon in future course structures.

(5) Progress
  Of seeing progress, however slight, take place in a mentally handicapped person taught by the student.

Professional skills deemed desirable
Competence, interest and enjoyment in the following:
(1) Observation, record keeping, assessment
  Being able to:
  (i) Observe behaviour in some detail and with some measure of objectivity.
  (ii) Use direct observation methods and relate them to known developmental scales in order to make some kind of systematic assessment of a child's current achievement. In training

observation skills (with some idea that one might finally try to relate what one observes to a developmental scale), one has to remind oneself constantly that some observed behaviour will not be specifically described on a scale but that if one jots it down as it occurs, it might indeed be seen to constitute a tiny step forward in a particular individual child's development; it might indeed awaken us to an order in development that we had not previously thought of before. One often finds those who train observational skills giving students/teachers/parents developmental scales in order to indicate *what* they are to look for. I prefer to help them record what they see and then use the scales later to focus their attention on the meaning (developmental-wise) of some of the observations they have recorded and to discuss the possible meaning of behaviour not particularly mentioned in scales.

(iii) Seek out/compile relevant tests to give to the children in order to find a starting point for teaching in a particular area (cf. page 117) and the possibilities for compiling tests using real objects and situations. It is perhaps important here to reiterate the words of Dr. Gunzburg[96] regarding the use of tests to find a starting point for teaching and to measure progress. 'Assessments must be carried out regularly and systematically with a view to *improving teaching efficiency* rather than to keep record files.' One of the very desirable qualities in any teacher working with the handicapped (perhaps with normal children too) is that the teacher should develop the skill of looking quite objectively, bi-annually at least, at the results of her work so that where results are minimal the teacher shall start asking herself why has this child not 'moved on;' why has this child not moved on as much as another child with the same degree of handicap and *not* compared with, as Dr. Gunzburg again writes, 'normal people?' 'Comparing the achievements of mentally handicapped children and adolescents with EACH OTHER is of far more pactical value to teachers than obtaining scores indicating the width of the gap between normal and subnormal attainments,' and again 'it would help the mentally handicapped child's development and the teaching effort in general if it were acknowledged that a mentally handicapped child can function on an *average* level of efficiency, that he can be *superior* and even more important that he can be *backward* when comparison is made with the average achievements of other *retarded people* of the same low intellectual level and age.'

(iv) Devise and use efficient methods of recording and storing cumulative information including photography, notebooks, tapes, audio/video systems, home/school diaries, etc. What we devise to keep such records will indicate our own thinking regarding the importance of whatever we decide to keep track of in terms of our own work with a child, the child's progress and the family problems.

(v) Profile strengths and weaknesses in order to construct programmes for individual children. I might add a word of warning here though for when we have done the necessary academic exercise to make a profile we still have to decide whether to concentrate on further developing the child's strengths or attempting to help him with his weaknesses. As Mary Lindsay was always saying in the various lectures she gave, 'teaching is always a matter of making skilful judgements.' Sometimes the decision is taken out of our hands and the child decides for us, that is to say, if we are sensitive to his needs.

(2) A variety of teaching methods

(i) Use structured play techniques (cf. Chapters 6 and 8).
(ii) Arrange social education programmes.
(iii) Apply and follow up the results of special methods such as behaviour modification techniques to VERY carefully selected children.
(iv) Practise *not* responding to negative behaviour.

(3) Involvement of other people

(i) Use classroom assistants effectively and constructively, finding out their particular gifts and exploiting them.
(ii) Confer with other specialists in diagnosing specific difficulties and arranging treatment whilst maintaining some degree of independent judgement, e.g. in deciding to use modified versions of unproven formal techniques such as those used by Delacato, Peto, Paget Gorman Sign System.
(iii) Enlist the active planned cooperation of parents in the education of their children and find ways of supporting the family.
(iv) Use specially selected volunteers—those who are not just curious but who want to give a long consistent period of service to these children.

(v) Confer with research workers and using direct communication* techniques, encourage them to spell out their findings in simple terms, encourage them to appreciate your contributions.

(4) Language development and teaching skills
  (i) Observe, interpret and respond to the meaning of non-verbal behaviour.
  (ii) Analyse and continually modify personal language behaviour to increase effective communication and to increase and promote the use of stored *passive* language. Here I am suggesting that we can train the skill of listening to our own language structures, the words we use, the length of our sentences, the speed and velocity of our own speech. Language becomes so automatic a skill that any attempt on our part to consciously think about it as we are using it is a hard discipline—a discipline it would seem to me that we need to undertake even though we will fail on many occasions. Take for example our continued use of the words 'it', 'they', 'them' in daily conversation. Perhaps we need to think of substituting nouns in place of these words, particularly in the child's early stages of acquiring language—a very difficult habit to acquire as adults.

(5) Concern with equipment
  (i) Design, construct (or make attempts to involve others who can) and evaluate effective teaching aids. Headteachers might decide to give responsibility posts to imaginative teachers who can help colleagues think about this aspect of education. Too few special education teachers at the moment have the habit and concept that some of their preparation will concern itself with the collecting of suitable teaching aids and cataloguing them in such a way that they are immediately available to them the minute they need them. Whilst the making of teaching aids was very much a part of training in the past, little time was available to evaluate its use in more objective terms. School Council projects might begin to do this now, e.g. look at *new* material and the children's response to it.
  (ii) Use resource centres to provide children with the best available commercial materials and influence educational suppliers.
  (iii) Gain the cooperation of engineers, engineering departments and Art and Design Departments of Colleges to design and produce special equipment for a group of children and even for an individual child.

---

* Just tell them you do not understand this/that.

(6) Community education
   (i) Disseminate knowledge about the mentally handicapped to lay groups and other professional groups in the community by lectures, kits available from MIND, exhibitions of dance, art, films, slides, etc.
   (ii) Distribute written information explaining the activities of the school to the immediate community around the school.
   (iii) Become concerned with the PREVENTION aspects of mental subnormality.

Knowledge of mental subnormality
The following is an amended outline of the content of theoretical knowledge deemed necessary and initially compiled by me for a particular College of Education course at Main Level (6-8 hours weekly over three years).
(1) The causes, identification and classificatory systems and prevalence of subnormality.
(2) An outline of genetics and physiological study of the central nervous system and the brain.
(3) Recent advances in the experimental analysis of behaviour (profiling, the sequence of early learning, measurement of social skills, knowledge of deviations and similarities in learning).
(4) The application of educational and psychological research to the management of the mentally handicapped.
(5) The structure and acquisition of language. Speech and language disorders. Language stimulation. Non-verbal communication.
(6) Principles of education relevant to the mentally handicapped and curriculum development with special reference to:
   (a) children under five;
   (b) adolescents;
   (c) hyperactive children;
   (d) the physically handicapped;
   (e) children with sensory defects;
   (f) the emotionally disturbed;
   (g) mongol children.
(7) History of the legal aspects of subnormality.
(8) Sociological aspects (public attitudes, the problems, attitudes and mental health of the families of the mentally handicapped, rearing practices, and the role of the handicapped member in the family and society, the role of the teacher, problems of institutional care, the role of the voluntary societies).
(9) Comparative studies in the education of the mentally handicapped (this would include the systems and attitudes current in other countries).

It will seem impossible to the average reader at any rate that the special needs of the teachers as I have outlined them can be satisfied in the present system of initial teacher education in this country (or in the proposed new structures envisaged in the James Report). The experiences of those more recently concerned might have helped them to reconsider the presumed inadequacies of present courses and work towards a *two-year* professional training after a two-year general course of education for, as Cyril Cave expressed to a study group of psychologists organized by Professor Clarke in 1971, 'any recommendations that diminish the professional skill of the teacher of handicapped children will render a poor service to special education.' They will indeed.

In 1971 Mr. Cave reported to a particular group of professionals that In-Service training courses for teachers of the mentally handicapped were increasing in number, particularly those organized by Local Education Authorities. The experience I have had as a freelance lecturer since that time (1972–4) does not give me the impression that these short courses are now either often enough; as well structured as they might be (of course there are always exceptions); or that any attempt to evaluate the effects of the short courses is being carried out by those organizing them; being seriously considered in the financial estimates of the committees concerned. In fact there even seems to be some verbal evidence at least that there have been cut-backs already in some places and that specialized courses for teachers of the mentally handicapped are in fact being discouraged from 'high' places.

Although medical research is always advancing our knowledge about mental subnormality, there is very little evidence that the teachers (those specially trained and those who have 'come in' from normal education) are in fact receiving up-to-date lectures on the medical and preventive aspects of mental subnormality—this might reflect attitudes on the part of all those organizing short courses, suggesting:

(a) that such knowledge is not relevant for teachers (Appendix 6);
(b) that they (the organizers) have not the time available to become knowledgeable themselves sufficiently to guide the doctors/thepsychiatrists to give the teachers what they are currently needing;*

---

* I remember Dr. Cunningham of the Royal Albert Hospital, Lancaster, telling me as a new Tutor in 1961 to TELL him what I wanted him to lecture to my students about. Of course I could not do this until I had read several books on subnormality. He was wise in his instruction for of course he was the one to give the lectures, and students trust the knowledge of real specialists more than 'book' specialists, but in deciding on the topics I had to acquaint myself with the material.

(c) that they believe there are few doctors able to explain in sufficiently clear terms to teachers the phenomenon of mental subnormality.

Whilst the annual refresher courses organized by the National Association for Mental Health from 1962 onwards were mostly educationally oriented, a week of study ALWAYS included one, sometimes two, lectures by outstanding doctors in mental subnormality. It is of vital importance for both professions always to get together on such occasions. They have so much to give each other in influencing one another's thinking about the problems inherent in the situations likely to occur.

Some of us feel that many mistakes were made in 1971 when the courses as we knew them were so undemocratically and drastically changed to conform to other kinds of teacher training and when there was little evidence that the NEW course would provide the 58 per cent deficit* of teachers needed. Some of us might possibly like to see the 'clock put back' for as Dr. Ravenette said† 'we found that the best way of getting good teachers to work in the former junior training centres was to take them in for two years without training and then *if they liked the work* (the italics are mine) to second them for training. I think that this is still the right way to go about it because the special schools for the severely handicapped are indeed very special.' [117]

Compromises will have to be made if the mistakes some of us feel were made are to be rectified and if the children are to get the special kind of teacher they need. These compromises might include:

(1) More opportunities for an extra full-time course devoted entirely to professional training along the lines that have been suggested for those presently receiving three-year training with mental handicap as a Main/Optional subject. This course might be taken after say one or two years of practical experience or as a post-training one-day-a-week course.

(2) Compulsory *examinable* Summer School Courses designed and examined by well-informed professionals (and these will include some of the outstanding teachers from the two-year courses) for all those wishing to advance professionally in this sphere of education—there is plenty of space available in the summer time in our Universities for such courses and there seems no reason why teachers ultimately wishing to seek personal advancement should not contribute a small nominal fee to attend such a course.

---

* Forty-two per cent of the teachers were qualified.
† Study Group 5, Institute for Research into Mental Retardation, 1972. Ed., P. Mittler.

(3) Seminars for external examiners to courses so that they can work together to understand the high quality of teaching that should be and can be expected; to establish common standards of professional conduct in this particular sphere of special education; to ensure as far as possible that these standards are demanded on all courses; to share ideas on new methods of training teachers. It is not my impression that a tradition yet exists of external examiners meeting to discuss their findings and their problems in a field of education that needs as much sharing of ideas as possible. Perhaps one or other of the present research organizations in England might initiate such a seminar on a regular basis.

One question that remains to be seriously examined is whether the mentally handicapped in England are to receive education or the special education to which our efforts have been directed over a long period of time. If they are to receive the latter and by this I mean skilled, *planned, individualized programmes with parent involvement* then they need:

(a) teachers with professional training that is different in many respects from that received by teachers of normal children unless we subscribe to the equal rights of all children to have prescriptive education;

(b) teachers wanting more than promotion (without special training) or a transitory experience of these children;

(c) teachers known to have conscientious, painstaking qualities.

My own deep involvement with teacher education in full-time training, In-Service work and special seminar work in the University of Manchester can only lead me to conclude that all specialized courses should be as unrestricted as possible by rigid regulations and fixed time-tabling arrangements, for they need to afford those running them opportunities to be imaginative, to reflect, to be spontaneous, to innovate and experiment, for these are the features most likely to be of value to them in thinking about the education of the mentally handicapped and of the methods to use in training their teachers. I see no reason at all why much of the time spent in study groups and on short In-Service courses should not be organized so that *all* concerned (those organizing and the organized) will be involved with the mentally handicapped themselves for *they really* are the best teachers of what is needed if we take the trouble to look.

Authors note. Many of the ideas in this chapter have been taken from papers I was invited to present in England (ref. 28, 24) in Warsaw (ref. 23) and Denmark (ref. 25).

Appendix 1
Suggested activities for stimulating very young handicapped children and some of those in special care units

These can be extended by using the Uzgiriz and Hunt Scale.
(1) Play with child with your own fingers. Touch him. Play with his fingers. Hide fingers. Hide hand.
(2) Bulge out your face and burst your lips. Let child feel. Use facial expression.
(3) Light a match or (safer) shine a torch and see if eyes follow. Play daily with this. Hide the light. Reveal it again.
(4) Play at hand gestures.
(5) Play with a handkerchief, carrying out all kinds of activities with it.
(6) Hang toys (which make a noise when touched) immediately in front of child's vision if lying down.
(7) Suspend toys near feet so that child has to try to stretch out to touch them.
(8) Comb your hair closely in front of child. Put on cream, lipstick, etc., using a mirror. Wear a hat.
(9) Pull out tongue.
(10) Wear a poppet necklet.
(11) At one and the same time hang a toy which makes a noise and a handkerchief on to a piece of string or elastic near the child's reach.
(12) Sing daily and keep a record of songs sung.
(13) Give child different objects to handle—paper, tissue paper, shiny paper, cardboard tubes, cloth toys, plastic toys.
(14) When toys suspended in front of child move them with a long stick from different angles.
(15) Hang ribbons of different colours.
(16) Have a range of different sounds, e.g. bell in a ball, stone in a safe tin.
(17) Play with sound—the sounds in front of/behind/at the side of the child/a long way from child/near child. Call to child from different positions in room.
(18) Carry or wheel child to several different positions in the room in any one day.
(19) Play with a pan and a lid.
(20) Get a stick and play at tapping different objects in front of the child, behind/near/far/etc.

(21) Get a cover and put over child. Repeat and respond to his actions. Now put over your head for him to pull off, over and over again.
(22) Place small objects on palm of child's hand. Play giving and taking, or just putting object on palm if child lets it go.
(23) Encourage child to grasp different fingers on your hand. Bend one, waggle one, poke thumb, etc.
(24) Play with a bandage. Let child pull it out. Repeat with small ball of string.
(25) Introduce bits of brightly-coloured material on a string. Blow at them through a tube, or fan them.
(26) Play at opening and closing your fists in front of the child.
(27) Put a mirror in front of a child. Fix to table if sitting in a chair.
(28) Pencil/stick. Play holding games.
(29) Introduce soft collar and belt.
(30) Rattles.
(31) Put doll near mouth. Put other safe toys near mouth.
(32) Put objects on child's chest.
(33) Give child unfamiliar objects to explore with mouth.
(34) Play with a tobacco pouch.
(35) Watch (large pocket watch if possible). Dangle and hold in all positions.
(36) Solid objects, e.g. spoon.
(37) Watch and doll. Put in all positions together and apart.
(38) A roll of tinfoil.
(39) Present a bulky and large object, e.g. a very large parcel of newspaper.
(40) A small solid object, e.g. india-rubber (care, safety).
(41) A chain.
(42) Cardboard roll.
(43) Keys on a ring. Key (large).
(44) A case.
(45) Dolls suspended on a string in a row in front of child. Swing dolls for child, with hands/with stick.
(46) Dolls suspended in a row near feet. Put at different heights.
(47) Attach string to the child's wrist going to objects suspended, e.g. dolls, cloth, tins, rattles (vary it). Do same with other wrist, then on both. Then on one ankle, etc.
(48) Attach a string to the string holding suspended objects (which makes a noise). Put near child's face. If nothing happens put string in hand of child (or even tie it).
(49) Use the sound experiences (page 93).

Appendix 2 A teaching notebook as an aid to observation, assessment and systematic work with individuals and groups

A soft-backed spiral-ringed notebook 12⅛ in. × 8 in. (308 × 203 cm.) seems to be a useful and practical size.

Suggestions
1. Number all pages in the right-hand corner. First page to contain name of class teacher.
2. Set aside a number of pages at the back of the notebook for recording the following:
   (a) A ruled out chart to indicate the dates you work with individual children; the numbers of turns you give them. Aim to work each day with three children in a planned systematic way. The chart should help you.
   (b) Individual work with each child. Brief notes *before* and after teaching. Each child to have several pages for such an ongoing record.
   (c) Stories told and aids provided. Specific reasons for telling a story. Date.
   (d) As for (c) regarding songs.
   (e) A broad outline of the programme, i.e. timetable.
   (f) Plans for Mother's Work tasks (if children under 10):
           Cookery
           Other home economic plans.
   (g) A page ruled with following columns:

   Date   Visit Individual Group Followup. Describe model Frieze. Talking (recorded on tape-recorder) Music. Drawing. Drama Movement.

   (h) Brief note weekly on the contents of home/school diary.
   N.B. Visits **out** of school are probably amongst the most vital on the programme. Try to see them in terms of language stimulation programmes. This means you have to work hard on the language during the visit. Don't always expect the children to use their own expression until they return. Helping them to represent their real experience is one of our most important tasks.

APPENDIX 2

3. Third and every following page cut off 2 in. (half-way through notebook)
   Columns on second and third pages
   Page 2

Name of child	Age	Birthday	Age of Mother Father	Siblings	Length of stay in hospital/school	Hearing aid
Spectacles	Sedation	Menstruation	Voice Broken		Shaving	

   Page 3

Draw a man Description	Eye Dom.	Handedness	Footedness	Height Weight	Special Abilities

   Special Weaknesses

   Pages 4, 6, 8, etc., will contain brief *daily* observations on each child.
   Pages 5, 7, 9 will contain the intended daily plan.

Possible model for intended daily plan

A. *Free choice* Aims
   Preparation N.B. It is not necessary to indicate the actual activities here or the materials. The additional materials will be recorded against line one. See Point 4.
B. *Names of individual children to have systematic work:*
   1.
   2.
   3.
   The preparation will be written up in another part of the notebook.
C. *Detailed preparation* for *two*/ more of the following group activities:
   1. Music   4. Home Economics
   2. P. Education   5. Outdoor studies
   3. Story   6. Visit
   according to the stage of children's development.
   The preparation should include a statement of what you intend the children to learn and a statement of objective/goal, content, methods, aids.
   Comments. Daily or weekly evaluation.
D. *Specific work for classroom assistant:*
   (1) with individual children
   (2) with a group
   (3) making aids
   (4) tidying/mending.
At the bottom of page 2, six lines could be left for the following headings:
Line One. Teaching materials added daily. Purpose.
   Two. Assessment of child's levels in various areas.
   Three. Interesting language heard.
   Four. Mother's work or jobs (Language intended to be introduced).
   Five. Outstanding event of the day.
   Six. Other information considered useful.
The above forms a continuous record which is easy to link to:
   (1) The observation records;

(2) The intended plans for each day.

Teachers will not be able to use everything the child 'gives' so it is necessary to keep on referring back to previous records. If this is carried out conscientiously and the teacher becomes skilled in observation she will find that her own records will help her in formulating a programme for whichever group she has.

The written entries on the above lines 1-6 should be on pages 4, 6, 8, 10, (even numbers).

4th page heading

First impressions of each child from own observation. 6th, 8th, 10th, 12th, etc., pages contain the daily recorded observations about each child.

5th Plans for following day.

Pages 5, 7, 9, 11, 13, and so on contain no ruling across. These pages might contain the intended plan (see above) for each day based upon the recorded findings re the individual child/the group on the opposite page.

As the teacher records *some detail* of a child's activity response in specific terms she might underline in red the activity which might be followed up in an individual session or group activity the following day.

Records on individual sessions

Records of sessions with each child should be continuous. Use several pages for first child and then another few for the next and so on. Some of the sessions with individual children should have a creative element in them.

Once such a notebook is ruled out the teacher should find little difficulty in filling it in. Records and plans of one kind or another are a necessary feature of all teaching. Whilst experienced teachers might very well be motivated to keep their own daily 'rough' plan notes and records of the children, younger teachers or those new to teaching this group of children will find a value in keeping a notebook such as the one described, for it will encourage a systematic orderly approach to their work.

Appendix 3 Play as a two-way communication theme

A. *Theories of play*
    Surplus energy
    Instinct practice
    Relaxation
    Recapitulation of the history of the human race
    Safety valve
    Assimilation.
B. *Forms of play*
    Looking and reaching towards objects (enactive level, Bruner)

Manipulation of objects
Sensory motor play
Gross body play
Imitative:
(a) immediate without intention
(b) after a delay (short, longer, longer time)
(c) with intention of an incomplete/complete sequence of seen actions (iconic level, Bruner)
Representational symbolic play, e.g. uses a stick to 'fish,' play golf, play billiards, uses screwdriver as a medical syringe
Reconstructing life activities with small more real size objects
Imaginative, dramatic, role play (cf. Appendix 4, 7–8 years)
Constructional. Making something and playing with it, e.g. I saw a boy in a mental subnormality hospital make a fishing line from bits of Meccano and string and then act out fishing
Use constructional materials both large and small to construct something to play with.

C. *Development in play*
Play alone in the pram
Play with an adult (cf. Appendix 4, 12 months)
Solitary play
Spectator play—child spends time 'looking'
Parallel—alongside another child but not with him
Associative—very fleeting periods of play in a group (perhaps in two's)
Cooperative—more sustained play with another child building with bricks, playing ball
Group play with no specific known result in view for the group, e.g. going on a slide, waiting for a turn on the climbing frame
Group play with a definite aim, e.g. table games, role play, tag, hide and seek
Group play with firm rules, e.g. football, that can be understood

D. *Some skills in thinking of play as communication—non-verbal/verbal*
Interesting the child in sounds/sound strings and inflections, his ability to steer the adult to carry out his wishes
Talking relevantly to/with the child
Making *positive* use of the child's actions and activities
Knowing how to present materials to the child
Innovating with anything at hand
Interpreting the meaning of the play to others
Recording observed spontaneous behaviour in some detail to compile assessment reports, to provide aids, toys appropriately to meet the play needs of the children, to note the changing quality of the play activities (cf. page 47 onwards)
Meaningful involvement.

E. *Attitudes*
Positive, curious about why children play, involvement, being uninhibited in the play situation, acceptance of play as a vehicle for learning.

These notes forming the theoretical basis for play workshop discussion amongst teachers on In-Service Training courses were compiled from my own involvement in children's play, preparation notes for lectures and observations, and from the following books:

Child Psychiatry. L. Kanner, 1948. Blackwell Scientific Publications, Oxford, Second Edition.
Modern Perspectives in Child Psychiatry, Ed. J. G. Howells, 1965. Oliver and Boyd, Edinburgh.
Children Growing Up, J. Gabriel, 1965. University of London Press, London.
The Psychology of Play, Susan Millar, 1968. Penguin Books, Harmondsworth, Middlesex.
The Origins of Intelligence, J. Piaget, 1966. Routledge and Kegan Paul, London.
Towards a Theory of Instruction, J. S. Bruner. Harvard University Press, Cambridge, Mass.
Fantasy and Feeling in Education, R. M. Jones, 1968. Penguin Papers in Education, Harmondsworth, Middlesex.

Appendix 4   Development of normal socialization

A process of adaptation through learning and following a pattern, viz:
  Complete dependence—babyhood
  Dependence—pre-school
  Growth of independence—first/middle school
  Mutual dependence—adolescence
  Independence—young adulthood
  Balance between dependence/independence—adulthood.

4 weeks	Watching mother.
6 weeks	Infant smiling. Indiscriminate smiling.
2 months	Response to human glances. Vocalizes.
3 months	Returning glance with smiling and cooing. Excited if shown moving toy.
4 months	Expression of displeasure if adult stops playing. Smiles at mirror image.
5 months	Likes and dislikes of food. Looks to see where cube has gone.
6 months	Actively seeks contact. Prattling, holding out arms. Distinguishes between angry and friendly tones.
7 months	Imitation beginning. Expectation in response to repetition of stimulus. Attracts attention by cough.
8 months	Responds to 'No.'
9 months	Becomes accustomed to friendly stranger. Understanding gestures. Attempts to hold on to adult's clothes.
10 months	Waves bye-bye; plays pat-a-cake; claps. Peek-a-boo.
11 months	Drops toys deliberately to be picked up.
12 months	Organized play with an adult. Growing ability to form lasting

18 months	relationships with others. Fear of strangers (range 25–50 week individual differences). Has sense of 'me' and 'mine.' People are a hindrance to his activities (usually forbidden). Interrupts activities to notice newcomers. Cries when they leave. Likes to be shown picture books.
2–3 years	Helps by fetching and carrying.
3–4 years	Helps in domestic tasks, e.g. clearing table, sweeping, dusting.

Interaction with children of same age

6–8 months	Other child treated as an object.
9–13 months	Tendency to fight. Will roll ball to another child.
14–18 months	Interest in other child. Social use of playthings. Taking toys away very roughly. *Solitary play.*
18 months–2 years	More social contact with a child if toys present. Games increase in number between children. *Solitary play.*
2–3 years	Child able to maintain active contact with one child at a time. Imaginative play. No rules in play. *Solitary and parallel play.* More aware of others. Taking turns on slide, swing.
3–4 years	Beginning to play fleetingly in groups. Staring when someone is hurt.
4–5 years	Rules change rapidly. Objects represent what is in child's mind. Groups of 3–4 children play. Can get a desired response from other children. Plays competitive games, e.g. tag, hide and seek, hopscotch. *Associative play.* Beginning to give sympathy. Reaching to others' distress. Enjoys entertaining others.
5–6 years	Plays simple table games. Games requiring taking turns. Observing rules. Dominoes. Tiddlywinks. Beginnings of *cooperative play*. Rivalry seen. Acts out stories heard.
7–8 years	Participates in pre-adolescent play. *Group play.* Boys engage in games with loose rules, unorganized football, floor hockey, follow the leader. Girls dramatic play symbolizing dramatic or social situations, e.g. playing house, school/doctor nurse, shop.
8–10 years	Growth of peer group activity. Brownies, Cubs, Clubs, team games, clubs with passwords, initiation ceremonies. Growth of ideas of competition (copied or natural).

Mutual dependence

(a) *Boys*

10–16 years	Individual 'best' friends but also groups. Mingle easily.
12 years	Lots of friends.
14 years	Whole gangs of friends. Sport main interest.
15 years	Beginning of dating.

(b) *Girls*

12 years	Have best friends. Some tend to have temporary difficulties in friendships. Tend to be critical.
14 years	Boyfriends. Dating.

Independence

18–20 years	Assumes personal responsibility. Directs own social affairs.
20–25 years	Assumes responsibilities beyond own needs. Contributes to support of others, 'is good to neighbour,' shares in the responsibility of others.
25+	Contributes to Social Welfare of others. Altruistic. Inspires confidence. Relied on in times of stress. Promotes Civic Progress. Contributes to public welfare of others. Has wide recognition.

Compiled in preparation for an In-Service course (June, 1973) by me from a variety of sources, including books by Gessell, Illingworth, Doll, Buhler, Gunzburg, National Extension College material (Cambridge), Muller, Ilg and Ames.

A number of useful developmental scales are in the process of being devised by the National Children's Bureau, 8 Wakley Square, London EC1V 7QE. These cover all areas of development between 0–5 years and 5–9 years. Whilst it would take a teacher a long time to complete the observational records in their present form, the points themselves reflect the kind of features we should be seeing in children's behaviour between 0–2, 2–5 and 5–9.

Another developmental scale which appears to be gaining some interest in this country since the mentally handicapped came under the education umbrella is *The Developmental Potential of Pre-school Children*, Else Haeussermann (1958), Grunwe and Stratton, New York. This looks at children between 2 and 6 years. The manual and materials are expensive but they can be obtained from the Methodist Bookshop, Sheffield.

Two useful scales of motor development compiled by Beth Stevens (U.S.A.) appear in the publication for the Copenhagen Seminar, 1973 (address, page 45). A third but more comprehensive general scale is used at the Cerebral Palsy Ryegate Assessment Unit, Sheffield.

An enterprising teacher at Heritage House School, Halders Road, Chesham, has compiled her own useful observational scale.

One of the difficulties of the future will not be that the teacher/nurse/parent has too few scales to work from in order to do a more competent job, but that she will need guidance to be able to select well from the mass of data being produced. Another difficulty might arise from schools using different observational scales, particularly if a child transfers from a school in one part of the country to another.

Appendix 5 Rates of Development in Educationally Subnormal (Severe) Children

Whilst the use of the I.Q. score as a predictor of future development has been largely discredited (at least in the last decade), the concept of rate of development is useful, particularly to young or inexperienced teachers, and to other adults concerned with children.

I.Q.'S OF EDUCATIONALLY SUBNORMAL (SEVERE)

AGE	30	35	40	45	50	55
	M E N T A L A G E S					
6	2·3	2·6	2·9	3·0	3·6	3·7
7	2·6	2·9	3·1	3·5	3·9	4·1
8	2·8	3·1	3·5	3·10	4·3	4·7
9	2·10	3·3	3·9	4·2	4·8	5·1
10	2·11	3·4	3·11	4·6	4·11	5·6
11	3·0	3·4	4·0	4·6	5·2	5·9
12	3·0	3·5	4·1	4·9	5·5	5·11
13	3·0	3·8	4·4	4·11	5·9	6·6
14	3·3	3·11	4·9	5·6	6·3	7·1
15	3·7	4·5	5·2	5·11	6·9	7·6
16	4·6	4·11	5·11	7·0	7·7	8·4
17	4·10	5·7	6·3	7·4	8·0	8·9
18	5·3	5·11	6·9	7·6	8·3	9·0

This chart was compiled for the many groups of teachers I have lectured to since 1972 on In-Service training courses. The idea of presenting the material in this way was mine. The material is taken from *Stanford-Binet Intelligence Scale*, M. Terman and Maud A. Merrill, Third Revision, 1960, Harrap and Co. Ltd. If for no other reason such a chart is useful for it can form the basis of meaningful, sometimes controversial discussion.

Appendix 6 Early attempts to evaluate teaching skills and initial suggestions to teachers for teaching practice assessment

Handed to a University Lecturer and to a College of Education Lecturer in Special Education in 1963, both helping me to assess a student's teaching ability.*

On meeting a student please ask to see:
(a) The teaching notebook;
(b) The observation of children notebook.

Each student has been given detailed instructions about the keeping of these notebooks. Helpful and encouraging comments and suggestions should then be written for the student concerned. Negative comments would be better left off the actual notebook and reported to the Tutor in confidence. Any difficulties which the student is having in the centre should be reported at once to the Tutor. It is suggested that a teacher of the handicapped will perhaps be successful to the extent that he/she is able to develop along some of the following lines:

(1) Is the student making an attempt to provide each child with something that is helping him to develop?
(2) Is the student providing wherever necessary and allowing the children *to use* basic materials like sand, water, dough, plasticine, a variety of toys, paper, wood, etc?
(3) Is the student able to discuss generally many of the children in the group and comment upon one or two at a deeper level with some appreciation of the problems involved?
(4) Can the student work with an individual child in the 12-16+ group whilst keeping an eye on the rest of the group?

---

* Mr. Asher Cashdan, now Open University Senior Lecturer.
Mr. Steve Jackson (cf. Acknowledgements).

(5) If a group of children gather spontaneously round the student during an activity period can this situation be spontaneously met in a constructive and interesting fashion, i.e. by playing a game, looking at a picture, starting a news sheet, singing a song, telling a story?
(6) How does the student deal with the child who cannot attend to what she wants?
(7) What signs are there of the student building on what the children have given in speech, action or by bringing something of interest?
(8) To what extent is she *showing* the children how to use their materials—water, sand, paper, cloth.
(9) To what extent is she spending time teaching dressing, washing, etc., to those who need such instruction in the actual situation.
(10) How does the student cope with the toilet situation if expected to?
(11) Are there any signs of indirect teaching during breaks or at home time or on arrival (dressing, speaking, keeping noses clean).
(12) To what extent has the student been able to plan and execute a visit of some kind in the very near vicinity of the Centre? Visit to a pillar box, phone box, public convenience (older children), the Centre kitchen, visit to a shop with one/two or more children.
(13) In which situation was the student *aware* of difficulties and problems even if not able to cope adequately with them?
(14) To what extent is the student providing individual work for those over 16 years or for those who have possibly come from the E.S.N. Schools?

Classroom environment
(1) Is it stimulating?
(2) Does it have any of the following which the student has introduced or developed: shop, house corner, dressing-up box, newspaper to tear or cut, waste materials (to give sensory experiences, knowledge of the environment and stimulus for creative activities), puppets of many kinds?
(3) Does it have a developing nature table, exploration table, music corner, mirror, clock?
(4) Is there a small part of the room which is perhaps screened off, and which is not stimulating for the child who cannot work at a quiet occupation if there is too much stimulus around him?
(5) Is the student's reaction to a mess, to noise, to movement in the room a positive one or an anxious one?
(6) Has the student worked out a satisfactory method of clearing away, with the children's help, materials, etc., at the end of a period? In the case of those under 12 years, is she encouraging them to do as much for themselves as possible?
(7) Has the student made good use of the walls of the classroom for displaying the *children's* efforts?
(8) Has the student put up large sheets of paper or found a board for the children to scribble on spontaneously?
(9) Has the student set up a quiet corner for looking at books, magazines, pictures?

Please note:
Students have been informed that:

(a) assessors are looking for successful spontaneous and additionally well-thought-out reactions in the teaching situation and for the provision that has been made for the children in the group;
(b) assessors are not looking for success in class teaching except in those activities which demand a group that is ready for group teaching, i.e. in music, dancing, physical education and movement.

Students will be taking with them into the centres what I have called a 'Language Development Box'. This is to be used primarily with those children:
(a) who do not speak;
(b) who have little speech.

A collection of carefully selected pictures is also being made by students. Assessors could note if these are being used.

It might be useful for assessors to remind students to collect drawings, group pictures, news sheets, scrap books and any other work that the children do not take home, for the discussion on children's work at the end of the practical period.

Notes written spontaneously to guide staff supervising students on teaching practice (1968)

Ideas for the next teaching practice and notes to Tutors (1969)

Give *verbal* encouragement to individual students through the use of words like excellent, satisfactory, etc.

Your notes in students' notebooks should reflect, generally speaking, a critical evaluation of (a) preparation, (b) teaching appropriateness, etc. They should also give positive specific suggestions about arrangement and presentation of work. The words 'excellent,' 'good,' 'satisfactory' should perhaps only appear if *the reasons* for the judgement are specified by you; otherwise a student does not know WHY you consider it excellent, good, etc. If *you know* what the student has been taught, some of the written remarks are not necessary for she is only doing what is expected of her and not something original. In helping students on the next practice with individual work encourage them to use their observations made about the free play/choice situations and to lead on the teaching from the child's INTERESTS by discussing their observation notes. Please read the *Planning for the Individual Child* hand-out. I would like to see a balance between:
(a) structured activities and table activities;
(b) working from the CHILD's spontaneous interests;
(c) creative ideas.

Encourage much more recording of language and speech sounds (the crash course in phonetics might be useful here). Encourage more reading for reference purposes by suggesting *specific books* to students. Indicate books please, to enable them to understand better the following:
(1) Development in human growth.
(2) The handicap (medical/intellectual).
(3) Teaching of specific skills.
(4) The *arrangement* of materials for learning.

The students *aims* for individual children are not nearly specific enough. Not enough correction from Tutors about this, e.g. to encourage language instead of to teach 'a particular word.'

APPENDIX 6   275

Encourage much more use of:
(1) Sheridan Scale.
(2) Gunzburg P.A.C.
(3) Structured list of Activities and Special Care Unit List.
(4) Any one scale you favour. Please specify.
(5) Your own additions to the Structured List of Activities (please share) immediately.

Please carry them around with you as you go to help students.

The good student is always one step ahead in the arrangement of her notebook.

Comments might be made by you alongside some of the actual observations in order to indicate how a student should use them or what is being learnt.

Some students have not yet gained the idea of continuity from one individual session to the next. Help is needed with this. Much more verbalization (in your supervisory session with her) on the part of the student might be encouraged about WHY they introduce an activity.

Each student's notebook needs to be checked and specific ideas given by you and written down as far as possible on each visit.

Try to encourage students to think in *positive* terms about a child's behaviour all the time, i.e. question them about CHILD'S purpose, needs, diffculties rather than supporting records such as 'she is stubborn' without questioning and discussion. Relate behaviour to student's knowledge of child development. Help them to think about their *own part* in being on the receiving end of a child's behaviour:
(1) Are they thinking sufficiently about means and levels of communication?
(2) Are they thinking sufficiently about their own language?
(3) Are they looking to see if child has a specific difficulty in addition to mental handicap?

The attitude we should be encouraging is that *we* as teachers must work hard towards gaining and using the positive behaviour by being POSITIVE ourselves. Will you ensure that each student is understanding the concept of mental age, i.e. its slow rate of change as the child grows older. Check if they put column Mental Age. Some of them are obviously copying the M.A. *at the time of testing* and not bringing it up to date. Show them how to do this by referring to the Stanford Binet I.Q. tables.

Sometimes phrases/descriptions written by students denote:
(1) negative attitudes;
(2) personal attitudes which need modifying because student is still holding on to them and they will hold up development as a teacher;
(3) insufficient relating of normal child development to the mentally handicapped;
(4) lack of understanding of theory.

Ask students if they ever look back at their own records. Can we devise a means whereby they must refer back? *At the end of each fortnight they could make a summarizing report (based upon previous recorded observation) of what they have been attempting to teach.*

Much more correcting of points on child development needed. Use the students *own* experience with the children in relating it to child development.

In preparing for session with a very handicapped child, specific detail in records must be encouraged, e.g. 'holding objects' needs to be expanded to 'holding pan,' 'holding spoon,' and 'holding teddy bear.' Encourage student to see that in doing this she is recording the experiences *she* is giving the child. She can see what extra new experiences she needs to give.

Please talk to students in your Tutorial group about collecting data on test results and presenting it in such a fashion as to be useful not only in telling one about an individual child but his response compared to others in the class. In this way you are helping the student to see the meaning of the underlying theory in action and stimulating imagination, etc.

Discourage students from using subjective words/phrases in their notes like 'intrigued,' 'proud of,' 'seemed to enjoy,' 'is good at,' 'is fair at.' Encourage specific description at all times (see list).

Ticks only tell the students that you have read their work. They do not indicate how they need to be developing their thinking. They do not indicate how we are thinking as helping Tutors about the observations made by the teacher in training.

If the students give you a practical example of something theoretical, give them the appropriate theoretical term. In this way you are attempting to relate the theory to their experience all the way through the course, e.g. 'Susan was able to act out the events in the right order—.' *Word given:* sequencing.

Write down more questions about the records in order to extend the student's thinking as she reads them. Reflective exercise.

Give the student specifc reading and ask her to write notes on it which she may hand in for checking if she so wishes.

When students set out to do a specific piece of teaching please refer them all the time to what is known of the normal child's achievement as well as the subnormals. Make constant reference to the books on development, e.g. Beard, Brierley, Lovel, Gunzburg.

Verbal urging should be used sparingly with weak students. What *they* need is concrete and practical written suggestions. In this way their own thinking will develop with experience and as they gain in confidence.

Phrases which should be discouraged in students' observation records

Reasons:
    too subjective;
    tell you nothing really;
    just as easy to be specific;
    they might indicate student's personality; we project our own feelings on to others on many occasions—sometimes even on to the children.

really pleased	for ages
enjoyed	tendency to be bossy
to enjoy	slightly obsessed
intrigued	thrilled with
not very good at	gets upset at slightest thing
she follows directions well	quite a lot of patience
managed quite well	listened enthusiastically
fascinated by	for a while

loves
fussy
did so and so but then

very excited
for a long time
bossy

Guide to observation and making of reports (nursery schools)
You will spend the first day of your week settling in. The remaining four days might be spent in the following manner:

(1) Half-an-hour each day will be spent (at the same time of the day) observing the activities of a child of three who has few difficulties. You will record all that you see and hear as you do in our observation sessions in College. If the child comes to see what you are doing tell him you are just writing stories and encourage him to go away from you. Teacher might need to help you here. You will observe the same child each day.
(2) Half-an-hour daily observing the spontaneous response of the *adult* who is with the children. She might be the teacher or the nursery nurse.
(3) Helping in the nursery in any way you can.
(4) Making a collection of examples of children's work from all over the nursery. These should be mounted and labelled. A little information about the work and the child who did it might prove useful in future discussion.
(5) Collecting information about the following:
   (a) kind of area in which nursery is situated;
   (b) number of children; boys, girls; ages;
   (c) number of staff; training, experience;
   (d) methods of cooking dinners; serving dinners; menu for each day; any special method of coping with dinners;
   (e) toilet and washing facilities; methods; teacher anticipation;
   (f) the daily programme.
(6) Plan of nursery. Indicate outdoor provision and use of large apparatus and experimental apparatus.
(7) When observing plan of classroom arrangement of equipment and materials, note methods for storing.
(8) Description of teaching materials and equipment which interest you. Obtain information about where to order such equipment.
(9) Observation and report of three music and three movement sessions in the infant department. Describe any story-telling sessions in the nursery department. Try to record pattern of sessions.

In addition to your report sections, your report should contain a final paragraph—'The value of my experience in the nursery school.' (This should be on a separate piece of paper so that it and the report can be assessed by two people.)

Author's note. On both one-year and two-year courses (1961-71), students spent at least a week in a nursery school or a day nursery. On two-year courses students spent a week in the same class in each year of study. During the first week in the first year they had to choose one particular child to observe especially and then to follow up the child a year later. In this way students were seeing development in action as it were.

Visit to school for educationally subnormal (and/or other type of special school)

You will be attached to your school for the duration of your course. Usually you will attend for a full day each week on a Thursday, 9.30 a.m.–4 p.m. So that you can see the work on other days as well as on Thursdays you will spend three consecutive days in the school. During this particular three-day period you will help the teachers as much as you can and in any way they ask. They know our students. See as much as you can of the school and if you meet two children (boy and a girl) in whom you become particularly interested note their names and classes. (Make sure as far as you can that they will be in the school for the next two years.) When you go again you will be working with these children and beginning a two-year study of their development.

The aim of your weekly visits to a school of this kind is:
(a) to meet and talk to experienced teachers who will be interested in you and your work and from whom you will learn many things about teaching;
(b) to practise teaching Movement and Music to some of the classes when you have had some lectures in each subject;
(c) to learn how to work with two individual children;
(d) to study these two children.

During this first visit discover the following (do not ask questions about these on the first day):
(1) the plan of the school (make a plan);
(2) number of children in the school (girls and boys);
(3) number of teachers;
(4) names of the staff;
(5) number and kind of other types of staff;
(6) number of classes;
(7) kind of activities going on in the school.

N.B. If you have a school dinner remember to pay for it. I expect some of you will prefer sandwiches. Offer to pay for the cups of tea and coffee you have. At the end of each day write a short description of what you have seen on paper the size of one of your loose-leaf files. (This should be kept for reports throughout your course.)

Name the report 'First Report on Special School'
Name —
Hand it in by the following Monday. When it is returned place in your Course Report File. Please do not arrive at school on Thursday of this week before 10 a.m. Have a happy time there.

Teaching in the E.S.N. school

You are expected to arrange the teaching of Movement to a class or classes with the Headteacher or teacher concerned. Remember to change. Use the notes given to you. You will practise taking Movement for the next few months. If you can fit in Music and have some ideas, try that with a small group. If you are not sure, leave this subject until later in the term. You will be given sample lessons.

If you feel you are ready to work with one or two children this week tell the teacher and begin to teach one (alone) for half-an-hour. As soon as you have finished the half-hour with one child spend ten minutes writing up your notes on what you have learnt about him and what you have prepared and carried out. Then work with the second child and record your findings. Your notes should be written on a report sheet which you will keep in your special Course Work File. I shall be asking for these at half-term.

The main aim of the *first* session is to discover some of the following:
(i) The age of the child chosen.
(ii) The story of his family. You can get him to talk about it (tape recorder), to draw it, to model it in paper, card, clay. What is his life like at home?
(iii) His interest(s) in school. How can you encourage these?
(iv) His interest(s) out of school. How can you encourage these and follow them up?
(v) Can he write his own story (never mind the spelling at first). Ask him to write you a little story. Give him *five* minutes only. Be strict with the time. Praise whatever the child gives.
(vi) If he cannot write something without help give him something to copy, e.g. about himself. You will have to prepare some good printing on a card.
(vii) What he likes to draw.
(viii) What can he tell you about a picture (have one ready to show him).

In your *second* session with your child you can give him:
(a) a standardized reading test;
(b) a standardized spelling test;
(c) the Draw-a-Man test;
(d) follow up some of his interests from the first session.

(a) Prepare for this by trying to get a copy of *The Psychology and Teaching of Reading* by F. Schonell (Oliver and Boyd). You will find the reading test on page 92, and the instructions for giving and scoring the test on pages 94–9.
(b) The words for the spelling test are attached. You will read them slowly, one at a time and give *no help*. You go on until the child has spelt five incorrectly. Encourage him by your attitude.
(c) Have a piece of paper and pencil ready and give the instruction to the child 'Draw me a man. Make it the best man you can.' No further help must be given. When the child says he has finished, ask, 'Are you sure? Is there anything else?' Give him a minute or two and then take away the paper after praising his attempts. Do not suggest that he has missed out anything. Bring back the drawings to College and we can discuss and score the drawings together.

If the teacher *has* time to discuss your children with you see what you can discover about the child's levels and difficulties. See if you can discover what illnesses he has had, when he was admitted to the school, and where he came from.

Use the *third* session in any way to help or interest the child. Report what you do carefully and the reasons. If you take something or make something for a child describe it.

Date all reports.

A visit to a mental subnormality hospital

Summer vacation project
The purpose of your visit is:

(1) To see as much as you can of the life of the wards during the daytime—children and adults.
(2) To spend time during the evening joining in with and evaluating the activities of the patients.
(3) To spend no more than half day in the school if there is one.
(4) To see patients with rare clinical conditions* of subnormality, e.g. gargoylism, de Lange syndrome, epiloia, phenylketonuria, hydrocephaly, microcephaly and macrocephaly. This should be done in as unobtrusive a way as possible with the nurses' help. There should be no discussion about a child or adult within his hearing (cf. page 31).
(5) To understand the organization of a large mental subnormality hospital.
(6) To find out about the Mental Health Tribunals.
(7) To discover what arrangements are made to encourage parents, volunteers to play an ACTIVE role.
(8) To see if any interesting experiments are being carried out in the hospital to improve the lot of the patients.
(9) To see what developments are taking place in the area to enable more and more patients to be cared for in the community.
(10) To discover what the hospital staff feel about any changes that are taking place.

You are expected to keep a daily diary of your impressions and some detailed observations and an account of your own ACTIVITY during the week. Try everything. We should like you also to observe one person sufficiently to design and make something which would be useful to him. Make a copy of this and be prepared to:
(a) bring it into College;
(b) talk about why you made what you did and what value it was to the person concerned.

Mr. — and Mr. — will be discussing these with you.† Have an interesting time.

Baby visits–first year
You will visit your baby every fortnight throughout the year. If you miss a visit for any reason try to make it up at another time so that you do not miss a vital stage in the development of your baby.

Try to get a baby as young as possible. Ideally he should be less than a month old.

On your first visit get some information about the baby and his parents. Make this the first page of your book:
    Baby's name
    Date of birth
    Mother's name
    Mother's age
    Mother's occupation before marriage
    Father's name
    Father's age

---

   * A useful book of reference for clinical conditions is Robinson and Robinson's The Mentally Retarded Child, McGraw-Hill, 1965, pp. 3–272.

   † A form of In-Service training for the staff concerned. In listening to the students experiences they were learning too.

Father's occupation
Brothers or sisters (with ages)
Address
Type of house
Number of rooms upstairs and downstairs
Description of district.

On each visit you will be:
(1) Talking to the mother about her baby. She may tell you about the birth for example to begin with and later on will tell you all about the things the baby is doing, eating and saying ($\frac{1}{4}$ hour).
(2) Watching the baby and recording all that he is doing. Do this for 10–15 minutes and make sure that you are watching the baby while *he is awake*. You will not get much of a picture while he is asleep.
(3) Doing little experiments and tests with the baby. I will discuss this with you later and give you a list of things to do with your baby.

Each visit should start on a separate page. Write the age of the baby and the date of the visit as a heading. Under this heading write up the details of your visit in three separate sections:
(1) Observation of baby (while he is playing freely in a non-test situation).
(2) Baby's responses to tests (and here you must describe the test AS WELL AS the baby's response to it).
(3) Interview with mother.

Make your books attractive so that anyone can see without opening them that they are baby books. Try to get as many photos as you can of the baby at different stages, to illustrate your book. It would be better if you took these photos yourself so that you have exactly the type of picture you want. If you take a little time and trouble over taking pictures you may be able to gather a pictorial record in your book of how the baby sat, crawled, crept, walked, climbed the steps, etc., at different ages. You could also show the development of his manipulative skills. Use corners to fix your photos into your book so that they can be taken out if necessary. I may ask you all to bring a photo of your baby into College from time to time so that we can make comparisons between babies of the same age.

Remember. Your reception in the home of the baby will depend entirely on you. Not only should you be your charming selves, but also be enthusiastic about the baby and be willing to offer to help if there is time at the end of your visit. If you offer to baby-sit, the mother will possibly fall over you in gratitude (once she has established that you can be trusted with her treasure).

If you are well prepared and organized, you will arouse great interest in the baby's mother and she will be less likely to interrupt you during your testing session, but (and this is more important) you yourselves will get the maximum benefit from this experience.

Compiled by Olwen Gregory.

First teaching practice notes
(1) The approach during your teaching practice is experimental. We shall be looking at the following:
   (a) Your relationship with individual children.
   (b) Your ability to understand that 'the teacher must be a provider' and to act upon it.

(c) Your understanding and provision of an ordered, interesting classroom environment in cooperation with your fellow student(s). Two or three of you will be working with a group of children in one classroom. It is important that you begin to think about the following points as soon as possible:

 (i) Age groups of children you will be working with, i.e. 5-9's, 9-12+, 12-16's.

 (ii) Organizing the classroom so that you feel that your contribution will be recognized by your Tutors. Refer to books about a learning environment. There are plenty in the library. Your lecture notes on the environment should be useful here.

 (iii) Planning an active daily programme together for the children concerned. You will visit the centre beforehand. Consult your own programme. See notes on the programme in the Junior Training Centres.

You will experience the following during this particular teaching practice:

(i) The reasons for taking these children individually in order to assess (discover) some of their needs, and their level of development.

(ii) Teaching individual children, seeing what is useful, what is not.

(iii) The preparation of materials and aids and thinking needed *beforehand* to teach successfully and meaningfully.

(iv) Using simple tests and your own observation records as starting point for your teaching.

(v) The determination and concentration needed by you to work with individual children when other activities are going on around you in the classroom.

(vi) How to organise the group for Movement, Dance, Drama, Storytelling, Music, Cookery.

(vii) How to organize free choice sessions each day for the children and use what you observe in them to develop the children's interests.

(viii) The organization of outdoor expeditions.

(2) Method of working in two's/threes:

 (a) Together you need to prepare the environment for learning—at the beginning of your practice. You need to continue to provide for the children throughout the five weeks, by making teaching aids, finding them in the centre, looking around for interesting materials.

 (b) One of you will teach individual children throughout the day and take group activity (Music, Storytelling) at the end of the day. The other one/two will be responsible for teaching the other group activities. If there are two of you, you will alternate day by day teaching the group or working with individual children. This means that in the first week one of you will have worked with individual children on three days, the other on two days. In the second week it will be the other way round.

 (c) Group teaching (three of you):

  (i) Free choice—(both of you) preparing for it, (both of you) teaching the children whilst it is going on;

  (ii) One of you take Movement (the other can be writing up notes, observing the lesson in Movement, making something for the classroom);

APPENDIX 6   283

(iii)   Take Music, Drama, Cookery, (where appropriate). If there are three of you, you will arrange it a little differently. See example below. Those of you in three's please present a similar programme to me and to your individual Tutor before Christmas.

Examples.

	Monday	Tuesday	Wednesday	Thursday	Friday
1st week	Ho.	B.	Ha.	Ho. a.m. / B. p.m.	Ha.
2nd week	Ho.	B.	Ha. / Ho.	B. a.m. / Ha. p.m.	Ho.
3rd week	B.	Ha.	Ho. / B.	Ha. a.m. / Ho. p.m.	B.
4th week	Ha.	Ho.	B. / Ha.	Ho. a.m. / B. p.m.	Ha.
5th week	Ho.	B.	Ha. / Ho.	B. a.m. / Clearing away.	Half term

When you have finished with your own children you will consult the notes of your fellow student and continue to work with her child following up her preparation. In this way the children will have lots of turns. You do not stop working with individual children just because you have worked with the ones you are particularly interested in. If you are responsible for individual teaching either for a whole day/half day, do not help the other student(s) in any way, e.g. by tidying up, by supervising the children during a group activity. Continue teaching, planning, preparing for the individual child. Leave your partner(s) to get on with her/their own work with the group and you get on with yours.

(3) Testing and assessing. During the first three days you should carry out the tests. Try to devise one test for the children. We shall give you the others. Record some exact examples of speech. Make a chart showing the results of your tests for the whole class. Do it with your partner(s). Try to assess the children's level all the time. It does not matter if you are wrong. We want you to try to discover ways and means for yourselves of finding the children's levels. Note any particular difficulties you have discovered. Describe in your records. Do not be afraid to ask other people to help you in this assessment. If experts visit the Centre—doctor, psychologist, M.W.O., research worker, speech therapist—ask the Head for a little time to talk to them. This should be recorded. Have questions ready for them about each child.

(4) Individual teaching. The word 'teaching' should be thought about in very wide terms. It is intended that you should experiment with doing something actively, continuously and systematically with each child in the group. This might mean:

> playing with the child (and observing what he does), building bricks, dressing dolls, playing shop, playing with puppets. Reading to the child, talking to the child. Writing down a child's story, exactly as he tells it, or recording it if you have a tape recorder. Telling the child a story, looking at picture books, objects and talking about them. Making models in cardboard, clay or wood. Practising a skill, throwing a ball, etc., threading a needle, cutting with scissors. Matching objects, pictures, words, etc. Painting with child. Encouraging the child to talk about or draw about or make a model about something on the nature table. Helping a child to listen to a specially made tape-recording of his voice—of words or a story. Recognizing coins. Playing a table game such as dominoes, snap, etc. Giving a child special instructions. Showing a child how to use a particular tool, a piece of apparatus, the cupboard. Cooking or baking with appropriate graded steps and aids.

The individual work session should be planned in brief beforehand and *written up* beforehand too. It is not necessary to write an essay to show what you intend to do. Brief points only showing the specific work you will do should be recorded. As soon as you have taken the child you should underline in red the point you intend to follow on with in the succeeding session. This should be done each time so that we can see how your thoughts about continuity for each child develop in this first practice. Comments on the results should be written down immediately the child goes away from you. If you are quick-thinking you could jot down the next session's plans. Think about Ivor:

1st Session	Playing in and discussing Mr. N's. car
2nd Session	1. Continued the above
	2. *Introduced him to 'car'*
3rd Session	1. Continued with playing
	2. *Got him painting his own 'car'*
	3. Playing on the platform on castors with him
4th Session	1. Complete the painting of car
	2. etc.

Think about the other children in our practical group, consult notes. There can be no continuity if you do not look at the sessions which have gone beforehand and cast your mind back to what you did with the child.

Work should be based on:
(a) your own observation of the child's needs and assessment of his level (because of your growing knowledge of child development);
(b) the responses to your tests; whilst giving them you might see a child's difficulties and prepare an aid, an experience to help him;
(c) his natural interests which he might convey in his free choice sessions, his language, his play;
(d) what you have come to understand you need to teach the child; the list of structured activities will be useful here; consult daily.

Each session should last no more than 20 minutes. Be strict with yourself. It should contain:

(a) a follow-up of something observed;
(b) something from the lists of structured activities appropriate to the assessed level of the child which will be repeated and extended in future sessions;
(c) an interesting new experience;
(d) something continued from previous session; remember you have underlined it either in the comments, notes or in the list of ideas written out beforehand.

Points to help you. Have your Individual Teaching Day Programme pinned up on the wall so that you know when you are going to do it. It will also help us to see who is responsible for the individuals and the group on the day we come to see you. Duplicate it in your group teaching notebook. The length of each individual session will depend upon the number of children in your class. Working with four and doing the preparation (in the centre) will be very satisfactory. *Date* all your sessions with your individual child and state times also:

e.g.   7-1-70   Time started   10.15 a.m.   Finished 10.35 a.m.
                              10.00 a.m. – 10.45 a.m.

You will divide up the class into two or three groups for the purpose of individual teaching and for making a study of the children you are particularly interested in.

(5) Observation and recording.

One personal notebook. Writing in it should take no more than half-an-hour daily. This should contain:

(a) Your daily observations of each child. Register-like method. Brief. Examples of language and description of behaviour and activities. 2 lines per child going across half the page.
(b) A list of teaching aids made with reasons and responses of child(ren).

Date	Teaching Aid, Made/Bought	Reason	Response

This list could be started before you go to the training centre and then added to as you see the needs of the children. The response column would be filled in later.

One notebook between the group. To be filled in immediately the child is taught. This will contain the preparation (BEFOREHAND) for each child and the comments after teaching him. It will be owned communally so that it can be consulted by both of you. Notes made about any child in an individual session could be read by the other student(s). They might lead to a follow-up in the free choice session. By having one notebook you can discuss the contents and help each other to understand the principles about individual teaching.

Evening preparation. Looking for and thinking about teaching aids. Making teaching aids. Thinking about group activities, but not writing it up. Consider continuity again here too.

(6) Visits. These should be planned and taken together (one afternoon/one morning a week). Make quite sure that you inform the Head and the class teacher of your intentions beforehand. You need to prepare for the visit beforehand by going where you intend taking the children.

(7) Other points. Talk to each other in loud clear tones whenever you can about the activities going on in the room. Remember to pronounce your words very clearly. Remember not to talk about any child's personality in front of him to other adults. This latter should be noted throughout your teaching life. This point is stressed because it can easily be forgotten that the S.S.N. mght understand what you are saying.

During the next week or two you should be cosidering some of the following:

Purchasing and arranging your notebooks in consultation with your partner/- your tutor.

Buy soft-backed exercise books with good paper in them. We do not want notes in files. They are too heavy to carry around or to post if we need to.

Collecting a varied amount of waste creative materials.

Collecting and preparing boxes and tins for storing pencils, crayons, waste materials. Making some printing equipment.

Recording some simple tunes on tape. We might be able to help here.

Collecting everyday objects and pictures of objects for sorting, matching, naming, etc.

Collecting or making some attractive large pictures for storytelling, for cookery.

Making up three-quarters of your own stories based upon what you imagine the children's experiences might be. We shall be pleased to read these for language suitability.

When you meet the children try to weave stories about them and their lives—very simple events are important to children.

Duplicating pictures of simple objects for testing, naming, colouring, cutting out, etc.

Visit by Tutors and Lecturers. You will be visited throughout the practice by your Tutors and several Lecturers. They will ask for your notebook so always have it ready. They will watch you teach in a variety of situations. They are there to help you. You will feel nervous at the beginning. Think of the child/children, then you will forget. You will be expected to write a report on one child using your records. This will be on your return and before Easter.

We shall be pleased for you to keep a note of the difficulties you experienced during this teaching practice, as well as the benefits gained, because there were two of you working together.

College will be open on Monday and Tuesday nights for music sessions (piano, guitar), painting and Social Club. Please come in to make teaching aids. You can buy sheets of white paper for 2p, grey for 1p, for teaching practice charts. You may take material from the store, provided you ask. There will be plenty more when you return.

Remember we are always ready at hand to help you if you get into difficulties. Please do not hesitate to call upon us for help if you cannot see how these difficulties can be solved.

No grades will be given to you for this practice. We shall naturally tell you where you have done well, where you need help.

Notes such as these were given to students before each teaching practice so that the various points could be thoroughly discussed in small groups with Tutors. We encouraged students to be adventurous with the children; to seek professional help from us as they needed it. We never suggested that they were visitors in the teaching practice school with the implication in this phrase that they were there to do as they were expected. We expected them to bring about change in one way or another. Over the years we were not disappointed.

Final teaching practice
You will probably find it very useful to refer to all the previous notes about teaching practice as well as to all your lecture notes in practical subjects including Education and Child Development. As this is finals we want you to devise your own teaching practice notebook based upon what you have read, seen of other students notebooks and discussed for your last practice. Notebooks should:
(a) indicate your observation skills of individual children—remember to include language for each child; record sounds wherever you can too;
(b) show the link between what you observe and record (including language) and what you teach (i) the individual child (ii) the group, and what you provide in terms of creative materials and teaching aids;
(c) contain a record (half the notebook) of your planning for the individual sessions—brief but specific—(refer to notes handed out);
(d) contain a description of the teaching materials you take, MAKE and obtain from the centre and your reasons for such provision;
(e) your programme; please refer to your programme notes and think of the group you have in relationship to the terminology you use, e.g. you will not use the term 'mother's work' if you have a senior group;
(f) show clearly the detailed preparation you make for each group session; thus it is of little value writing that the children will move to records or sing songs; we want to know which songs, which records, the reasons for choosing them and an evaluation of their appropriateness;
(g) be soft-backed and no larger than 7in. × 9in. (18 × 23 cm.);
(h) indicate that you have discussed the children with the teacher from a variety of angles, e.g. if any child is having specific sessions in reading you do not ignore it completely; there should be some follow-up link with teacher's individual work.

Further considerations regarding notebooks
They should not contain odd slips of paper which fall out when we look at the books. Although they are working notebooks they should be attractive to look at and the writing should as far as possible be in uniform ball pen, i.e. items should not be in scribble or in pencil or coloured inks. Underlining in colour might be useful to indicate language.

The notebooks should not contain separate charts.

We should not have to se magnifying glasses to read your notes and we should not have to spend hours on them to gain the order of your thinking—so aim for brevity and clarity.

Please let the Head of the Centre see your teaching book *at least once a week*. Discuss this with her. She will not have a lot of time to spend reading it but it will give her some idea of what you are doing with the children in her school.

Visits from Tutors and External Examiner
You will all have several visits from your personal Tutor. In addition some of you will be visited by me and Mr. J. Ward, Dept. of Education, University, Manchester. (He trains the educational psychologists but he has been a teacher and he is very, very interested in the mentally handicapped child.) We shall be making brief visits to many students so that he can get an idea of general standards. Then he will be spending longer periods of time with specially chosen students. Your notebook should be easily available for he will want to see it.Unless he indicates that he wishes to talk to you (and this really applies to all Tutors too) please go on teaching as though we were not there (we know you will be nervous but think of the children and then you will forget us).

Dinner Duty
We do not expect you to do this more than once a week for you have to prepare for the afternoon sessions. Of course, if the Head needs you in an emergency this is different. If you do regular dinner duty in order to gain a free dinner this is your own concern—but remember there is a limit to energy and you need it to teach.

Lateness or absence
This should be reported to us immediately. If you will not be at the Centre on a particular day (illness or Centre outings) please let me know. I usually set out by 8.30 a.m. I will then inform your personal Tutor.

If you have any difficulties let us know. Remember we are here to help you. Best wishes.

The third and final teaching practices were carried out without a partner. In the years immediately preceding the Education Act (1970) some students were fortunate to have a classroom assistant on their last two practices.

Special care unit guide (2nd year; 8 supervised morning sessions)
Each time you visit:

(1) Observe the child for ten minutes wherever he happens to be. Detailed records.
(2) State what you are going to do. Remember you will be there for $1\frac{3}{4}$ hours with the child so you must plan for the whole morning.
(3) Describe each event in detail:
    (a) if you are going out—mention those things which may affect his response, e.g. weather, how he's dressed, what he's riding in/on, how you are dressed, where you are going, reactions of other people to him;
    (b) if you are in the special care room—mention what you are wearing, where he is in the classroom, upright, recumbent, and what is going on around him.
(4) State what you have made for each session—how you used it and the

response to it.
(5) Say how you follow up each session.
(6) If you can think of any piece of equipment that might help this child (even if you cannot make it) do a diagram explaining why you think it useful.
(7) Any other information from teacher, physiotherapist or Head.
(8) Remember to use your list of structured activities and special care list and the games you've played with your normal babies described in your own fortnightly reports.

Compiled by Olwen Gregory, 1968.

Special Care Units
During the second year of the course, students spend one half-day per week for a period of six weeks in Special Care Units, under the supervision of a Tutor. In the case of the Miles Platting Special Care Unit (since renamed Leacroft School) this introduction to the problems of the child with multiple handicaps has been of particular value in view of the fact that the Unit Teacher is an ex-student (distinction, 1970) of this Course. In addition, the school physiotherapist makes valuable contributions to the students' training. The pattern of the six-week course is as follows:
(1) Each student selects one child to study over the period. This choice must be one out of the six most handicapped children in the Unit. All are physically handicapped.
(2) The student has a session with the child and the physiotherapist in which the child's individual physical problems are demonstrated and explained. Basic simple physiotherapy techniques appropriate to the individual child are taught, and the student carries out these movements under the supervision of the physiotherapist.
(3) The student then works with the child and gains probably her first experience in handling a severely physically handicapped child.
(4) The student then observes the child for a few minutes and records her observation until she recognizes in the child's behaviour a 'growth' point for a structured programme of work. It is generally found that the initial experience with the physiotherapist is of great help at the beginning stage (e.g. if the student wishes the child to put out a hand to touch an object, then she already knows that the child should be held or positioned in a certain way in order that the maximum conditions for success are achieved).
(5) From this point on, the student is encouraged to observe and evaluate the child's responses, and to devize items of equipment in order to secure a greater degree of stimulation and response. This may cover a wide field, e.g. Language and Movement combined, Language and Demonstration, Storytelling with 'picture questioning' to follow, etc.
(6) The ultimate objective is to see if the students can follow through the following sequence as a 'skeleton' for their educational programme:
   (a) observe—decision and execution as a result.
   (b) response to decision and execution;
   (c) observation of response;
   (d) observe—decision and execution, etc.

The whole relationship thus ideally becomes self activating and allows great scope for the individual student to pursue her own line of enquiry in a way best suited to her own interests. However, the students are expected to integrate their 'physiotherapy knowledge' and their 'educational knowledge' into a unity when dealing with the children. Full records of all work are kept on indexed cards.

Compiled by B. Narey.

Ideas collected from post-graduate students and others on a Summer School, Block Programme, New Brunswick University, Canada, 1972

Essay title: Write about four clinical conditions in Mental Retardation. State how this knowledge is useful to the teacher.

The following ideas were extended as I read the essays and as they triggered off my imagination. Sharing ideas is an attitude we must encourage in the field of mental retardation. We all need them if we are to help the child and its parents and do a good job ourselves. I collected some of the ideas from the essays and duplicated them for all the members of the class.

(1) Dietary procedures in children having metabolic disorders. Possible short attention span and hyperactivity in some children with phenylketonuria.
(2) Respiratory problems of mongols—blowing noses; much exercise in the open air.
(3) Heart conditions possible in mongols—*regular* check-ups. Consultation with doctor regarding specific activities—lifting heavy items, physical education, exercise in early months (refer Brinkworth).
(4) Teachers of the cerebral palsied child need to have some of the knowledge and perhaps the skills of the other experts, e.g. physiotherapists, speech therapists.
(5) To be knowledgeable when parents (i) talk about the condition and (ii) want to know more about the condition.
(6) Meningitis—consider effect upon parents. Possibly different from that upon parents who know from birth that the child is handicapped. Perhaps a different problem for teacher to cope with.
(7) Microcephaly. Secondary causes—higher achievement expected so our planning will be different.
(8) Tuberous sclerosis. Teacher noticing ash leaf shape rashes (after five years) refer to the doctor. T.S. is associated with epilepsy—teacher to know what to do in the case of convulsion.
(9) A knowledge of the medical aspects might make us question all the time the stereotypes in physical type and personality. It should make us QUESTION all the time as more is discovered in education as well as medicine.
(10) Cerebral palsy—the whole field of children in this group might make the teacher more curious about such a child's emotional state, e.g. is he depressed on account of being deprived of adequate stimuli? This in turn should make us more aware of the possible emotional states of normal children in some situations.
(11) Spina bifida. Bowel and elimination problems. Problems of odour from the child—social aspects with others here—adults, children.

(12) Epilepsy associated with various kinds of clinical conditions—if teacher is aware of the conditions where likely, she will be prepared and learn how to cope. Best plan is to visit a school of epileptics and see how experienced teachers cope.
(13) Acceptance of child's disabilities.
(14) More likely to make the teacher aware that the child might need:
   (i) medication;
   (ii) physiotherapy;
   (iii) speech therapy;
   in addition to appropriate well-structured language stimulation programmes.
(15) Will reduce teacher's fear.
(16) The teacher will be an educator in the community to:
   (i) help others;
   (ii) have a realistic view of the conditions;
   (iii) reduce fears in them;
   (iv) get the community involved.
(17) Hydrocephaly—be aware of possible eye troubles. Possible use of more auditory/tactile experiences.
(18) Will increase teachers' feelings for and towards the parents because we know more acutely the seriousness and the underlying sadness of their problems and their need for our continuous support.
(19) Will give teachers in the field more professionalism. When they are asked about the conditions they will have confidence about:
   (i) some of the information they can give;
   (ii) where to find other useful information.
(20) Will enable teachers to have more positive attitudes towards a child regressing because of his medical condition, e.g. Tay-Sachs disease or onset of epilepsy as part of hydrocephaly—they will understand that it is not their fault.
(21) It will enable teachers to consider the parents' needs when they have a child with a condition of a deteriorating nature.
(22) Enables the teachers to understand more fully the individual nature of problems in mental retardation.

Appendix 7 Colleges of Education offering courses (main/optional/B.Ed.) in mental handicap

Leeds Polytechnic (including a course for postgraduates).
City College of Education, Sheffield.
Harris Polytechnic/Chorley College of Education.
Maria Grey College, Chiswick.
Didsbury College of Education, Manchester.
Trent Polytechnic, Nottingham.
Matlock College of Education.
Wall Hall College of Education, Watford.
Avery Hill College of Education, London.
King Alfred's College, Winchester.
Culham College of Education, near Abingdon, Oxfordshire.
C.F. Mott College of Education, Liverpool.
Caerleon College of Education, Wales.
West Hill College, Birmingham.
Kingston-upon-Hull College of Education.
Redlands College of Education, Bristol.
Keswick College of Education, Norwich, Norfolk.

Some College Tutors have been able to gain more time than others for students to have on-going weekly contact with the mentally handicapped throughout the three years of teacher training. If students are interested in this essential practical aspect of their work they should enquire about this when writing for the syllabuses of the colleges applied to.

References

1. WINSCHELL, J. F. (1970) *Teacher Training and the Plague.* Proceedings of the 1st International Seminar of Special Education and Rehabilitation of the Mentally Retarded (I.A.S.S.M.D.), Malmö, Sweden.
2. GUNZBURG, H. C. (1968) *Social Competence and Mental Handicap,* Baillière, Tindall and Cassell, London.
3. CLARKE, A. M. AND CLARKE, A. D. B. (1973) (eds.) *Mental Deficiency, The Changing Outlook,* Methuen, London. Third edition.
4. O'CONNOR, N. AND TIZARD, J. (1956) *The Social Problem of Mental Deficiency.* Pergamon Press, Oxford.
5. TIZARD, J. AND GRAD, J. C. (1961) *The Mentally Handicapped and Their Families.* Oxford University Press, London.
6. TIZARD, J. (1964) *Community Services for the Mentally Handicapped.* Oxford University Press, London.
7. PENROSE, L. (1949) *The Biology of Mental Defect.* Sidgwick and Jackson, London.
8. HILLIARD, L. T. AND KIRMAN, B. H. (1965) *Mental Deficiency.* Churchill-Livingstone, Edinburgh and London. Second edition.
9. WOODWARD, W. M. (1972) *The Development of Behaviour.* Penguin Books, Harmondsworth, Middlesex.
10. HOLT, K. S. (1958) The Influence of a Retarded Child upon Family Limitation, *Journal of Mental Deficiency Research,* **2,** 28–36.
11. *Scott Report. The Training of Staff of Training Centres for the Mentally Subnormal* (1962). H.M.S.O., London.
12. HERRIOT, P. AND THOMAS, B. (1972) *Jim's People.* Learning Developments Aids, Wisbech, Cambs.
13. BERRY, P. (1971) *Language Imitation Test.* Hester Adrian Research Centre, Manchester University, Manchester.
14. STEVENS, MILDRED (1964) *Training Observation in Teachers of the Severely Subnormal.* Proceedings of the International Association for the Scientific Study of Mental Deficiency, Copenhagen, ed. B. W. RICHARDS, Harberbury Hospital, St. Albans.
15. CUNNINGHAM, C. C. AND JEFFREE, DOROTHY M. (1971) *Parents Workshop.* National Society for Mentally Handicapped Children, North West Region, Manchester.
16. JEFFREE, DOROTHY M. AND MCCONKEY, R. J. (1973) *Developmental Scales* (unpublished). Hester Adrian Research Centre, Manchester University, Manchester.
17. WARD, J. (1970) On the Concept of Criterion Referenced Measurement, *British Journal of Educational Psychology,* **40,** 314.
18. WHELAN, E. (1973) Developing Work Skills: A Systematic Approach. In *Assessment for Learning in the Mentally Handicapped,* ed. P. MITTLER. Churchill-Livingstone, Edinburgh and London.
19. GREGORY, OLWEN (1972) *The Characteristics of Profoundly Handi-*

REFERENCES

capped Children in Day Centres in Glasgow. Unpublished M.Ed. Thesis, Manchester University, Manchester.

20. LEESON, JOYCE (1960) A study of Six Mentally Handicapped Children and Their Families, *Medical Officer*, **104**, 311–314.
21. WISEMAN, A. (1963) *Special Care Units.* Teaching and Training. National Association for Teachers of the Mentally Handicapped. Apply to Mrs. E. Hughes, Delamere House School, Stretford, Lancs.
22. STEVENS, MILDRED (1968) *Observing Children who are Severely Subnormal.* Edward Arnold, London.
23. STEVENS, MILDRED (1970) *Some Basic Techniques in Training Teachers of the Severely Subnormal.* Proceedings of the 2nd Congress of the International Association for the Scientific Study of Mental Deficiency, Polish Medical Publishers, Duga 38/40, Warsaw.
24. STEVENS, MILDRED (1971) *The New Pupils.* Conference Report, National Society for Mentally Handicapped Children, Taunton.
25. STEVENS, MILDRED (1973) *The Special Needs of Students Training to be Teachers of the Mentally Handicapped—A Matter of Controversy.* Seminar Report Sam 1, Danish National Association of Teachers in Special Education, Copenhagen.
26. FORREST, M. (1973) Training Courses for Teachers of Mentally Handicapped Children, *Froebel Journal*, **27** (Autumn).
27. STEVENS, MILDRED (1974) A Mother and Baby College for Parents of the Mentally Handicapped, *Social Services Free Magazine* (Manchester), December.
28. STEVENS, MILDRED (1969) *Transfer or Transformation.* Guide Lines for Teachers No.7. February. College of Special Education, Pembridge Hall, 17 Pembridge Square, London, W2 4EP.
29. MITTLER, P. (1974) *Research and the Teacher.* Published by the National Council for Special Education, Birmingham.
30. BRUNER, J. S. (1966) *Towards a Theory of Instruction.* Harvard University Press, Cambridge, Mass.
31. MARSH, L. (1970) *Alongside the Child in the Primary School.* A. and C. Black, London.
32. DEWEY, J. (1966) in *Selected Educational Writings*, ed. F. W. GARFORTH. Heinemann, London.
33. OLECHNOWICZ, H. (1974) (ed.) *The Socialisation of Severely and Profoundly Retarded Children.* Nasa Ksiegarnia, Warsaw. Copies free to those applying to the editor.
34. HEAVEY, R. (1973) *Creative Drama and the Mentally Handicapped Child.* Obtainable from Mill House School, Newton-le-Willows, Lancs.
35. SINSON, JANICE (1973) *Assessment and Social Education of Severely Subnormal Children in a Pre-school Unit.* Seminar Report Sam 1, Danish National Association of Teachers in Special Education, Copenhagen (cf. page 45).
36. PIAGET, J. (1966) trans. MARGARET COOK. *The Origins of Intelligence in the Child.* Routledge and Kegan Paul, London.
37. CARROL, H. M.C. (1972) in *The Education of the Mentally Handicapped*, ed. A. LAING. Faculty of Education, University of Swansea.
38. GILLHAM, W. E. (1974) in *Special Education*, **1** National Council for Special Education, London.

39. ISAACS, SUSAN (1970) in *The Origins and Growth of Modern Education*, ed. ELIZABETH LAWRENCE. (pelican Original) Penguin Books, Harmondsworth, Middlesex.
40. KEPHART, N. C. (1971) *The Slow Learner in the Classroom.* Charles E. Merrill, Columbus, Ohio. Second edition.
41. VERNON, M. D. (1962) *The Psychology of Perception.* (Pelican Original) Penguin Books, Harmondsworth, Middlesex.
42. FITCH, JOAN (1968) *Storytelling for Slow Learners.* National Council for Special Education, 17 Pembridge Square, London, W2 4EP.
43. LUNZER, E. AND HULME, I. (1966) Play, Language and Reasoning in the Severely Subnormal Child, *Journal of Child Psychology and Psychiatry and Allied Disciplines*, **7**, 107–23.
44. BUNDEY, SARAH (1970) *Genetic Counselling in Relation to Tuberous Sclerosis.* Proceedings of the International Association for the Scientific Study of Mental Deficiency, Warsaw.
45. TANNER, J. M. (1964) *Physical Growth and Education.* University of London Press, London.
46. WHELAN, E. AND MAIER, I. (1972) *Assessment and Behaviour Modification in the Mentally Handicapped. An operant approach to the Treatment of Overactive Children.* Hester Adrian Research Centre, Manchester University, Manchester.
47. SCHONELL, F. (1942) *Backwardness in the Basic Subjects.* Oliver and Boyd, London and Edinburgh.
48. GREGORY, OLWEN (1973) *The Use of a Piagetian Assessment Technique in the Assessment of Profoundly Handicapped Children* (unpublished). I.A.S.S.M.D., The Hague. Obtainable by writing to her personally at Belmont School House, Sandringham Avenue, Newton Mearns, Renfrewshire, Scotland.
49. PIAGET, J. (1967) *The Child's Conception of the World.* Routledge and Kegan Paul, London.
50. KIRK, S. A. AND MCCARTHY, J. J. (1961) *The Illinois Test of Psycholinguistic Abilities.* Institute for Research on Exceptional Children, Illinois University, Illinois.
51. VAN OUDENHOVEN, N. J. A. (1973) *Cognitive Styles in Imbeciles.* Proceedings of the 3rd Congress of the International Association for the Scientific Study of Mental Deficiency, The Hague. (cf. note page 59).
52. HEWETT, SHEILA (1970) *The Family and the Handicapped Child.* Allen and Unwin, London.
53. OLECHNOWICZ, H. (1973) *Studies in the Socialization of the Severely and Profoundly Retarded.* Warsaw. Obtainable free from Nasa Księgarnia, Warsaw.
54. HARGROVE, APHRA (1967) *Serving the Mentally Handicapped.* National Association for Mental Health, 22 Harley Street, London, W.1.
55. FAULKNER, R. E. (1971) Opportunity Classes: Study of a Group of Voluntary Integrated Nursery Classes for Handicapped and Normal Children, *Community Medicine*, **126**, 213–7.
56. BOWLEY, A. AND GARDENER, K. (1957) *The Education of the Young Handicapped Child.* Churchill-Livingstone, Edinburgh and London.
57. DALE, D. M. C. (1967) *The Deaf Child at Home and at School.* University of London Press, London.

58. BRINKWORTH, R. AND COLLINS, J. (1969) *Improving Your Mongol Baby.* National Society for Mentally Handicapped Children, London.
59. JEFFREE, DOROTHY, M. AND CASHDAN, A. (1971) The Home Background of the Severely Subnormal Child: A Second Study, *British Journal of Medical Psychology*, **44,** 27–33.
60. MOGFORD, KAY (1974) *The Communication of Young Severely Handicapped Children.* Child Development Research Unit, University of Nottingham, Nottingham.
61. STEPHENS, ELSPETH (1973) *Appraisal of and Programming for Early Development.* Seminar Report Sam 1, Danish National Association of Teachers in Special Education, Copenhagen (p. 45).
62. REYNELL, JOAN (1973) Planning Treatment Programmes for the pre-school Handicapped Child, In *Assessment for Learning in the Mentally Handicapped*, ed. P. MITTLER. Churchill-Livingstone, Edinburgh and London.
63. DOLL, E. A. (1947) *Vineland Social Maturity Scale.* American Guidance Service, Minnesota, U.S.A.
64. GARDENER, D. E. M. AND CASS, J. E. (1965) *The Role of the Teacher in the Infant and Nursery School.* Pergamon Press, Oxford.
65. BERRY, P. (1976) *Language and Communication in the Mentally Handicapped.* Edward Arnold, London.
66. MOLLON, R. (1967) *The Nursery Book.* Pan Books, London.
67. PICKARD, P. M. (1965) *The Activity of Children.* Longmans, London.
68. MILLAR, S. (1968) *The Psychology of Play.* Penguin Books, Harmondsworth, Middlesex.
69. BEREITER, C. AND ENGELMANN, S. (1966) *Teaching Disadvantaged Children in the Pre-school.* Prentice-Hall, Englewood Cliffs, New Jersey, U.S.A.
70. WOODWARD, MARY (1959) The Behaviour of Idiots Interpreted by Piaget's Theory of Sensori-Motor Development, *British Journal of Educational Psychology*, **29,** 60–71.
71. STEPHENS, ELSPETH AND ROBERTSON, JEAN (1972) *Growing Up in Hospital. Occasional Papers 4, Institute for Research into Mental Retardation.* Butterworths, London.
72. ABBAS, K. A. AND DONOGHUE, E. C. (1973) Improving the Children's Play, *Special Education*, **62,** No. 4. National Council for Special Education, London.
73. MORGENSTERN, M. AND MORGENSTERN, H. (1966) *Practical Training for the Handicapped Child.* Heinemann Medical Books, London.
74. STEPHENS, ELSPETH AND ROBERTSON, JEAN (1972) *Occasional Papers 2 and 3. Institute for Research into Mental Retardation.* Butterworths, London.
75. LUNZER, E. (1959) Scale for Measuring Adaptiveness in the Use of Play Materials. Intellectual Development in the Play of Young Children, *Educational Review*, **11,** 205.
76. TIZARD, J. (1960) Residential Care of Mentally Handicapped Children, *British Medical Journal*, **1,** 1041.
77. KUSHLICK, A. (1965) Community Services for the Mentally Subnormal. A plan for Experimental Evaluation, *Proceedings of the Royal Society of Medicine*, **58,** 374–80.

78. ROBINSON, H. B. AND ROBINSON, N. B. (1965) *The Mentally Retarded Child. A Psychological Approach.* McGraw-Hill, New York and Maidenhead.
79. MOGFORD, KAY (1974) *Development Play and Handicap.* Child Development Research Unit, University of Nottingham, Nottingham.
80. NEALE, MARIE AND CAMPBELL, D. (1963) *Education for the Intellectually Limited Child and Adolescent.* Ian Novak, Sydney.
81. HERMELIN, B. AND O'CONNOR, N. (1960) Reading Ability of Severely Subnormal Children, *Journal of Mental Deficiency Research,* **4,** 144-7.
82. GILDER, ANNE (1965) Reading Games—An Experiment with Mentally Handicapped Children, *Medical Officer,* **113,** 179-81.
83. MOSLEY, D. (1971) *Research into Training Techniques Using the Talking Typewriter.* National Society for Mentally Handicapped Children, Barnet Branch.
84. HOUGHTON, V. P. AND DANIELS, J. C. (1966) The Phenomenon of Eulexia, *United Kingdon Reading Association Bulletin No. 6,* July.
85. HEWETT, SHEILA (1972) *The Need for Long Term Care. Occasional Papers, Institute for Research into Mental Retardation.* Butterworths, London.
86. GUNZBURG, H. C. (1966) *Progress Assessment Charts.* National Association for Mental Health, London. Extended now to one especially for mongol children.
87. JACKSON, S. (1968) *A Teacher's Guide to Tests.* Longmans, London.
88. HARRIS, D. B. (1963) *Children's Drawings as Measures of Intellectual Maturity.* Harcourt, Brace and World, New York.
89. PASCOE, T. W. (1968) *Introductory Handbook on the Severely Subnormal.* Guide lines for Teachers, No.3. College of Special Education, London.
90. CURZON, WINIFRED (1967) *Training Teachers of the Mentally Handicapped.* Paper read at Spastics Society Conference, Oxford.
91. DAVIES, B. D. AND GIBSON, A. (1967) *The Social Education of the Adolescent.* Unibooks, University of London Press, London.
92. WHELAN, E. (1974) *Report of the Research Projects.* Hester Adrian Research Centre, Manchester University, Manchester.
93. BARANYAY, EILEEN (1971) *The Mentally Handicapped Adolescent.* Pergamon Press, Oxford.
94. MARSHALL, ANN (1967) *The Abilities and Achievements of Children Leaving Junior Training Centres.* National Association for Mental Health, London.
95. MITTLER, P. (1970) (ed.) *The Psychological Assessment of Mental and Physical Handicaps.* Methuen, London, pp. 631-3.
96. GUNZBURG, H. C. (1970) *The Application of an Operational Philosophy for the Education of the Trainable Mentally Retarded.* Proceedings of the 1st International Seminar of Special Education and Rehabilitation of the Mentally Retarded, Malmö, Sweden.
97. HOLT, W. AND REYNELL, J. (1970) *Observation of Children.* National Association for Mental Health, London.
98. CONNOLLY, K. (1973) Ethological Techniques and the Direct Observation of Behaviour. In *Assessment for Learning in the Mentally Handicapped,* ed. P. MITTLER. Churchill-Livingstone, Edinburgh and London.

99. TANGERUD, H. (1970) *The Education of the Educable Mentally Retarded.* Proceedings of the 1st International Seminar of Special Education and Rehabilitation of the Mentally Retarded, Malmö, Sweden.
100. STANDING, E. M. (1957) *Maria Montessori. Her Life and Work.* Hollis and Carter.
101. NEILL, A. S. (1962) *Summerhill.* Penguin Books, Harmondsworth, Middlesex.
102. KUSHLICK, A. (1968) *Residential Care for the Mentally Retarded.* Fourth International Congress, International League of Societies for the Mentally Handicapped, Hebrew University, Jerusalem.
103. MITTLER, P. AND WOODWARD, M. (1966) The Education of Children in Hospitals for the Subnormal: A Survey of Admissions, *Developmental Medicine and Child Neurology,* **8,** 16–25.
104. DEY, J. (1970) *Down's Syndrome. Review of 500 Children. Some Interesting Facts.* Proceedings of the 2nd Congress of the International Association for the Scientific Study of Mental Deficiency, Warsaw.
105. CORIAT, LYDIA F., FERREYRA, MARIA, E. AND ALFONSO, J. F. (1970) *Familial Down's Syndrome.* Proceedings of the 2nd Congress of the International Association for the Scientific Study of Mental Deficiency, Warsaw.
106. EGG, MARIA (1969) *The Different Child Grows up.* John Day and Co., New York.
107. CORTAZZI, D. (1968) The Bottom of the Barrel, *Journal of Mental Subnormality,* **15,**
108. WHALLEY, T. AND HEWARD, J. (1973) No Stagnation at Sandhill Park, *Special Education,* **62,**
109. BANK-MIKKELSEN, N. E. (1971) *The Quality of Services for the Mentally Retarded in Denmark.* National Society for Mentally Handicapped Children, London.
110. SLETVED, H. (1970) *Basic Principles in the Education of Severely and Profoundly Mentally Retarded Children.* Proceedings of the 2nd Congress of the International Association for the Scientific Study of Mental Deficiency, Warsaw.
111. TOFFLER, A. (1971) *Future Shock.* Pan Books, London.
112. SIEJKO, MARIA (1974) In *Studies in the Socialization of Severely and Profoundly Retarded Children,* ed. H. OLECHNOWICZ Nasa Ksiegarnia, Warsaw.
113. KIRMAN, B. H. (1968) *Mental Retardation.* Pergamon Press, Oxford.
114. MITTLER, P. (1973) (ed.) *Assessment for Learning in the Mentally handicapped.* Churchill-Livingstone, Edinburgh and London.
115. JORDAN, J. E. (1970) *Attitudes Towards Mental Retardation in Five Nations.* Proceedings of the 2nd Congress of the International Association for the Scientific Study of Mental Deficiency, Polish Medical Publishers, Duga 38/40, Warsaw.
116. STEVENS, MILDRED (1954) *Some Aspects of an Active Approach in the Junior School.* Unpublished M.Ed. Thesis, Manchester University, Manchester.
117. RAVENETTE, A. T. (1973) Planning Treatment Programmes for School Age Children. In *Assessment for Learning in the Mentally Handi-*

capped, ed. P. MITTLER. Churchill-Livingstone, Edinburgh and London.

118. FLANDERS, B. (1973) *The Training of Teachers of Mentally Handicapped Children.* Seminar Report Sam 1, Danish National Association of Teachers in Special Education, Copenhagen, (cf. p. 45).

119. BRAGE, N. (1970) *Instructional Materials for the Mentally Retarded.* Proceedings of the 1st International Seminar of Special Education and Rehabilitation of the Mentally Retarded, Malmö, Sweden.

120. CAVE, C. (1973) in *Mental Retardation and Behavioural Research,* eds. A. D. B. CLARKE AND A. M. CLARKE. Churchill-Livingstone, Edinburgh and London.

Further useful reading

This short selection of books and articles has been useful to me as a teacher. Everything that I have mentioned below has a *practical* implication for all those living with/working with handicapped children. If you have something to share with me, please contact me.

(A) Parents

BAGNALL, N. (1974) (ed.) *Parent Power.* Fontana, and Routledge and Kegan Paul, London.
BRINKWORTH, R. (1973) The Unfinished Child. Effects of Early Home Training on the Mongol infant. In *Mental Retardation and Behavioural Research*, eds. A. D. B. CLARKE AND A. M. CLARKE. Churchill-Livingstone, Edinburgh and London.
BROWNING, ELIZABETH (1972) *I Can't See What You're Saying.* Elek, London, (Aphasia).
BURTON, L. (1974) *Care of the Child Facing Death.* Routledge and Kegan Paul, London.
CLAIBORNE PARK, CLARA (1967) *The Siege.* Colin Smythe, Gerrards Cross, Bucks, (Autism).
CLARKE, A. D. B. AND CLARKE, A. M. (1969) *Practical Help for Parents of Retarded Children.* National Society for Mentally Handicapped Children, Hull.
CRAFT, M., RAYNOR, J. AND COHEN, L. (1967) *Linking Home and School.* Longmans, London.
DEAN, JEAN (1976) *Parents' Expectations of Education for Profoundly Handicapped Children.* Unpublished Thesis, Department of Education, Manchester University, Manchester.
DOUGLAS, J. W. B. (1967) *The Home and the School.* Panther Books, 3 Upper James Street, London, W.1.
FOTHERINGHAM, SKELTON AND HODDINOTT (1975) *The Retarded Child and His Family.* Monograph Series, 11. The Ontario Institute for Studies in Education, Canada.
FURNEAUX, B. (1969) *The Special Child.* Penguin Education Special, Harmondsworth, Middlesex.
HANNAN, C. (1975) *Parents and Mentally Handicapped Children.* Penguin Mind Special, Harmondsworth, Middlesex.
HUNDLEY, M. J. (1971) *The Small Outsider.* (Autism). Angus and Robertson.
MCKEITH, R. (1974) The Feelings and Behaviour of Parents of Handicapped Children. In *The Handicapped Person in the Community*, eds. D. M. BOSWELL AND J. M. WINGROVE. Tavistock Publications in association with The Open University Press, Milton Keynes.
PARFIT, J. (1971) *Spotlight on Group Work with Parents in Special Circumstances.* National Children's Bureau, 8 Wakley Street, London, E.1.
ROITH, A. I. (1963) The Myth of Parental Attitudes, *Journal of Mental Subnormality,* **9,** 51–4.

WEST, P. (1973) *Words for a Deaf Daughter.* Penguin Books, Harmondsworth, Middlesex.
WILKS, J. AND WILKS, EILEEN (1974) *Bernard. Bringing Up Our Mongol Son.* Routledge and Kegan Paul, London.
WOODS, G. E. (1970) *The Blind Mentally Retarded Child.* Proceedings of the 2nd Congress of the International Association for the Scientific Study of Mental Deficiency, Warsaw. (A must *before* you begin to teach.)
YOUNGHUSBAND, E., BIRCHALL, D., DAVIE, R. AND KELLMER, P. (1970) (eds.) *Living with Handicap.* National Children's Bureau, 8 Wakley Street, London, E.1.

(B) Mental Subnormality Hospitals
BLAND, G. (1964) *Education in Hospital Schools for the Mentally Handicapped.* College of Special Education, London.
CORTAZZI, D. (1973) *Illuminative Incidents as a Technique for Team Building.* Seminar Report Sam 1, Danish National Association of Teachers in Special Education, Copenhagen.
CORTAZZI, D. AND ROOTE, S. (1975) *Illuminative Incident Analysis.* McGraw-Hill, New York and Maidenhead.
GUNZBURG, H. C. AND GUNZBURG, A. L. (1970) *Social Education and the Institution: The Shaping of a Therapeutic 'Non-Institutional' Environment.* Proceedings of the 2nd Congress of the International Association for the Scientific Study of Mental Deficiency, Warsaw.
MORRIS, P. (1970) *Put Away.* Routledge and Kegan Paul, London.
RICHARDSON, HELEN (1969) *Adolescent Girls in Approved Schools.* Routledge and Kegan Paul, London.
STEVENS, MILDRED (1965) Breakthrough to Kenneth. In *Breakthrough,* December. National Society for Mentally Handicapped Children, Brazennose Street, Manchester, 2.
STEVENS, MILDRED (1976) (In preparation) A Language Survey in a Mental Subnormality Hospital School—An In-Service Training Technique. National Council for Special Education, Bradford.

(C) Play
BROWN, MARY AND PRECIOUS, N. (1968) *The Integrated Day in the Primary School.* Ward Lock, London.
GABRIEL, J. (1965) *Children Growing Up.* University of London Press, London.
HARTLEY, R., FRANK, L. K. AND GOLDENSOHN, R. M. (1952) *Understanding Children's Play.* Routledge and Kegan Paul, London.
MELLOR, E. (1956) *Education Through Experience in the Infant School.* Blackwell, Oxford.
METTERSON, E. A. (1964) *Play with a Purpose for the Under Sevens.* Penguin Handbooks, Harmondsworth, Middlesex.
POCOCKE, S. E. (1966) *Children of Today.* University of London Press, London.
ROBINSON, C. M., HARRISON, J. AND GRIDLEY, J. (1970) *Physical Activities in the Education of Slow Learning Children.* Edward Arnold, London.
STEVENS, MILDRED (1960) Play and the Adolescent, *Teachers World.* Journal National Union of Teachers.

STEVENS, MILDRED (1964) *They Like to be Busy.* Teaching and Training. Editor Frances M. Dean, 22 Chandos Road, Harrow, Middlesex. National Association for Teachers of the Mentally Handicapped.

(D) Medical and Practical Nursing Aspects
The busy teacher only needs a point of reference here. The five books following should perhaps be part of EVERY teacher's personal library:
CLARKE, A. M. AND CLARKE, A. D. B. (1972) (eds.) *Mental Deficiency, The Changing Outlook,* Methuen, London. Third edition.
HEATONWARD, W. A. (1975) *Mental Subnormality.* Wright, J. 44 Triangle West, Clifton, Bristol. Fourth edition.
MORLEY, M. E. (1972) *The Development and Disorders of Speech in Childhood.* Churchill-Livingstone, Edinburgh and London. Third edition.
PRIMROSE, D. A. (1974) *Mental Subnormality.* No. 15 Modern Practical Nursing Series, Heinemann, London.
ROBINSON, H. B. AND ROBINSON, N. M. (1965) *The Mentally Retarded Child.* McGraw-Hill, New York and Maidenhead.

(E) Useful Organizations
Why not join as a group? They all need your support and your money.
Association for ALL Speech Impaired Children, Room 14, Toynbee Hall, 28 Commercial Street, London, E1 6LS.
Fair Play for Children, 237 Pentonville Road, London, N.1.
National Children's Bureau, 8 Wakley Street, London, EC1V 7QE.
Opportunity Play Group Movement, Dr. R. Faulkner, 1 Weston Road, Stevenage, Herts.
Toy Libraries Association, Sunley House, 10 Gunthorpe Street, London, E1 7RW.

The book *No Child is Ineducable* (1967) by Stanley Segal (Pergamon Guides, Oxford) contains perhaps one of the most comprehensive lists of useful organizations dealing with handicapped children. 1976